AS IT PLEASES GOD® MOVEMENT

ASITPLEASESGOD.COM

THE SPIRITUAL M✝DDLEMAN APPROACH

Copyright © 2021 by R.O.A.R. Publishing Group. All rights reserved.

Visit www.DrYBur.com or www.AsItPleasesGod.com for more information. No part of this publication may be reproduced, stored in a retrieval system, or transmitted in any way by any means, electronic, mechanical, photocopy, recording, or otherwise, without the prior permission of the author except as provided by USA copyright law. All rights reserved.

R.O.A.R. Publishing Group
581 N. Park Ave. Ste. #725
Apopka, FL 32704
ROAR-58-2316
762-758-2316
www.RoarPublishingGroup.com

Send Questions or Comments to:
CustomerService@RoarPublishingGroup.com

Published in the United States of America
ISBN: 978-1-948936-59-0
$22.88

ASITPLEASESGOD.COM

ASITPLEASESGOD.COM

Send *As It Pleases God* ®

Book Series and *Workbook* **Testimonies, Donations, Questions, or Orders to:**

Dr. Y. Bur
R.O.A.R. Publishing Group
581 N. Park Ave. Ste. #725
Apopka, FL 32704
ROAR-58-2316
762-758-2316

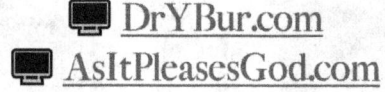 Dr.YBur@gmail.com

Visit Us At:

AsItPleasesGodMovement
AsItPleasesGod

DrYBur.com
AsItPleasesGod.com

Please Donate

Please DONATE to this *Missionable Movement of God* as a GIVE-BACK to the Kingdom. Thanks for your support. Many Blessings.

AIPG Donation Link

Scan to Pay

AVAILABLE TITLES

ASITPLEASESGOD.COM

www.DrYBur.com

TABLE OF CONTENTS

Introduction	13
Chapter One	21
Divine Expectations	21
Emotional Intelligence	23
Spiritual Gird	25
The Fairytale of Warfare	28
DNA Hiccups	31
Chapter Two	35
Winning the War and Losing the Kingdom	35
Spiritual Mantles	40
Toe Stubbing	42
Who or What are you investing in?	45
Contingency Clause	52
Kingdom Order	54
Chapter Three	61
Rockable Diamonds	61
Examining Cleanser	63
The Drawing Board	66
Signs Of The Time	68
Winning in the Eye of God?	70
Chapter Four	75
The Four Corners	75
The Change	80
The Facts	82
The Chance	84

 The Power of Exchange 85
 Show Me 87
Chapter Five 89
 Spiritual Nutrients 89
  Title Blockage Analogy 92
  Spiritual Tares 94
  The Systemic Glitch 97
  Bread of Life 97
  Spiritual Benefits 99
  Spiritual Strength 104
Chapter Six 105
 Kingdom Weights 105
  Unveiling The Pharisees' Spirit 106
  Spiritual Training 110
  Spiritual Refreshers 114
  Spiritual Snares 119
  Justifiable Ammunition 120
  Spiritually Sharp 125
Chapter Seven 127
 The Way 127
  The Twist 131
  Straight Way Faith 133
Chapter Eight 139
 The Spiritual Middleman Approach 139
  Specific Instructions 144
  Awakening Effect 144
  Spiritual Walk 147
  Spiritual Lenses 151

    Voice of Mockery 154

    Spiritual Language 157

Chapter Nine 163

    Divine Agreement 163

    Direct Connect 166

    Spiritual Crown 169

    Age of Faith 173

Chapter Ten 175

    Heavenly Perception 175

    Slighted Perception 179

    Unspeakable Joy 181

    Set Aside For Him 186

Chapter Eleven 189

    Spiritual Hedge 189

    Wall of Fire 192

    Wall of Hope 195

    Wall of Obedience 197

Chapter Twelve 199

    Divine Instructions 199

    Word Pictures 201

    Divine Guarantees 203

    Spiritual Transformation 206

    Olive Tree Anointing 207

    Spiritual Refinement 211

    The-Lord-Is-Peace 215

INTRODUCTION

"For there is one God and one Mediator between God and men, the Man Christ Jesus." 1 Timothy 2:5.

The MAN from above or the ONE in the middle is indeed here for us, even if we are in denial of Him. *"For in Him we live and move and have our being, as also some of your own poets have said, 'For we are also His offspring.'"* Acts 17:28. Regardless of how we see ourselves, we are here for a reason, and it is our responsibility to understand what that reason is or is not. Thus, with *The Spiritual Middleman Approach*, the goal is to break the self-imposed limitations that we do not realize we have. How can we not know? When we are Spiritually Veiled, we will not know about our untapped potential until Divine Order is established, *As It Pleases God*.

Even if we are Holy Ghost-Filled and Fire-Baptized, there are certain things we will not know about ourselves unless we position ourselves to glean from the Vestibule of Divine Wisdom from the Heavenly of Heavens. Why? We must Spiritually Till our own ground, with humility, selflessness, and obedience. If not, the veil must remain for our protection or to avoid the misuse of our Spiritual Gifts.

Although some may go to the dark side to obtain a simulation of Spiritual Gifts or learn through mimicking, conditioning, or adaptation, it still may not be from the Holy of Holies. Plus, there are consequences and repercussions for not following the Spiritual Protocol, *As It Pleases God*. Why do we need to follow Spiritual Protocol? It is how we were created in the first place. Simply put, without Spiritual Protocol, we would not exist, nor would there be the bonding of DNA or protoplasm (composed of the nucleus and the cytoplasm).

Please allow me to break this down: In *The Spiritual Middleman Approach*, we need to know that DNA and protoplasm are both essential components of all living organisms. DNA is the genetic material that contains the instructions for the development, growth, and reproduction of organisms. It is a complex molecule made up of four nucleotide bases, adenine (A), cytosine (C), guanine (G), and thymine (T), which are arranged in a specific sequence.

Protoplasm, on the other hand, is the living substance that makes up the cell. It includes the cytoplasm, which contains all the organelles of the cell, and the nucleus, which contains the DNA. While DNA provides the BLUEPRINT for life, protoplasm is the medium through which life is expressed. In essence, DNA is the information, and protoplasm is the middleman machinery that carries out that information.

In the Eye of God, we are no different in the Realm of the Spirit, and if someone says that we can bypass Spiritual Protocol, doing whatever we like, whenever, and however, we are sadly mistaken. Remember, we can only bypass a lower law by a HIGHER one. Regardless of whether we are dealing with protoplasm or Spiritual Protocol, they have a job to do, and we cannot stand in its way, or it will turn on us by Divine Design. If we think we are powerful enough to beat the Divine System established by our Heavenly Father, it will make an example out of us in due season. Before going any further, please know this: *"For by Him all things were created that are in heaven and that are on earth, visible and invisible, whether thrones or dominions or principalities or powers. All things were created through Him and for Him."* Colossians 1:16.

Whether known or unknown, HOLINESS is a part of our Spiritual Journey or Heaven on Earth Experience hidden underneath what we call righteousness. When proclaiming holiness in a state of unrighteousness, we inadvertently create Spiritual Interferences or Static within the human psyche, instigating a secret battle or warring of the flesh, deepening the hole within us. Once this happens, we can rarely articulate what is going on unless we have some form of Divine Insight, Spiritual Discernment, or Spiritual Intervention.

Righteousness is indeed the most sacred part of our Spiritual Relations that we often overlook, going unattended and ungoverned to our detriment. Then again, operating in the Spirit of Righteousness is rarely discussed, *As It Pleases God*. Why? First and foremost, we often confuse ordinary righteousness (man-induced) with Spiritual Righteousness (God-Involved). Secondly, it is due to the lack of Divine Illumination on how it applies to the Spiritual System of God and how it works together for our good.

Well, with *The Spiritual Middleman Approach*, we will share how to operate in the System of God by properly adding the Holy Trinity into the equation of our lives, *As It Pleases Him*. At the same time, we should not settle for ordinary righteousness but go for the Spiritual Jugular (The Spiritual Lifeline).

From my perspective, it makes perfect sense to adhere to God's Divine Plan for our Spiritual Growth if we are to invest time and energy in cultivating ourselves, *As It Pleases Him*. By following our Divine Blueprint, we can avoid the pitfalls of trial and error or operating in a Spirit of Error.

Why must we work on or cultivate ourselves to avoid pitfalls? First, we are all a work-in-progress, and the moment we see someone unwilling to become better, stronger, wiser, or avoid growth altogether...RUN! Secondly, *"For we are His workmanship, created in Christ Jesus for good works, which God prepared beforehand that we should walk in them."* Ephesians 2:10.

As life would have it, if we are not sure about our Divine Mission, *As It Pleases God*, we become easily condescending in the areas we fail to understand. Or, we may play the blaming game like Adam and Eve in the Garden of Eden, wallowing in our very own Pool of Bethesda of our choosing. Now, based on who we blame, our Pool of Bethesda can become a place of grace, mercy, healing, and compassion, or it can become a place of shame, disgrace, wallowing, or sickness.

How can we change the trajectory of our pool? In the same way that God clothed Adam and Eve in righteousness amid their acts of disobedience in Genesis 3:21, He has done the same for us. How? By allowing Jesus to become a formal SACRIFICE and

ATONEMENT for us, releasing the Holy Spirit to do what we cannot do for ourselves. In the Eye of God, all we need to do is just come into AGREEMENT, *As It Pleases Him*, and pick up your mat and walk like the man healed at the Pool of Bethesda in John 5:1-15.

Here is what we must know: *"In Him also we have obtained an inheritance, being predestined according to the purpose of Him who works all things according to the counsel of His will."* Ephesians 1:11. Having the pool of Grace and Mercy in mind, God is shifting the blame elements to Kingdom Responsibility for a time such as this with *The Spiritual Middleman Approach.*

All in all, regardless of whether we are dealing with an Upper or Lower Pool, in or out of the Kingdom, irresponsibility and recklessness have become our pastimes without us realizing what is happening. More importantly, based on my observations and according to the Signs of the Time, it has become easy to point the finger when we are guilty of the same behaviors listed under a more tolerable label. To add insult to injury, we hide our hands as if we are without blemish after slinging dirt at the guilty or blameless without any form of mercy, understanding, or compassion for another being. Nor do we take the time to repent or work on ourselves to become better, wiser, and stronger, *As It Pleases God.*

In Psalm 64:1-8, David has a conversation with God about those who throw rocks and hide their hands. Here is what it says, *"Hear my voice, O God, in my meditation; Preserve my life from fear of the enemy. Hide me from the secret plots of the wicked, From the rebellion of the workers of iniquity, Who sharpen their tongue like a sword, And bend their bows to shoot their arrows—bitter words, That they may shoot in secret at the blameless; Suddenly they shoot at him and do not fear. They encourage themselves in an evil matter; They talk of laying snares secretly; They say, 'Who will see them?' They devise iniquities: 'We have perfected a shrewd scheme.' Both the inward thought and the heart of man are deep. But God shall shoot at them with an arrow; Suddenly they shall be wounded. So He will make them stumble over their own tongue; All who see them shall flee away."*

Label or not, I am here to say, 'Respect the Spiritual Journey of another,' regardless of how it appears to the naked eye. What is the purpose of doing so? God has a reason for everything, and we are not usually the ones who handle judging how He trains or transitions His sheep. We are merely Spiritual Vessels that He uses in the assisting process, not the judging! For me, if we cannot talk someone up, we should not talk them down or drag them through the dirt, as if God does not have a Divine Plan for their lives.

Why would someone drag another person through the dirt? The reasons will vary from person to person, situation to situation, drama to drama, bias to bias, trauma to trauma, and so on. Nevertheless, the underlying reason is associated with negative emotions such as fear, anger, jealousy, envy, pride, greed, covetousness, revenge, hatefulness, or competitiveness. Dragging someone through the dirt is never acceptable behavior, regardless of the situation, circumstance, or event.

However, regardless of the reason behind it, dragging someone through the dirt can cause significant emotional harm and should be avoided. Instead, conflicts and differences should be resolved healthily and respectfully. By choosing to take the higher road, we can build stronger relationships and create a more positive, productive, fruitful, and peaceful environment.

Do we not have free will to say and do whatever we like? Absolutely. Thus, in the Eye of God, it does not absolve us from accountability, especially when bringing shame to the name of another without having the facts. Then again, when airing out someone's dirty laundry to cover up the stench of our own dirty deeds, or when we are outright playing dirty.

Do we not have the right to play dirty, especially when getting the short end of the deal or when thrown under the bus? Absolutely! We have free will to do whatever, whenever, and however, but we still must remain accountable for the choices we make, whether good or bad, right or wrong, just or unjustly, and so on. Here is what we must know when playing dirty: *"Whoever digs a pit will fall into it, and he who rolls a stone will have it roll back on him."* Proverbs 26:27.

So, when using *The Spiritual Middleman Approach*, make sure that you are using the Fruits of the Spirit to keep everything copacetic. What if we have been wronged? Should we still use the Fruits of the Spirit? Absolutely. In the Eye of God, our strength is determined by our obedience, humility, kindness, and self-control. On the other hand, their absence reveals weakness, even when appearing strong. So, if we have an issue with someone, we should never publicly blast them without telling them face-to-face. Really? Yes, really! Here is what the Bible says about this matter: "*Moreover if your brother sins against you, go and tell him his fault between you and him alone. If he hears you, you have gained your brother.*" Matthew 18:15.

What if they do not listen? Forgive them anyway and move on in the Spirit of Excellence. Why should we be the bigger person, especially when made to feel small or repulsive? In *The Spiritual Middleman Approach*, regardless of how we feel, "*A soft answer turns away wrath, But a harsh word stirs up anger.*" Proverbs 15:1.

More importantly, if you are feeling slighted in any way, the problem is not within them; it is within you! Therefore, according to the Heavenly of Heavens, you must rectify this negative emotion quickly before it becomes leverage that can be used against you. Really? Yes, really. Galatians 6:1 says, "*Brethren, if a man is overtaken in any trespass, you who are spiritual restore such a one in a spirit of gentleness, considering yourself lest you also be tempted.*"

In *The Spiritual Middleman Approach*, we must remain in a state of peace to maximize the Divine Empowerment contained in this book. What if we are not at peace and we are really on edge? We must do our best to bring ourselves into a state of relaxation by making a *Spirit to Spirit* Connection with the Holy Trinity to usher in a peaceful state of mind. Why? If we are at peace with ourselves, we can be at peace with others.

On the other hand, if we are NOT at peace with ourselves, it becomes challenging to be at peace with others because this negative energy will follow us, doing what it does...becoming a magnet. Therefore, "*If it is possible, as much as depends on you, live peaceably with all men.*" Romans 12:18. Above all, "*Be angry, and do not sin: do not let the sun go down on your wrath, nor give place to the devil.*" Ephesians 4:26-27.

In this book, we cannot take for granted that someone knows what they need to do, *As It Pleases God*. For this reason, we take the soft approach of sharing this information for the GREATER GOOD. Nonetheless, it is always best to approach any situation or circumstance with extreme caution, having the Whole Armor of

God in full effect, using the Spiritual Principles and Tools set forth by our Heavenly Father. What is the reason for doing so as Believers? We never know when the enemy will shoot his best shots to disable, distract, or outmaneuver us with a known or unknown element of kryptonite.

What if we do not have kryptonite? Unfortunately, we all have our type, and no one is beyond temptation. Thus, we cannot exhibit condemnatory behaviors as if we do not have any Spiritual Home Training or Etiquette while *Winning the War and Losing the Kingdom*.

According to the Ancient of Days, we must stay on READY in the Spirit of Righteousness and fully repent to ensure the Kingdom of Heaven has our backs! As *God Promised*, if we use our God-Given Spiritual Tools with *The Spiritual Middleman Approach*, redirecting all things back to the Kingdom, the Light of God will illuminate the way or our next step, guaranteed.

The Way of our Heavenly Father has *Kingdom Weights* associated with our Spiritual Journey. Even if we do not know or understand them, we must PROTECT and ALIGN ourselves in a *Spirit to Spirit Relationship, As It Pleases Him*. For this reason, it is crucial to muster enough courage to prune what is blocking our *Rockable Diamonds*, preventing our Internal Growth, or zapping our *Spiritual Nutrients*.

The Keys to God's Heart is available to all, yet it is only used by a few in Divine Totality, the way He intended from the Garden of Eden.

For those who desire to Spiritually Capitalize on the Promises of God with an undefiable *Spiritual Edge*, we must learn the *Divine Expectations* needed in the Commissioning Process, according to the Word of God. Understanding the Kingdom in such a manner provides us with an *Olive Tree Anointing* that will put our enemies to boot, making our Spiritual Journey worth the effort, along with the *Divine Instructions* and Provisions to sustain us in Earthen Vessels.

As we all know, we all have strengths and weaknesses. Yet, it is quite common to develop a system to cover them up instead of dealing with them to become better, stronger, and wiser. Why does this occur within the human psyche? We often think our weaknesses make us unwise; however, if we dare to work on them consistently, they will inadvertently make us WISE by default.

How can weaknesses make us WISE? We have weaknesses for a REASON, and if we take the time to put in the work, we are better equipped to help another in the same condition with humility, understanding, and compassion. By sharing in such a manner, activating the Law of Reciprocity, God gives us more to determine how well we can convey and forgive simultaneously as a formal Spiritual Test. Why? Our Gifts, Callings, Talents, Purpose, Blessings, and Birthrights are hidden in our weaknesses, disabilities, quirks, traumas, and so on, causing us to doubt, downplay, or second-guess our Predestined Blueprint. Therefore, we must become quick to repent and forgive, leaving no stone unturned while gleaning the underlying WISDOM.

On the other hand, if we continue to hide our weaknesses without working on them to become better, we become condescending, judgmental, uncaring, biased, unforgiving, and hateful. In my opinion, the most frightening thing about this...is that the person with the undealt with or overlooked hidden weaknesses, or who is exhibiting negative charactorial traits, does not realize they are behaving in such a manner.

Frankly, this is similar to the *'Throwing the rock and hiding our hands'* analogy, or when repeating the same repented behavior, desensitizing the conscience further. How does this relate to being condescending, judgmental, uncaring, biased, and hateful? This behavior is often hidden or exhibited behind masks, carried out behind someone's back, or when we spit in the face of those who had our best interests at heart.

When we become Spiritually Blind, Deaf, and Mute to our conscience, we think we are doing others a favor when it is indeed a disservice in the Eye of God. Why? We are focused on pleasing ourselves without realizing it, instead of PLEASING God! I am not revealing this information to make anyone feel bad because we must all go through this phase of life; however, we DO NOT want to remain in this phase of our Desert Experience.

If you are ready for *The Spiritual Middleman Approach* to rock your world, restructuring it to adequately accommodate your Heaven on Earth Experiences, without any further ado, let us go DEEPER!

CHAPTER ONE
Divine Expectations

"What purpose then does the law serve? It was added because of transgressions, till the Seed should come to whom the promise was made; and it was appointed through angels by the hand of a mediator." Galatians 3:19-20.

As we move throughout, living our best lives, it is imperative to question ourselves on whether we are presenters or Vessels of God. What is the purpose of this question? It is easy to become a presenter, trained by a man in a self-led system of conveyance, making it easy for anyone to put on a show regardless of their level of expertise, education, or wealth. As a presenter of faith, even if our motives are Godly and righteous, when the mask falls off, so does the energy, causing us to become exhausted, frustrated, or insecure while appearing to have it all together.

On the other hand, according to the Heavenly of Heavens, to become a Vessel used by God in MIRACULOUS ways with *The Spiritual Middleman Approach*, we must become trained by the Holy Spirit. If not, we will waver in and out of faith depending upon how we feel, what is going on around us, or whether we are getting what we want, when we want it, and how.

How do we recognize if we are one of the two? In my opinion, if we can pinpoint our temper tantrums, outbursts, fits of rage, incomplete tasks, insecurities, or what causes us to run away or shut down, we can determine if we are presenters or Vessels of God. Is this not a little biased here? Everyone is entitled to their opinion; however, I am here to do a job, bringing forth Divine AWARENESS and PREPAREDNESS to those willing to receive.

Suppose we are on a Mission for God and are NOT on a learning curve regarding ourselves from the inside out consistently, then what happens to us? In this case, we subject ourselves to the Spirit of Arrogance, Defeat, or Error, causing us to miss our cues that lead to Spiritual Delays similar to when a video is buffering. If we buffer for too long, we can lose our Spiritual Edge, leaving room for the enemy's wiles. Or, we may interject worldliness into our system of conveyance due to our inability to hear, discern, or feel the nudging of the Holy Spirit.

How is it possible to hear a nudge? When it comes down to the Realm of the Spirit, we can Spiritually See, Hear, and Understand the audible and inaudible nudges of the Holy Spirit. So, we must pay attention to what is happening around us. Plus, we must be attentive to what is being said or omitted in the people, places, and things in or out of our circle. Why? The Voice of God is not limited to the communicable efforts of man; therefore, we must step outside of our fleshly being to connect with God, *Spirit to Spirit, As It Pleases Him.*

When using *The Spiritual Middleman Approach*, the Voice of God is not something we should take lightly, nor should we confuse His Voice with our self-talk or a voice of another kind. If we fail to understand the Voice of God, we can easily confuse the MESSAGES from the Kingdom, presenting them from an angle of manipulation instead of Godly Edification. What does this have to do with anything? Manipulation leads all things back to SELF with diversified options to benefit or please us. On the other hand, Godly Edification points everything back to the Kingdom of Heaven through the Blood of Jesus with the ONENESS of the Holy Spirit, *As It Pleases Him.*

What if we are on the right track, providing Spiritual Edification, and are rejected? If we are operating in the Spirit of Righteousness, rejection is a part of the learning process, and if we cannot handle a little rejection like the CHAMPION that we are, then it is time to step back into the Spiritual Classroom. Why? Spiritual Training requires us to gird up our loins, and if we can be easily broken, we become a prime target of sifting, manipulation, and trauma to our detriment.

Emotional Intelligence

To be clear, we all have weaknesses, and if brokenness causes us to run from the Vicissitudes of Life with our tails in between our legs, we can become prey due to the Cycle of Life. What does this mean? Predators in the Animal Kingdom take out the weakest for breakfast, lunch, and dinner at any opportunity! Frankly, we are no different in this Spiritual Cycle.

Still, we do have a slight twist in the process...our predators target us from the inside out, causing us to create our own Spiritual Taboos, Yokes, or Demise through our character, responses, behaviors, attitudes, thoughts, words, arrogance, disobedience, dullness, lukewarmness, stiffneckness, and so on. All of this happens without us realizing what is taking place as we become the enemy's laughingstock. To add insult to injury, with all of this junk in our trunks, we still think we have it going on and are on top of our game, not realizing in the Eye of God that the game is on top of us with rotten fruits all over the place.

Why would our enemies laugh at us? They see our weaknesses a mile away. Meanwhile, we are up close and personal with ourselves, knowing nothing about who we really are. All in all, we are still in denial of our weak spots while appearing strong and lying to ourselves, knowing nothing about the *Divine Expectations*. Then again, they see us blaming the Devil or others for self-induced or self-led issues while unawaringly giving him justifiable access to us through emotional unintelligence.

Clearly, I am not calling anyone emotionally unintelligent. I am only referring to a condition the enemy uses to gain access to cause us to turn on ourselves unawaringly by shattering the *Divine Expectations* of the Kingdom of God.

Here is the deal: Emotional unintelligence refers to a lack of awareness and understanding of one's own emotions, as well as the emotions and well-being of others. Unfortunately, it can lead to inappropriate emotional responses, emotional meltdowns, emotional rollercoasters, difficulty in managing emotions, a keeled Spiritual Compass, and a silencing of the conscience. All of these produce challenges in building and maintaining conducive relationships, effective communication, and wise decision-making.

Now, developing emotional intelligence, *As It Pleases God*, involves recognizing and regulating one's own emotions, as well as empathizing with and responding appropriately to the emotions of others with kindness, empathy, respect, and sincerity. In addition, to accurately perceive and respond, the psyche must be put in check, *As It Pleases God*, to prevent our emotions from being all over the place due to our selfish wants, needs, and desires.

Through self-regulation of our sensory faculties and understanding *Divine Expectations*, we can monitor ourselves on a moment-by-moment basis to unlock our full potential and take charge of our lives. Furthermore, we must do this for ourselves; we cannot expect someone else to do this for us...God expects us to put in the necessary work to keep the enemy from gaining leverage over the psyche.

Why must we do this for ourselves, especially when help is available? Yes, help may be available, but in the Eye of God with *Divine Expectations*, we must put in the work, Spiritually Tilling our own ground, using the Fruits of the Spirit, and behaving Christlike. If not, we can become a toxic cesspool with rotten fruits all over the place without realizing it or thinking we are the victim.

For example, if our emotions are a negative cesspool, they will spill over into the lives of others, sucking them in by default. How is it possible to become a cesspool, especially as a Believer? Without pointing the finger, let us talk about a cesspool for a moment. Picture this: A cesspool is a sizeable underground vessel that is used for the temporary storage of sewage and wastewater and is designed to be emptied periodically by a vacuum truck. If it is not vacuumed out, it will overflow its walls, contaminating the ground surrounding it and spreading disease with an unpleasant, putrid odor. Not only do cesspools pose serious health risks, but they also contribute to environmental pollution, and they are septic. In short, this is what negativity does to the human psyche, making it a dumping ground for toxicity, and this is NOT what God has in mind for us.

Thus, in *The Spiritual Middleman Approach*, it is our responsibility to convert a negative cesspool into a stream of palatable, flowing water, quenching the thirst of all mankind for the GREATER GOOD. *"But whoever drinks of the water that I shall give him will never thirst. But the water that I shall give him will become in him a fountain of water springing up into everlasting life."* John 4:14.

In the Eye of God, to be successful in personal, professional, and Spiritual settings, developing emotional intelligence is crucial in perfecting the Fruits of the Spirit and being Christlike with self-awareness, self-regulation, self-mirroring, self-motivation, and self-correcting with a work-in-progress mentality. Plus, by opting out of this process, the enemy can gain leverage.

How is it possible to give the enemy accessible leverage in our lives? Does the enemy not already have access, especially if we behave like them, indulging in unrighteousness without repentance? I am not here to pass judgment...so I will plead the 5th on this one.

Amid all, we should exercise extreme caution if we find ourselves running around playing pretend, becoming provoked or manipulated easily, compromising what the Word of God says, stuck on negative, and indulging in all types of foolery. Why? Behaving in such a manner gives the enemy leverage to use their strengths to pounce on, accuse, and manipulate what we are in denial of, breaking or oppressing us to the core, to satiate their ego. Believe it or not, when we are broken to the core, it becomes difficult for a wounded person to fight back or take responsibility without Divine Intervention.

What is the purpose of Divine Intervention? We are Spiritual Beings having a human experience; therefore, we must connect back to the SOURCE, *As It Pleases God*, and not as it pleases us. If not, we will lose ground Mentally, Physically, and Emotionally until we come to ourselves, awakening from our slumber. In so many words, we must look toward Heaven from whence our strength cometh, cover ourselves with the Blood of Jesus, and invoke the Holy Spirit to help amid our weaknesses, frailties, mistakes, quirks, or whatever.

Spiritual Gird

In the same way that the enemy uses their worldly tools against us to oppress, torment, divide, and weaken on their behalf, we can do likewise. With *The Spiritual Middleman Approach*, we must exercise our God-Given rights to use our Spiritual Tools as leverage according to the Word of God to deliver, comfort, unite, and strengthen. For this reason, when we become transparent about our weaknesses, repenting and working on them consistently, *As It Pleases God*, using the Fruits of the Spirit, and exhibiting Christlike Character, we inadvertently build and strengthen our Spiritual Girds by default. In addition, it causes all things to work in our favor, sometimes turning our weaknesses into our greatest strengths.

What is a Spiritual Gird? It is the Spiritual Means or Garment of Divine Training and Positioning as a Believer in the Faith of the Holy Trinity with the Word of God according to our Blueprinted Destiny. What does all of this mean? We gain Spiritual Strength and Mobility through the Head Chief in charge by putting on the Whole Armor of God to withstand the enemy's wiles. If we ignore Him and our reason for being, we defy Divine Order according to the Heavenly of Heavens.

Here is what the Bible says, *"The LORD reigns, He is clothed with majesty; The LORD is clothed, He has girded Himself with strength. Surely the world is established, so that it cannot be moved."* Psalm 93:1. *"Let your waist be girded and your lamps burning; and you yourselves be like men who wait for their master, when he will return from the wedding, that when he comes and knocks they may open to him immediately. Blessed are those servants whom the master, when he comes, will find watching. Assuredly, I say to you that he will gird himself and have them sit down to eat, and will come and serve them. And if he should come in the second watch, or come in the third watch, and find them so, blessed are those servants."* Luke 12:35-38.

In essence, we must stay on READY, period! According to the *Divine Expectations* from the Heavenly of Heavens, we must put our flesh under subjection to avoid unreadiness or disqualification in the Eye of God. *"But I discipline my body and bring it into subjection, lest, when I have preached to others, I myself should become disqualified."* 1 Corinthians 9:27.

How do we put ourselves under Spiritual Subjection as Believers? We need our Father in Heaven, the Blood of Jesus as a formal sacrifice, and the Holy Spirit to guide us on the path of righteousness. Suppose we omit any one of the three. In this case, we will find ourselves fighting against each other over religion, mistreating others, speaking waywardly, degrading people, competing against everyone, being hateful, consumed with ungratefulness, blinded by greed, and the list goes on, while appearing right in our own eyes.

Why would we appear right in our own eyes when we are all so wrong in the Eye of God? Regardless of how well we paint the picture of our lives, when we do not place God first, *As It Pleases Him*, it will result in some form of idolatry and selfishness, even if we are holier-than-thou. In all simplicity, knowingly or unknowingly engaging in idolatry causes us to become Spiritually Disarmed in areas where we need to be fully armed with the Weapons of Warfare.

Here is what God wants us to know about *Divine Expectations*, even if we get nothing else from this chapter. "*I am the LORD, and there is no other; There is no God besides Me. I will gird you, though you have not known Me, That they may know from the rising of the sun to its setting that there is none besides Me. I am the LORD, and there is no other; I form the light and create darkness, I make peace and create calamity; I, the LORD, do all these things.*" Isaiah 45:5-7.

As Believers, most often, we do not understand how to apply Spiritual Principles correctly to ward off the oppressive nature of the enemy. What does this mean? The enemy plants seeds of discord or deception, similar to what happened to Adam and Eve in the Garden of Eden. If we do not understand what the Word of God says about unrighteous seeds, we will allow them to germinate within the human psyche, like sipping up slimy slop, thinking it is the best thing since sliced bread.

Without uprooting, regrafting, or counteracting it with righteousness and positivity, we will begin to deceive ourselves without realizing what is happening. From experience, it is easy to say the enemy is defeated or under our feet...but what do we do when the enemy's foot is on our neck or has yoked our children? What do we do when we are sleeping with the enemy? What do we do when the enemy is within? Wait, wait, wait...do not answer this; let us go deeper.

From my perspective, as a Child of the Most High God, I do not want to hear what you say...I want to see what you do, how you behave, what you sacrifice, and how you treat another human being who can do NOTHING for you. What is the big deal, especially when we know the Word of God, and that is all we need? Unfortunately, this is how we are deceived.

For the record, the enemy knows the Word of God better than we proclaim. Plus, they also use Spiritual Principles to turn us against ourselves because we lack the application of the Divine Truth. As we sit on our hands or twiddle our thumbs, we do not know what to do when the enemy comes for us or our BLOODLINE.

Then again, we think grace is going to save us when we are behaving like hellions on wheels, knowing nothing about the Fruits of the Spirit, behaving Christlike, correctly applying the Blood of Jesus, and becoming ONE with the Holy Spirit. To add insult to injury, we are unable to self-correct, repent, forgive, or exhibit respectfulness, breaking our homes with our bare hands without realizing it.

This cluelessness cannot happen on my watch, not now and not ever...we need to KNOW the *Divine Expectations* for our Heaven on Earth Experience, *As It Pleases God* to protect ourselves and those around us. It is imperative to know what to do, going toe-to-toe with the enemy with the Word of God, breaking any form of stronghold sent to steal, kill, and destroy.

The Fairytale of Warfare

Most think that Spiritual Warfare is a fairytale, not realizing they are living a full-blown lie. So, my question is, 'Where is the fairytale really residing?' Exactly! The fairytale is within us, especially if we are full of lies or trying to prove ourselves worthy to people, especially when leaving God out of our equational efforts! Here is what we need to know: *"But the hour is coming, and now is, when the true worshipers will worship the Father in Spirit and Truth; for the Father is seeking such to worship Him. God is Spirit, and those who worship Him must worship in Spirit and Truth."* John 4:23-24. Please allow me to break this down into layman's terms with *The Spiritual Middleman Approach* in mind:

- ☐ God requires us to KNOW the Signs of the Time.
- ☐ God requires us to UNDERSTAND the value associated with worshiping Him.
- ☐ God requires a *Spirit to Spirit* Relationship for us to RECEIVE the Divine Wisdom, Secrets, and Mysteries from the Ancient of Days.
- ☐ God requires TRUTH and transparency to ATTAIN the Spiritual Seals from the Heavenly of Heavens.
- ☐ God requires us to BECOME CLEAR about His Divine Expectations.

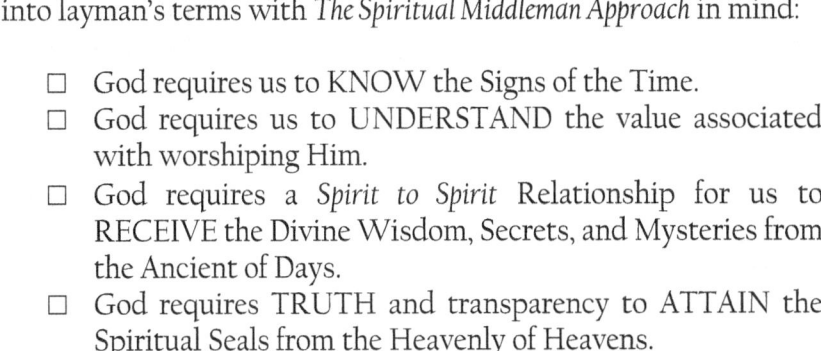

Fairytale or warfare, God does not hide His *Divine Expectations*; it is a matter of whether we will heed to them. Attempting to contend with the enemy using debauched tactics will place us into a state of déjà vu or ultimate compromise. Listen, we need to use the Fruits of the Spirit and operate with Christlike Character to ward off the enemy's wiles, understanding we are all a work-in-progress.

In *The Fairytale of Warfare*, we must continually work on ourselves on a moment-by-moment basis. Why do we need to put in the work, mainly when Jesus paid the price on the cross for us? We can forgive ourselves, repent, and self-correct midair when we err. Unfortunately, it is not a matter of if we err; it is a matter of when. Even if we pretend to be perfect, in the Eye of God, this is not the case. Here is the truth about this matter: *"Where do wars and fights come from among you? Do they not come from your desires for pleasure that war in your members?"* James 4:1.

Whether we are Believers, holier-than-thou, humbly serving the Kingdom, a hellion on wheels, a Spiritual Outlaw, or however we classify ourselves, we must all walk in the Spirit, *As It Pleases God*. Why? We are Spiritual Beings having a human experience, so we must approach God in Spirit and Truth. Doing so enables the conscience or Spiritual Compass to clue us in on when to self-correct to avoid division, debauchery, strife, and overcome whatever with whomever. Can this really help us? Absolutely!

Here is the Spiritual Seal: *"I say then: Walk in the Spirit, and you shall not fulfill the lust of the flesh. For the flesh lusts against the Spirit, and the Spirit against the flesh; and these are contrary to one another, so that you do not do the things that you wish. But if you are led by the Spirit, you are not under the law."* Galatians 5:16-18.

According to Kingdom Standards, we can better train the human psyche to behave appropriately in public or private when strategically aligned with the Fruits of the Spirit and governed by the Holy Spirit. The moment we attempt to operate with rotten, negative fruits as Spiritual Ammunition without the Holy Trinity, we inadvertently shoot ourselves in the foot, especially when thinking we can overcome the enemy with his method of operation.

Come on...once again, the enemy knows Scripture better than us, so they know how we should behave, and if we operate out of character, they already know they have the upper hand.

Our behavior is considered seeds to the sower, regardless of whether it is positive or negative, right or wrong, just or unjust, and so on. How is this possible when the seed to the sower is referring to the Word of God? The Word of God is written on the heart of everyone; therefore, no one can say they do not know; they are simply NOT aligned or AWAKENED to it due to some form of Spiritual Blindness, Deafness, or Muteness. Here is what we need to know: *"Then His disciples asked Him, saying, 'What does this parable mean?' And He said, 'To you it has been given to know the mysteries of the Kingdom of God, but to the rest it is given in parables, that seeing they may not see, And hearing they may not understand.' Now the parable is this: The seed is the Word of God."* Luke 4:9-11.

Here is what happens to the Word of God, determining what type of fruits it will bring forth based on one's stance:

- ☐ *"Those by the wayside are the ones who hear; then the devil comes and takes away the word out of their hearts, lest they should believe and be saved."* Luke 4:12.

- ☐ *"But the ones on the rock are those who, when they hear, receive the word with joy; and these have no root, who believe for a while and in time of temptation fall away."* Luke 4:13.

- ☐ "Now the ones that fell among thorns are those who, when they have heard, go out and are choked with cares, riches, and pleasures of life, and bring no fruit to maturity." Luke 4:14.

- ☐ "But the ones that fell on the good ground are those who, having heard the word with a noble and good heart, keep it and bear fruit with patience." Luke 4:15.

What is the purpose of knowing this information? Regardless of whether we live a life of fairytale or reality, nothing goes unnoticed, even if we are experts at hiding things. According to Scripture, *"No one, when he has lit a lamp, covers it with a vessel or puts it under a bed, but sets it on a lampstand, that those who enter may see the light. For nothing is secret that will not be revealed, nor anything hidden that will not be known and come to light."* Luke 4:16-17.

In *The Fairytale of Warfare*, it is best to come clean with God in our *Spirit to Spirit* Connection, ensuring we can get rid of the weeds, seeds, and deeds of deception and debauchery to avoid any DNA Hiccups.

DNA Hiccups

We all desire the Promises of God, but why are some of His Divine Promises held up? Could it be that we are not surrendering, *As It Pleases Him*, and want Him to bow down to us? Is it possible that we need to understand His *Divine Expectations* better to properly ALIGN ourselves with His Promises, *As It Pleases Him*? Then again, are we not ready, are we not adequately equipped, or do we have a DNA Hiccup?

We can sit around laughing, doubting, pouting, or criticizing, but when it is all said and done, *"God is not a man, that He should lie, nor a son of man, that He should repent. Has He said, and will He not do? Or has He spoken, and will He not make it good?"* Numbers 23:19.

The Promises of God are real, and if the Holy Spirit has not confirmed this from within, we have work to do. Why? If we do not know our place in the Kingdom, we become overlooked by Spiritual Omission due to the lack of Spiritual Growth, outright Spiritual Error, or *DNA Hiccups*.

According to the Heavenly of Heavens, due to our Spiritual DNA, without the elements of growth in and out of the Kingdom, it becomes challenging to WIN in the Eye of God, even if we are in denial. Listen, if we are growing in the things of the world and NOT growing in the Kingdom, we create Spiritual Deficits by default, depriving ourselves of our Blueprinted Benefits. How is this possible, especially when everything we need is already? We choose our course in life of our own free will, even if we have been PREDESTINED for a specific mission.

Here is what we need to know: *"I call Heaven and Earth as witnesses today against you, that I have set before you life and death, blessing and cursing; therefore choose life, that both you and your descendants may live; that you may love the LORD your God, that you may obey His voice, and that you may cling to Him, for He is your life and the length of your days; and that you may dwell in the land which the LORD swore to your fathers, to Abraham, Isaac, and Jacob, to give them."* Deuteronomy 30:19-20.

In the Promises of God, our Predestined Blueprint will NOT impede upon our self-made or self-willed plans. Why? What God has for us requires us by the sweat of our brows to WANT it, TILL for it, UNDERSTAND it, PREPARE for it, and POSITION ourselves accordingly. Blasphemy, right? Wrong. *"In the sweat of your face you shall eat bread Till you return to the ground, For out of it you were taken; For dust you are, And to dust you shall return."* Genesis 3:19.

If we do none of them (If we do not want, till, understand, prepare, or position ourselves for it), we become limited by default. And due to this *DNA Hiccup*, our lives become a cycle of déjà vu until we come to ourselves or awaken from our slumber.

On top of the repetitive cycles with various characters, Heaven and Earth become witnesses to our Seasons, Seeds, and Vicissitudes. At the same time, they do what it takes to get our attention, allowing the Winds of Life to shake us to the core. Or, they may even do a number on the human psyche to awaken the desire to seek help, pushing us out of our comfort zones and blocking us from particular Spiritual Gardens, similar to the Adam and Eve Experience.

What do Heaven and Earth have to do with anything, especially when we have the right to live our lives the way we desire? First and foremost, we did not create ourselves. Secondly, this is a God-Ruled Nation, even if it does not appear as such to the naked eye. Thirdly, we are all children of God, even if we fail to admit it. Lastly, if everything in Heaven and on Earth obeys God, what makes us any different? Or do we think we get a FREE PASS?

Unbeknown to most, DISOBEDIENCE contributed to the *DNA hiccups* within mankind in the first place. Therefore, if we do not WILLFULLY obey God, we cannot blame anyone or anything for the reality in which we experience. Why must we assume responsibility? When we are disobedient, it does not begin or end with God; it is a manifestation leading to all manner of self-deficiency. What does this mean in layman's terms? We overlook a human plague that cannot be seen with the naked eye until the damage is done from the inside out, even affecting the innocent until it is Spiritually Contained.

What does all of this have to do with the Promises of God? Once again, we are Spiritual Beings having a human experience in Earthen Vessels. If we fail to understand this fact, Divine Wisdom avoids us, and our Spiritual Blueprint lays dormant until we are ready. Furthermore, we become Spiritually Blind, Deaf, and Mute in Kingdom Formalities, heeding to the people, places, and things of our worldly system without restraint.

To add insult to injury, we fall into the trap of thinking everyone around us has issues without taking a second look in the mirror. Listen, if we fail to see ourselves clearly from God's Divine Perspective, omit His *Divine Expectations*, or fail to examine ourselves correctly while lacking humility and gratefulness, we commit Spiritual Purgery upon ourselves without realizing it.

If we do not RESPECT who we are in Spirit and Truth, the Realm of the Spirit will not trust us with its Divine or Mysterious Secrets and Powers. Why do we get deprived? Due to the probability of its selfish misuse. For example, this is similar to King Saul's selfish misuse of power, which put a *DNA Hiccup* into his Bloodline. While, at the same time, secretly coveting God's Elect

(The Prophet Samuel and King David) and attempting to change the trajectory of God's Divine Will to fit his wants, needs, and desires, feeding the lust of the eyes, the lust of the flesh, and the pride of life.

As It Pleases God, I am not here to point the finger; I am here to Spiritually Guide us on properly using our hands in the Eye of God. What does this mean? I am Divinely Appointed to bring a Supernatural Awareness, giving the Spiritual Tools needed to help us become Kingdomly Mindful. What is the purpose of becoming MINDFUL in such a manner? Frankly, we all have a little bit of this Saul Spirit running through our veins; however, once again, this plague must be Spiritually Contained, especially when God's Promises are involved.

Our Heaven on Earth Experience has genuinely BLESSED us beyond imagination, even if we are Spiritually Blind, Deaf, or Mute to the Plans or Purposes of God. What is more, God's Divine Ways and Mercies are granted to us daily, even if we choose not to pay attention or lift our fingers to praise Him—He is FAITHFUL. Nevertheless, our Creator stands at full attention, watching and waiting to see what we will do and how we will respond to what we have dominion over, especially when it comes to our Divine Blueprint.

According to the Heavenly of Heavens, the *Divine Expectations* of the Kingdom are hidden in the 360-Degree Internal View we have of ourselves. Once we understand what God expects from us, we can solidify our performance methods, *As It Pleases Him* to avoid *Winning the War and Losing the Kingdom.*

So, if you are ready to become a Spiritual Ambassador for the Kingdom, *As God Promised*, let us go deeper to develop the *Spirit to Spirit* Connection together as ONE.

CHAPTER TWO
Winning the War and Losing the Kingdom

"But now He has obtained a more excellent ministry, inasmuch as He is also Mediator of a better covenant, which was established on better promises." Hebrews 8:6.

Amid living life to the full comes with ups and downs beyond what we could care to imagine, which are commonly referred to as the Vicissitudes, Cycles, or Seasons of Life. Yet, in our daily lives, if we are Winning Wars and losing the Kingdom, then one must eventually ask, 'What is the purpose of fighting?'

Are we fighting to be seen? Are we fighting for an image? Are we fighting to have the last word? Are we fighting for control? Are we fighting to support our hidden or open biases? Are we fighting to stay on top? Are we fighting to appear as if we have it all together? Are we fighting to prove ourselves worthy, especially when we know we are rotten to the core? Are we fighting with ourselves, contending with the critic from within? Are we fighting to keep our tongues from sinking ships? Are we fighting to play clean up out of a mess we made due to the lack of discipline or self-control? Are we fighting for power, money, or ungoverned lustful pleasures?

One would ask, 'What is the purpose of asking these questions?' Most often, we are fighting battles we do not have a clue about the reasons why. In so many words, we are wasting energy, cluelessly working against ourselves, thinking we are right in our own eyes.

Yet, in our obliviousness, our motives, thoughts, words, biases, and desires are unrighteous in the Eye of God, contradicting Kingdom Standards and Principles we may already know but choose to ignore.

For the record, the heart's denied or ignored underlying motives have God absolutely livid with us! Why would God become livid, especially when we have free will to do whatever, with whomever? It is because we are laying foolery and folly at His doorstep or using His Holy Name in vain, capitalizing when we should be Spiritually Strategizing with Kingdom Principles.

Frankly, among the Saints proclaiming HOLINESS, they do not realize that their behaviors, thoughts, words, actions, attitudes, and demeanor are straight from the PIT! Nor do they take the time to understand Kingdom Prerequisites while proclaiming that the Holy Spirit is saying this or that. In all actuality, it is a familiar Spirit speaking to incite chaos, confusion, or disrespectfulness to provoke, accuse, abuse, use, reject, or defame.

With all due respect, 'Have we NO shame about how we conduct ourselves amongst the sheep, from our houses to the pulpit and abroad?' Yet, we care about putting on a show, pretending to be more than we are, mainly before people, but giving a rat's tail about how we are appearing in the Eye of God.

Listen to me, and listen well: The known and unknown sheep who are in a fold and the field are meticulously watching us based on our presentations. What does this mean? Depending upon how we make people feel, we initiate the feelings of being worthy or unworthy, valuable or invaluable, accepted or rejected, supported or unsupported, and so on, based upon the fruits of our lips, behaviors, and actions. For this reason, in the Kingdom, we do not bank on lip service; we look for the FRUITS of the Spirit, period.

Understandably, no one is perfect, but we all stand to be corrected, we are all trainable, and we all determine the types of fruit we will bear, regardless! Clearly, this does not mean we have to kiss up to anyone, play the fool, or indulge in unrighteousness; it means we should exhibit KINDNESS and COMPASSION in our words, deeds, thoughts, and demeanor in the Spirit of Excellence, with outright integrity, while keeping it moving in the Spirit of Righteousness.

Sadly, if we take an honest poll, we will find that many of us DO NOT know the DIFFERENCE between positive and negative behaviors, words, beliefs, character traits, thoughts, demeanor, and body language. Why do we not know the difference, especially when educated? Education has nothing to do with knowing the difference between the two from a Spiritual Perspective, according to Divine Laws. It is knowing how to, when to, why to, where to, and with whom to apply the differences to varying experiences, *As It Pleases God* and not to please ourselves.

Unfortunately, it means it is not about reading it in a book; it is about actively applying it to real-life situations, circumstances, and events at the right time with Spiritual Discernment that comes through practical USE. Frankly, the usability of positives and negatives, as well as the counteractions, will vary from person to person based upon their traumas, background, conditioning, biases, perspective, religious dogmas, and the list goes on. For a time such as this, the Oracles of God are ordained to call this behavior to the forefront for corrective action. If not, the warring within the human psyche will continue to zap our innocent children right before our very eyes.

Personally, it breaks my heart to see innocent victims needing help from the inside out being led to the slaughter due to unresolved or rotten fruit from the Shepherds called to lead the flock. Thus, they lack the Spiritual Finesse, Pristineness, and Savvy to implement or penetrate the core of individuals, *As It Pleases God*.

What is the big deal as long as we are Believers and deliver the Word of God? Delivering the Word to please ourselves or our agenda and living by example, *As It Pleases Him*, is not the same in the Eye of God. I was one of those sheep led to the slaughter by those proclaiming to be sent from God. Yet, they possessed internal wickedness and debauched character without realizing it, with a long trail of rotten fruits that appeared good in their own eyes.

In addition, they were gung-ho about telling me what to do but providing ZERO know-how, how-to, why-to, why-not, where-to, when-to, or with whom to do or not to. Meanwhile, manipulation was provided as a guise to cover up the lack of Spiritual Wisdom, Understanding, and Restoration when queried or when their behavior was called into question.

On the other hand, only to have the ungodly with good hearts pick me up out of the mud, dusting me off with a helping hand of hope. Once again, it was the outright non-believing individuals who took it upon themselves to set me back on the path toward the Kingdom to become the Leading Oracle of God for a time such as this, with outright humility. For this reason, we should never judge who God uses to help us get back on our feet.

Is it not a bit arrogant to proclaim to be the Leading Oracle of God? Maybe or maybe not, but I carry myself in a way that only the Holy Spirit will reveal this to someone in totality. Whereas, with all other means, they will only have limited knowledge and understanding of my Spiritual Positioning. By far, this allows me to see straight through them, gleaning the necessary information I need to EXTRACT and CONVERT into Divine Wisdom to feed God's sheep.

In exposing the truth, once the ungodly realized who they were helping, they wanted to recruit me for their mission of folly after the fact. For this reason, we must become rooted and grounded in the Word of God with the Fruits of the Spirit, exhibiting Christlike Character without fail or compromise. If I did not know I was Divinely Called and Spiritually Marked from a young age, I could have been swept away in an alternative direction or compromised my integrity.

How can someone possess good fruits and be ungodly at the same time? Having good fruits and exhibiting the Fruits of the Spirit are two different entities in themselves. Poshness is trainable, but when it comes down to motives, the ungodly will make their requests known in due time; we only need to listen long enough, setting a Spiritual Guard over our tongues. As a forewarning, if we talk too much, we will miss our Spiritual Cues of when to hold, fold, or walk away. Whereas, with the Fruits of the Spirit, the Holy Spirit is doing the training to fine-tune our motives from ungodly to Godly, unrighteous to righteous, negative to positive, wrong to right, and so on.

In or out of our transitional phase or fall from grace, it is imperative to become GRATEFUL for everyone, everything, and each experience, capturing the Spiritual Lessons hidden in them all. What is the purpose of doing so? We never know who is designed to help, inspire, nurture, teach, mentor, or direct us toward our

Divine Blueprint or Destiny Enriched Provisions. For the record, God will use anything or anyone to accomplish His whatever. Plus, the ungodly know when to back up from an Anointed One who knows who they are. It is the Godly appearing righteous, wearing a mask, in training, or a wolf in sheep's clothing who ignores Divine Revelation, not knowing who is whom or what is what.

What would cause this to happen, primarily if we are sold out to the Kingdom? We need the Holy Spirit to reveal this information for Divine Clarity in our *Spirit to Spirit* Relations. What about the ungodly? They also receive revelation from a familiar Spirit or the Spiritual Apparatus called the conscience, letting them know it is better to move on to a weaker vessel. Plus, they would rather digress than contend, subjecting themselves to a curse or getting themselves cast into the Abyss.

To be clear, just because we are caught up does not mean God will not use us, especially if our hearts are righteous. Unbeknown to most, those caught up usually know the value encapsulated in helping those in the commission of their Divine Destiny. While at the same time, receiving the Divine Blessings that would cover them amid their ungodliness. From my perspective, this is similar to Rahab, who was labeled as a prostitute by most and rejected by many. More importantly, regardless of her label, she had a righteous heart in helping the spies with the Mission of God to save her family. Through this one act of faith, she became the wife of one of the spies, marrying into the Tribe of Judah, which put her into the lineage of Jesus. We can read about it in Joshua 2-6.

Here is what we need to know: *"But the LORD said to Samuel, 'Do not look at his appearance or at his physical stature, because I have refused him. For the LORD does not see as man sees; for man looks at the outward appearance, but the LORD looks at the heart.'* " 1 Samuel 16:7. For this reason, as long as I have breath in my body, the Devil is a liar, and we are going to slay the internal giants crippling our legacy and children once and for all! So, let us go deeper.

Listen, unbeknown to most, defamation of character runs rampant among the operation of familiar Spirits to secretly assassinate the truly righteous individuals who possess the Fruits of the Spirit and Christlike Character, *As It Pleases God*. However, when knowingly or unknowingly operating in such a manner, it can lead to an aborted Blueprint, lost Spiritual Mantles, and Generational Curses. Why? If we are making a conscious effort to thwart the Spiritual Blueprint of another, do we think that for a minute, we will not become affected by the negative seeds sown? They will bear fruit!

Even if we do not understand the impact or importance of Seasons, Vicissitudes, or Cycles and how they operate, they have a job to do. What type of job would they have? According to the Heavenly of Heavens, their Divine Purpose is to establish balance, weed out imbalances, and do what they are designed to do without our permission, bringing about Divine Order.

Actually, this is similar to what happened to the older generation of the Children of Israel when they were forbidden to go into the Promised Land because of the negative bickering, fussing, fighting, complaining, and operating in a Spirit of Bondage instead of Spiritual Liberation. Amid all, regardless of whether the Seasons, Cycles, or Vicissitudes rain on our parades, create drought in our deserts, or put us in time-out. When *Winning The War*, as long as the sun rises in the east and sets in the west, there is always hope for us if we dare to get an UNDERSTANDING, *As It Pleases God*, not man.

Spiritual Mantles

Spiritual Mantles have transferred from one Bloodline to another throughout the Bible due to known and unknown acts of willful disobedience. Of course, there are many presumable reasons documented in the Scriptures. Still, indeed, most are not, as they become our hidden secrets and unresolved traumas with a continuous cycle of déjà vu.

When dealing with *Spiritual Mantles*, whether we are exposing or hiding whatever or with whomever, they all link back to the inherent vices of disobedience, especially when we are taking advantage of a person, place, or thing, banking on grace or forgiveness to bail us out. Simply put, just because God bails us out in our folly does not mean we will not be absolved of responsibility, especially when we continue to exhibit the same behaviors over and over without repenting, forgiving, and changing for the better.

What does responsibility have to do with grace and forgiveness? From my perspective, this is similar to continually filling a bucket with rocks, hoping it will never break. Then, when we least expect it, the bucket gives way due to the NATURAL LAW of Thermodynamics (wear and tear) and the Law of Gravity, pulling everything to the earth's core and causing the rocks to fall out. Unbeknown to most, once a Natural or Spiritual Law is broken, regardless of the reasonable or unreasonable wear and tear, another Natural or Spiritual Law comes into play, irrespective of whether we understand it or not.

The funny thing about *Winning Wars and Losing Kingdoms* is that God proactively sends a forewarning. In my opinion, it is like He gives us a heads-up on what to do or not to do before any formidable action takes place. Why would God do such a thing? He does it to see if we are worthy of the *Spiritual Mantle*, primarily if we are gleaning from another man's reservoir. What does this mean? When we are gleaning from another man's Divine Gifting, Calling, or Creativity, who is also in Purpose on purpose, it is like we are gleaning from God Himself. Therefore, we must exhibit the utmost respect.

What does respect have to do with anything? Suppose we do not respect another man's Spiritual Gifts or Journey. In this case, the *Spiritual Mantle* we think we are worthy of having, we inadvertently relinquish to another Bloodline due to some form of Spiritual Omission or Negligence.

Without being Spiritually Unveiled, we may not know or recognize what or who God is using in our own strength. Therefore, we need the Holy Spirit and the covering of the Blood of Jesus to place respective filters and discernment in the appropriate places. More importantly, it behooves us to be on our best behavior at all times with the Fruits of the Spirit, exhibiting Christlike Character. Even if we do not feel like it or think someone or something is not worthy of our respectfulness, do it anyway! Plus, we never want to lose our Spiritual Crowns over negative foolery or provocations.

Spiritually Engaging, *As It Pleases God*, helps us build value and consistency in what we are doing and why. More importantly, it prevents inner folly, frugality, or cheating ourselves out of what is already in our DNA. What is the purpose of knowing this information? When dealing with *Spiritual Mantles* or using *The Spiritual Middleman Approach*, possessing an inferiority complex contributes to all other forms of negative actions, behaviors, and thoughts. Really? Yes, really! *"But after you shall arise another kingdom inferior to yours; then another, a third kingdom of bronze, which shall rule over all the earth. And the fourth kingdom shall be as strong as iron, inasmuch as iron breaks in pieces and shatters everything; and like iron that crushes, that kingdom will break in pieces and crush all the others."* Daniel 2:39-40.

We are designed to rise and build, not oppress and tear down ourselves or others. So, if we think we have the upper hand in life and are still battling with envy, jealousy, pride, greed, coveting, and competitiveness, it is fair to say that one's *Spiritual Mantle* is hanging in the balance. For this reason, it is imperative to examine ourselves according to the expectations set forth by our Heavenly Father. Why? Now is not the time to become reckless with anything or anyone. According to the Heavenly of Heavens, we do not want any form of unfavorable Spiritual Judgment causing us to become delayed or denied of the Promises of God or His Divine Benefits.

Toe Stubbing

As It Pleases God, it is always WISE to place the Kingdom first and then the war, instead of warring it out, thinking about the Kingdom on the backend or as a point of manipulation. What is the purpose of operating in such a manner? Some battles are best left alone, and if we do not involve the Holy Trinity, *The Spiritual Middleman Approach*, or the Kingdom in the matter, we are left to our own devices. At the same time, it appears to the naked eye as if we are winning, but with the Spiritual Eye of God, we have stubbed our big toe.

What does *Toe Stubbing* have to do with Winning, Wars, or Kingdoms? From a human perspective, we look at toes as being repulsive, not understanding the actual Spiritual Value hidden within them. I have always wondered why we have one big toe and four small toes and not all five big or small toes. Here is what I found: First and foremost, we can quickly lose our balance without having a big toe as the foundational backbone or maneuvering support for the small ones.

Secondly, having all big toes, our mobility would be drastically inhibited. If one does not believe this, try tiptoeing without using the big toe for support and watch what happens. Thirdly, having small toes will not provide enough strength to keep us from wobbling all over the place, especially in adulthood, unless we become conditioned during childhood. Yet still, the way shoes are made in today's day and age, we will have a slight disadvantage as opposed to operating according to the natural design of God's Divine Reasonings for having one big toe and four small.

Remarkably, and fourthly, if we accidentally step on someone's big toe, it will often cause them to expose their true colors or fruits while temporarily making a strong man weak. I do not know what it is about this part of the body that causes us to lose our sense of reasoning or instantly forget about our superficial masks, but it works! As a forewarning, DO NOT go about stepping on someone's toe to see their reaction. Theoretically, this is only an analogy provoking our memory of our very own personal responses to having someone step on our toes.

All in all, God knew what He was doing when He created us! Suppose we do not willfully attempt to balance ourselves Mentally, Physically, Emotionally, and Spiritually. In this case, we will begin to trip over ourselves by default, as if we are missing our big toe. Or better yet, we may find ourselves operating without God's Divine Guidance as the Kingdom's Backbone.

In the Ancient of Days, the tip of the ear, thumb, and big toe on the right were sprinkled with blood as a form of consecration. We have been conditioned to judge certain parts of the body and misuse others negatively; however, the ear, thumb, and big toe contain powerful Spiritual Principles we overlook because we are not Spiritually Trained to go DEEP.

For the maximization of *The Spiritual Middleman Approach*, let us go real DEEP for a moment. Suppose we compare our ears with our Spiritual Ear...can we hear the power? Hearing the authentic Voice of God with our Spiritual Ear is key to our Victories and Greatness, paving the way to our *Spirit to Spirit* Relationship, trumping anything known to man.

For example, if we take our thumb, does it not leverage the natural hand? Of course, it does. Well, the same applies to us Spiritually. As a matter of fact, our symbolic thumb bone power gives us even more Spiritual BACKBONE Power and Dominion when using our Spiritual Hand and utilizing our Spiritual Gifts, *As It Pleases God*. How do we make this make sense? In the Realm of the Spirit, approaching God, *As It Pleases Him*, gives us a Supernatural or Spiritual Trombone effect that penetrates the Heavenly of Heavens.

Let us take this a little further: With the big toe, does it not give way to where we place our feet? But suppose we dare to ANOINT the Spiritual Big Toe with humble obedience, the Blood of Jesus, be led by the Holy Spirit, and use the Fruits of the Spirit. In this case, we become a Spiritual Force to be reckoned with, possessing Kingdom Commissionability and Authority without having to say one word.

As we fast forward to our present-day situations, if we surrender the Spiritual Ear, Hand, and Feet to *The Spiritual Middleman Approach, As It Pleases God*, we are subjected to the MOLDING PHASE of the Kingdom. What does this mean for us? The Heavenly of Heavens gets involved and is fully vested in the initiation or outcome of our Divine Blueprint.

How do we surrender the Spiritual Ear, Hand, and Feet? We must get involved in the Spiritual Tilling process, helping ourselves become better and more transparent about our strengths and weaknesses to learn, grow, and sow back into the Kingdom when called upon. Frankly, there are Levels of Spirituality, even if we pretend as if we have arrived. Listen, to graduate from one level to the next, we must become lifetime learners, stepping into the Spiritual Classroom at the drop of a dime, gleaning the relevant information required for our next move, strategy, boost, or bailout.

Fortunately, after this Spiritual Unveiling, we will never look at our toes the same again. Here is the Spiritual Seal that we must know about our toes and the power hidden within them as we move on. *'Whereas you saw the feet and toes, partly of potter's clay and partly of iron, the Kingdom shall be divided; yet the strength of the iron shall be in it, just as you saw the iron mixed with ceramic clay. And as the toes of the feet were partly of iron and partly of clay, so the Kingdom shall be partly strong and partly fragile. As you saw iron mixed with ceramic clay, they will mingle with the seed of men; but they will not adhere to one another, just as iron does not mix with clay. And in the days of these kings the God of Heaven will set up a Kingdom which shall never be destroyed; and the Kingdom shall not be left to other people; it shall break in pieces and consume all these kingdoms, and it shall stand forever."* Daniel 2:41-44.

What if our Divine Promises, Birthrights, and Benefits are irrevocable? As a Word to the Wise, how would we know about them if they are Spiritually Veiled, right? My point exactly...we cannot miss what we cannot measure; therefore, it behooves us to Spiritually Align ourselves with our Heavenly Father on His Terms. From experience, doing so allows Him to Divinely Unveil *What, When, Where, How, Why,* and *With Whom* we must place a Spiritual DEMAND to obtain our Full Portion. For example, the *As It Pleases God* Book Series and Program has always been an Irrevocable Promise. Still, I had to become Spiritually Trained, Tested, and Commissioned to the Divine Unveiling, conferring to my Predestined Blueprint in order to POSSESS it.

For the sake of our Divine Unveiling, *The Spiritual Middleman Approach* is designed to steer us in the right direction to possess all God has for us without settling for a portion or trickles of His Divine Goodness. Besides, if we have to endure the Vicissitudes, Cycles, and Seasons of Life, we may as well get ALL God has for us with no sorrow attached.

Who or What are you investing in?

Are you investing in yourself? Do you know what investing in yourself means from God's Divine Perspective? Will you invest in others? Are you willing to invest in the Kingdom of Heaven? Investing in yourself from the inside out is crucial in the Eye of God. However, investing from the outside only to please yourself or others while doing nothing about your internal well-being DOES NOT impress Him. Why? He does not think like us; He prefers wisdom over superficial images or materialism. *"Wisdom is the principal thing; therefore get wisdom: and with all thy getting get understanding."* Proverbs 4:7.

We are quick to invest in outward appearances without involving God in the equation, especially when He is the Creator of it all. What an insult, right? How would you feel if you created something for someone, and once they got up on their feet, they booted you out, forgot about you, or seemingly spat in your face? Regardless of how Spiritually Grounded you are, it could leave a bad taste in your mouth, especially if you are NOT doing whatever with whomever for the right reasons.

One of the most overlooked commodities is the inability to invest in ourselves, *As It Pleases God*. Then again, according to the Heavenly of Heavens, the obliviousness associated with *Spiritually Investing* in our Spiritual Gifts or Divine Blueprint has placed us in the hot seat with Him. Why are we in the hot seat, mainly when we have free will? It distorts our self-discovery efforts by not seeing ourselves, our fruits, and our character clearly.

According to the Heavenly of Heavens, putting time, money, and effort into improving your skills, knowledge, understanding, and overall well-being to become the best version of yourself for the Greater Good is ideal in the Eye of God. *"How much better to get wisdom than gold, to get insight rather than silver!"* Proverbs 16:16. In addition, becoming wise, *As It Pleases Him*, can lead to better opportunities, career growth, home stability, and Kingdom Usability. By staying up-to-date with the latest trends and developments in your field, according to your Predestined Blueprint, you can position yourself to become a more valuable, noteworthy, and viable person, parent, sibling, mate, friend, partner, employee, entrepreneur, or Believer.

In the Eye of God, acquiring knowledge and wisdom helps you to achieve your goals and desires, maintaining a quality of life to your liking. Here is the desired mindset: *"Whatever you do, work at it with all your heart, as working for the Lord, not for human masters, since you know that you will receive an inheritance from the Lord as a reward. It is the Lord Christ you are serving."* Colossians 3:23-24.

How do we know if we are on the right track? Our desires will give us the lead-in. Really? Yes, really! *"The heart of the discerning acquires knowledge, for the ears of the wise seek it out."* Proverbs 18:15.

We are all unique and have our own set of strengths, weaknesses, desires, interests, and ambitions. Nevertheless, we must put in the work to become wiser and stronger while constantly upgrading our knowledge, skills, talents, abilities, and attitudes, both for our personal growth and to fulfill God's Divine Purpose.

The moment we stop investing in ourselves or refuse to learn, we become stunted Mentally, Physically, Emotionally, Spiritually, or Financially. What is the big deal about investing in ourselves from the inside out as Believers? We claim to love God, but often forget about the learning, growth, and sharing aspects of our reason for being. Instead, we allow negative characteristics to supersede the positive, productive, and fruitful ones.

Here are a few reasons why we avoid investing in ourselves, but not limited to such:

- ☐ Lack of self-awareness.
- ☐ Fear of failure.
- ☐ Lack of motivation.
- ☐ Busy schedules.
- ☐ Financial constraints.
- ☐ Procrastination.
- ☐ Lack of discipline.
- ☐ Negative self-talk.
- ☐ Prioritizing others over ourselves.
- ☐ Lack of external validation.
- ☐ Not knowing where to start.
- ☐ Lack of support from others.
- ☐ Fear of change.
- ☐ Feeling overwhelmed.
- ☐ Perfectionism.
- ☐ Lack of confidence.
- ☐ Feeling unworthy.
- ☐ Believing we know everything already.
- ☐ Not seeing the value in investing in ourselves.

As we meander through life, when investing in ourselves, we tend to forget about the people, places, and things contributing to where we are today, when it only takes a fraction of a second to become grateful. When we are privileged to have something or someone, it is in our nature to seek more outside of the Will of God without realizing it. For this reason, we must add Him to the Spiritual Equation to ensure our Kingdom Capital does not become liabilities in Earthen Vessels.

Furthermore, in all due respect, if we have not taken the time to understand or *Spiritually Invest* in our WHY, then why are we disrespecting the WHY of another or attempting to circumvent it? Here again, amid all, we must ask ourselves a few questions, but not limited to such:

- ☐ Are we *Spiritually Investing* in regrafting our soulish nature?
- ☐ Are we *Spiritually Investing* in having a Positive Mindset?
- ☐ Are we *Spiritually Investing* in our Spirit Man?
- ☐ Are we *Spiritually Investing* in our Spiritual Temple?
- ☐ Are we *Spiritually Investing* in our *Spirit to Spirit* Relations?
- ☐ Are we *Spiritually Investing* in our character?
- ☐ Are we *Spiritually Investing* in our fruits?
- ☐ Are we *Spiritually Investing* in our Divine Blueprint?
- ☐ Are we *Spiritually Investing* in our Dreams, Calling, Talents, Creativity, and Desires?
- ☐ Are we *Spiritually Investing* in our People Skills?

According to the Heavenly of Heavens, if one has answered 'No' to any one of these questions, there is still HOPE. How is this possible? As long as we breathe the Breath of Life, we have another opportunity to get it right in the Eye of God. However, while doing so, we must equip ourselves with Spiritual Tools to prevent unnecessary do-overs that we can get right the first time around.

As life would have it, we are quick to invest in the worldly people, places, and things leading us away from the Kingdom instead of toward it! So, what do we do? We must redirect the Mind, Body, Soul, and Spirit toward Kingdom Standards and Principles, doing a clean sweep of all the known and unknown worldliness, negativity, and debauchery.

Here is the deal: Our *Spiritual Investments* determine whether we are a Profitable or Unprofitable Servant in the Kingdom. Although we can go through the motions, appearing to be one of the two, our Spiritual Fruits and Character reveal the truth, regardless of whether we pay attention or not. Listen, overlooking our Spiritual Fruits and neglecting to exhibit Christlike Character prevents us from *Spiritually Investing* in ourselves, people, places, and things as we should. Why is this the case? It is due to our hidden, overlooked, or denied biases. In addition, it can also be a result of our cultural differences, limiting beliefs, selfishness, jealousy, envy, covetousness, greed, pride, or competitiveness. Even if we sugarcoat the truth, it does not negate the underlying root of whatever, with whomever, or our real WHY.

According to the Heavenly of Heavens, with our Spiritual Investments, we exhibit a form of Godliness, but not the Godliness from the Kingdom of Heaven. What is the difference? If our Godliness is dedicated to destroying, breaking down, hurting, or traumatizing others, we must rethink WHAT we are doing and WHY. When we find ourselves negatively repeating or mirroring how we were treated or traumatized, making others feel the same way we secretly feel without correcting this form of behavior, we cannot lay this at the doorpost of the Kingdom. Why? If we think being nasty, rude, violent, disrespectful, and obnoxious represents the Kingdom, then we are sadly mistaken, regardless of the mask that we convey in the presence of others.

In the Kingdom, we deal with Righteousness, not unrighteousness! For this reason, it is imperative to *Spiritually Invest* in ourselves, developing our Spiritual Fruits and Character, *As It Pleases God*. Of course, this does not make us perfect; actually, it makes us a work-in-progress, being able to apologize, repent, forgive, or self-correct at the drop of a dime. What makes this so important? It helps prevent the negative festering or manifestation of debauched charactorial fruits.

The bottom line is that playing pretend does not get us brownie points in the Kingdom; we must put in the work for ourselves. The Fruits of the Spirit and Christlike Character do not come pre-packaged on a shelf. They are already within us; we must dust them off and put them to work in our favor. More importantly, no one can do this for us; we are the best *Do-It-Yourself* Project known to man.

If we want all God has to offer us, we must do our due diligence. If not, we will settle for a portion of our Birthright, Promises, or Blessings, especially when it takes the same amount of energy, if not more, to walk away than it would to walk toward it. Really? Yes, really! For starters, we must *Spiritually Invest* in the Fruits of the Spirit, which gives Spiritual Leverage while filtering out the old man.

What are the Fruits of the Spirit? According to Galatians 5:22-23, they are Love, Joy, Peace, Patience, Kindness, Goodness, Faithfulness, Gentleness, and Self-Control. Why do we need to use the Spiritual Fruits as a part of our *Spiritual Investment*? *"Against such there is no law."* In so many words, they will take us from a victim mentality to being the VICTOR, causing ALL things to work together for our good, regardless of how it appears to the naked eye.

Listen, a real Champion in the Eye of God possesses the Fruits of the Spirit and exhibits Christlike Character with outright humility. However, it also helps us differentiate the wolves in sheep's clothing or when to exercise extreme caution. If we miss the Spiritual Cues naturally embedded in the Fruits of the Spirit, we can get sucker-punched or tossed around with the Vicissitudes of life easily. So, we must pay attention, get out of our feelings, and tame our thoughts; if not, we can become royally played in the Game of Life. How is this possible when we are on top of our game? Whether we are at the top or bottom of our game, it is a matter of perception. The enemy can smell our weaknesses a mile away, and if we hide, deny, or overlook them, they will hang us out to dry.

As a *Spiritual Investment* into ourselves, we must adequately align everything about ourselves with the Will of God or our Divine Blueprint, covering them with the Blood of Jesus. Why? We can put on the Whole Armor of God with confidence, knowing we are operating with clean hands and a pure repenting heart. Doing so prevents the enemy from using our secrets as an uppercut to knock the breath out of us or provide a breeding ground for compromise.

On the other hand, if we are out of Purpose, in denial, or contradicting the reason for our being, then we must ask, 'Are we really on top of our game?' 'Were we positioned by luck?' 'Are we riding on God's grace and mercy?' Or, 'Are we playing ourselves short?'

What is the importance of the Fruits of the Spirit and Christlike Character? It helps us become and remain Spiritually Righteous in the Eye of God, NOT in the eye of man. Here is what we need to know about our Spiritual WHY: *"And this I pray, that your love may abound still more and more in knowledge and all discernment, that you may approve the things that are excellent, that you may be sincere and without offense till the day of Christ, being filled with the fruits of righteousness which are by Jesus Christ, to the glory and praise of God."* Philippians 1:9-11.

Although God loves us all, *"For He makes His sun rise on the evil and on the good, and sends rain on the just and on the unjust."* Matthew 5:45. However, for those who listen, understand, learn, and obey the Will and Word of God, *As It Pleases Him*, their Spiritual Eyes become open to what the Spiritually Blind cannot see or comprehend. Plus, it helps us to establish ONE MIND with the Kingdom of Heaven, ensuring we are not intentionally dividing ourselves and others with selfish ambitions. Here is what Philippians 2:1-5 says: *"Therefore if there is any consolation in Christ, if any comfort of love, if any fellowship of the Spirit, if any affection and mercy, fulfill my joy by being like-minded, having the same love, being of one accord, of one mind. Let nothing be done through selfish ambition or conceit, but in lowliness of mind let each esteem others better than himself. Let each of you look out not only for his own interests, but also for the interests of others. Let this mind be in you, which was also in Christ Jesus."*

Now, the question is, how do we become like-minded? We must *Spiritually Invest* in ourselves using the Fruits of the Spirit as a formal guide to consciously gauge what we are doing and why. When CAPITALIZING on the Fruits of the Spirit, they help us in every area without fail, creating a Cycle of Reciprocity with everyone we encounter; even if nothing is mentioned, it goes unnoticed, or others downplay it. Really? Yes, really. It is in our nature to remember how people made us feel, and if we use the Fruits of the Spirit, it unveils the truth in the Eye of God, even when those around us are forming lies against us.

Personally, when using the Fruits of the Spirit, *As It Pleases God*, they create a worry-free environment, giving me the leverage to approach people, places, and things with a Righteous Spirit. At the same time, it granted me the Spiritual Authority from the Heavenly of Heavens to invite the Holy Spirit to speak the language of another, positively. Why? It creates a common ground of relatability to meet people where they are, where they are going, or where they have been, ensuring they do not develop a deaf ear, even if they pretend to do so. More importantly, it helps my natural talents collide with my Spiritual Ones, making an impact on those needing what God has BLESSED me to offer. In addition, it also helps me become appropriately equipped with the Spiritual Tools and Know-How to feed His sheep, *As It Pleases Him*.

Contingency Clause

As we go deeper into the Spirit of Gratefulness, pleasing God is a free-will choice. Contrary to what most would think, He will not force Himself on us or bogart our lives, even if we find ourselves blaming Him for our decisions, having a pity party, wallowing in mediocrity, or indulging in temper tantrums.

Before we go any further, regardless of our choices, to keep Divine Favor flowing, it is always best to Honor and Respect the SOURCE of our being. It does not matter whether we agree with them or understand their method of operation or reasoning; we must keep our hands clean in this area. Why is this so important in Kingdom Formality? When we are GRATEFUL to the Life-Giver (God and our Parents), we graft in long LIFE and PEACE.

On the other hand, disrespectfulness shortens our life span from the inside out, zapping our peace. According to Scripture, it says, *"Honor your father and your mother, as the LORD your God has commanded you, that your days may be long, and that it may be well with you in the land which the LORD your God is giving you."* Deuteronomy 5:16.

The free will exchange of Respectfulness in or out of the Kingdom of God is real, nor should it be taken lightly. Why? There is a *Contingency Clause* hidden in plain sight in Deuteronomy 5:16 (*that it may be WELL with you in the land which the LORD your God is GIVING you*). As a word to the Wise, whenever we lack Peace, it is best to look for the areas of disrespectfulness, ungratefulness, disobedience, or pompousness. What makes this so crucial for Believers? God frowns upon the overlooked, selfish, or undealt with self-inflicted initiations of the heart.

According to the Heavenly of Heavens, when it comes down to possessing the Promises of the Kingdom, we must prioritize God and His Business. In the Kingdom, Divine Order and the Will of God matter to Him! If we place ourselves before God or exclude Him from the equation for instant gratification, we are out of order, period. As a result, our lives will reflect likewise, regardless of how well we think we have it together or how anointed we think we are.

Unbeknown to most, the disorder is always reflected in our fruits, attitudes, habits, lusts, words, thoughts, beliefs, biases, and character, masked under superficial layers or masks of our choice. How do we pinpoint the erring process? Red flags or the conscience should always alert us when there is a lack of humility, bragging, disobedience, selfishness, envy, jealousy, greed, coveting, contention, or recklessness in the camp, distorting our perceptions. If we are not getting the internal alerts, it means that our Spiritual Compass is keeled, distorting our senses, or due to a break in the *Contingency Clause*. All this means is that we have work to do from the inside out, *As It Pleases God*, to get the psyche or our selfish nature under control.

On the other hand, if we place others before God, here again, we are out of order as well. Are we not supposed to love our neighbors? Absolutely! Yet, there is a *Contingency Clause* in loving our neighbors as well. According to Scripture, '*Love your neighbor as you love thyself.*' Matthew 19:19. It is imperative to love ourselves first to love others properly. Why? If we lack love for ourselves, jealousy, envy, greed, pride, coveting, competitiveness, and hatefulness will spoil our fruits and character, contributing to undercover or underhanded people-pleasing, fakeness, debauchery, showboating, and disrespectfulness.

Regardless of how we pretend, God is looking for authenticity because we never want to find ourselves *Winning the War and Losing the Kingdom* because of a lack of understanding.

Kingdom Order

Establishing *Kingdom Order* in our lives is essential for achieving a life of true purpose and fulfillment. Aligning ourselves with the Divine Will of God brings harmony, joy, freedom, and peace. Acknowledging the Holy Trinity, *As It Pleases God*, using the Fruits of the Spirit, and behaving Christlike will assist in guiding us. Then again, we can make wise decisions and take actions that lead to a balanced and meaningful existence and experience a sense of balance and clarity. Without *Kingdom Order*, rest assured, we will find ourselves *Winning The War and Losing the Kingdom*.

What is *Kingdom Order* in the Eye of God? It is placing God first, self and family next, and then others. Really? Yes, really! When living our lives, *As It Pleases God* allows the Holy Spirit and the Blood of Jesus to cover us while we are in a Spiritual Classroom of Kingdom Development. More importantly, placing God first helps us love Him as He loves us, then sharing it abroad without imposing offenses on others. In addition, it also keeps us from setting superficial or selfish conditions with ourselves and others, having nothing to do with God. What does this mean? It is when we use the Word of God to manipulate and control others for selfish gain, lustful desires, discredit other Believers, or make God a liar.

Truly loving God in the good and the bad teaches us how to endure and love ourselves while allowing us to deal with and understand our Divine Blueprint and Genetic Makeup. Obtaining this type of understanding helps us manifest the training, lessons, regrafting, cleansings, or unyoking needed to possess the Promises of God.

Once we understand who we are and why, we can love our neighbor, putting aside our quirks, biases, and cultural differences and doing what we are called to do. What if we are rejected? Listen, regardless of whether or not we are rejected, we are called to do our due diligence in the Spirit of Excellence.

Listen, we are designed to make an impactful difference, and if we are hateful, rude, arrogant, or disrespectful, the Promises of God can pass us by. How is this possible when the fight is fixed? If we do not recognize the fight, we are not equipped, or we are defeated in it, then Spiritual Blindness, Deafness, and Muteness will become our portion until we come to ourselves.

We are created in the Image of God, and if we downplay our Blueprint, Birthright, or His Promises, forfeiture is placed on the horizon. How do we make this make sense in the real world? We are at risk of losing what rightly belongs to us, especially if we do not step up our game. How is this a game? If we do not make the right moves, move slowly, meander unwisely, or become pompous, we subject ourselves to befalling the elements of defeat.

Frankly, no one in their right mind wants to fall short, especially when they can stand tall in the Eye of God. For this reason, we must become equipped with the Spiritual Tools to contend with the enemy's wiles. How do we go about doing so? We must stay in the 'As It Pleases God' Realm of the Spirit or under His Wing. Here is what Psalm 91:1-4 shares with us: *"He who dwells in the secret place of the Most High Shall abide under the shadow of the Almighty. I will say of the LORD, 'He is my refuge and my fortress; My God, in Him I will trust.' Surely He shall deliver you from the snare of the fowler and from the perilous pestilence. He shall cover you with His feathers, and under His wings you shall take refuge; His truth shall be your shield and buckler."*

Unbeknown to most, disobedience leads to recklessness, pompousness, dullness, lukewarmness, and a stiff neck, along with the squandering of what is designed to BLESS us to become a Blessing while providing Spiritual Provisions for all involved. Indeed, ungratefulness has tainted the human race without us giving it a second thought. Yet, for this very reason, *As It Pleases God*, He shows Divine Favor to those who are GRATEFUL and who show RESPECT for His Divine Creation, as well as their Divine Blueprint.

Everything has a Divine Purpose for being here and contributing to the Cycle of Life, regardless of whether we understand it or not. To master the Power of Responsibility as a human being in Earthen Vessel, we must understand the AUTHORITY encapsulated in *Kingdom Order* beyond a shadow of a doubt, *As It Pleases God*.

According to our Divine Blueprint, when MOVING for the Kingdom as a Vessel, we must become focused, strategic, humble, obedient, and usable, even if it makes us uncomfortable. Most would consider being uncomfortable as something negative, but from a Spiritual Eye, it is positive. For example, something has to change if we want water to become ice or when reverting ice to water. Suppose we want to expand our Mind, Body, Soul, and Spirit, *As It Pleases God*. In this case, something has to change, break, or give way to the newness of something else, especially with what has authority over us Mentally, Physically, Emotionally, or Spiritually, to please ourselves.

Without having the proper authority amid our daily engagements, we will be denied access to Kingdomly Wisdom, Understanding, Secrets, and Know-How. As a result of our denial, we will find ourselves forcing others to do what we are unwilling or cannot do for ourselves, or we will discover that we are outright pulling for straws.

Even if we feel superior in our own eyes, it does not make it so in the Eye of God. As a matter of fact, lacking humility in or out of Kingdom Order or operating with a stiff neck will cause us to get a side-eye from our Heavenly Father. Getting a side-eye in such a manner will cause us to turn on ourselves from the inside out. It does not matter if we have mastered the ability to control ourselves in the public eye; behind closed doors, the enemy from within will wreak havoc, even if we are Believers.

Now, here is the deal: As a Believer, we come up with all types of unbiblical rules and laws to satiate our hidden agendas and desires, having nothing to do with God or *Kingdom Order*. Yet, we pass the information along from generation to generation without consulting with our Heavenly Father for the TRUTH, especially when there is underlying hopelessness, doubt, and questions within the human psyche that we cannot tell a soul about.

If the TRUTH is told, the things we attempt to condemn others for doing, we are guilty of doing the same things without realizing it. Then again, we may find ourselves blaming the hiccup in the system on the efforts we created with our bare hands or pointing the finger. For example, if something goes awry when we have created a coherent system to beat someone else's system, when the system goes down, we cannot lay the blame elsewhere, right?

Essentially, it behooves us to involve God in the system, *As It Pleases Him*, or use *Kingdom Order* to start. Why is *Kingdom Order* so important? When God gives us something freely, we can give freely. For example, when God loves us when we feel unlovable, we can give it back to His sheep freely, placing a Spiritual Seal on the love we are receiving. When God offers us mercy amid our wrongness or erring, we can give mercy freely to the next person, gleaning another Spiritual Seal. As God forgives us, we can do likewise without holding grudges, racking up a profound Spiritual Seal. Even though God allows the ability to attain Spiritual Seals, it does not make us above the Laws of the Land, nor give us the right to abuse the Spiritual System or defy *Kingdom Orders* that are designed to save us.

Of course, we all have a little shade somewhere regarding something or someone. Says who? Says the heart, says the core, says the psyche! Need I go any further? The contents of the heart, our thoughts, words, and behaviors, reveal everything. However, according to Kingdom Standards, we are out of order if we violate the FREE WILL of man to prove ourselves as being correct or superior. Although we have limits and boundaries set to govern the Laws of the Land, when it comes down to the Temple of God, there is a different set of Spiritual Rules according to the Heavenly of Heavens.

What is the difference, primarily when the Temple of Man dwells in the land? DOMINION is the difference! Here is a viable question: 'Did God give us Dominion over man?' No! He did not, nor will He ever! Yet, we are trying to control people as if we own them, leading us to our own detriment. And, for the record, we have been set aside for God and not for man. In *Kingdom Order*, He allows us to work through Him as a VESSEL used for man, *As It Pleases Him*. We should not work through man to serve Him as if He were our last choice to please ourselves. In *The Spiritual Middleman Approach*, He is our FIRST choice, *As It Pleases Him*.

How can we make the first choice, dominions, and systems make sense in layman's terms? Simply put, we have manmade things on the lower platform, and then we have God Created on the higher level, similar to using lowercase letters vs. Uppercase as formal or informal distinctions. Firstly, let us take this back to the Beginning to get an understanding, *"Then God said, 'Let Us make man in Our image, according to Our likeness; let them have dominion over the fish of the sea, over the birds of the air, and over the cattle, over all the earth and over every creeping* thing that creeps on the earth.' So, God created man in His own image; in the image of God He created him; male and female He created them. Then God blessed them, and God said to them, 'Be fruitful and multiply; fill the earth and subdue it; have dominion over the fish of the sea, over the birds of the air, and over every living thing that moves on the earth.' " Genesis 1:26-28.

And secondly, in ALIGNMENT with the Promises of God, here is what we must know: *"And in that day I will set apart the land of Goshen, in which My people dwell, that no swarms of flies shall be there, in order that you may know that I am the LORD in the midst of the land. I will make a difference between My people and your people. Tomorrow this sign shall be."* Exodus 8:22-23. For this reason, it is imperative to repent and forgive daily, make a conscious effort to become better consistently without making life difficult for ourselves and others, and know that God deals with each of us individually. In addition, *"But know that the LORD has set apart for Himself him who is godly; the LORD will hear when I call to Him."* Psalm 4:3.

What is the big deal about having and allowing others to have free will? First, God did not create robots. And, please do not confuse discipline with having free will. We are required to train our children, but we cannot forget to set them FREE! Secondly, to SHINE brightly in or out of the Kingdom, extracting GREATNESS, we must learn how to work out our own salvation, *As It Pleases God.*

What does this mean, especially when we are taught we cannot lose our salvation? If we desire Kingdom Power, we must INVEST in our Earthen Vessels from the inside out, cover ourselves with the Blood of Jesus as Spiritual Atonement, become ONE with the Holy Trinity, use the Fruits of the Spirit, and behave Christlike. If we do not use the FREEWILL OFFERING, that is indeed our choice, nor can we condemn someone into the PIT based on our perceptions without God's Divine Perspective.

Why can we not determine someone's salvation? First, we are not God Almighty. Secondly, we do not know what He is using to train us unless He gives us Spiritual Discernment, *As It Pleases Him.* Thirdly, the last time I checked, *"God has chosen the foolish things of the world to put to shame the wise, and God has chosen the weak things of the world to put to shame the things which are mighty; and the base things of the world and* the things which are despised God has chosen, and the things which are not, to bring to nothing the things that are." 1 Corinthians 1:27-28.

Salvation is available to everyone. In all simplicity, if we do not use it, take it for granted, or forfeit it for something or someone who appears better, it may feel like a loss. Yet, in the Eye of God, it is still available if we follow the *Kingdom Order* in the RESTORATION or RECOVERY process. Listen, God will take the least likely and make them likely, even when they are thrown into the Pit and out to the wolves. How do I know? I was one of them; I was called everything but a Child of God, and now here we are! *"The stone which the builders rejected has become the chief cornerstone."* Psalm 118:22.

In *The Spiritual Middleman Approach*, if you cannot build others up, DO NOT break them down with your words, thoughts, deeds, or biases, making them feel worthless, shameful, fearful, or guilty. If you cannot communicate effectively or lack people skills, then it is time to step into the Spiritual Classroom for updates on how to motivate, inspire, and encourage.

Why do we need updates or have to play nice, especially when they need a blasting out? Could it be that while you are tearing people apart, your salvation is hanging in the balance based on your next move? Is this not judging? Absolutely not! I am Dr. Y. Bur, The WHY Doctor, for a reason. I am asking if the seed that you are sowing will provide restoration, recovery, or renewal. If not, you must RETHINK what you are doing before the deed is done. *"Do not be deceived, God is not mocked; for whatever a man sows, that he will also reap. For he who sows to his flesh will of the flesh reap corruption, but he who sows to the Spirit will of the Spirit reap everlasting life."* Galatians 6:7-8.

Unfortunately, this is how we 'get got' for the lack of understanding from a Divine Perspective! According to the Heavenly of Heavens, salvation is not just for our benefit or circle, but it is also used for the restoration of those around us. Thus, it is imperative to use a Spiritual Approach, *As It Pleases God*. Why? To prevent us from looking like boo boo the fool, proclaiming to be something or someone we are not when our fruits, words, and behaviors tell all without saying one word, as we selfishly please ourselves to the detriment of another.

Here is the deal in the Eye of God: Becoming Spiritually Blind, Deaf, and Mute takes on the effect of losing our salvation, making us clueless about Spiritual Principles, Protocols, and Solutions while appearing right in our own eyes. Frankly, this is how the enemy is turning the Church against itself because we do not KNOW what we should know about how Spirituality operates, *As It Pleases God*.

As a result, we think we are winning for the Kingdom and rejoicing when we are only setting ourselves up for the ultimate takedown or takeover because we are once again Spiritually Blind, Deaf, and Mute, but love God with all our hearts.

As human beings, we are prone to making mistakes and going astray from the path that God has for us, especially when the unresolved traumas of the psyche are involved. As a result, we often find ourselves in situations where we feel broken, lost, confused, frustrated, and in desperate need of restoration. We do not realize that our salvation is an essential part of the restoration, recovery, and rebuilding process of unveiling our Predestined Blueprint, using the Fruits of the Spirit, and building Christlike Character.

In *Kingdom Order*, salvation is a GIFT from God that is FREELY given to all who believe in Jesus Christ as their Lord and Savior. Through this, we are reconciled back to God to restore our *Spirit to Spirit* Relationship with Him, going from selfishness to selflessness, *As It Pleases Him*. More importantly, the process of restoration, recovery, and rebuilding is not only Spiritual. But it also affects every aspect of our lives, including the healing and transformation of our Emotional, Mental, and Physical well-being, restoring what was broken, recovering what was lost, and rebuilding what was destroyed. *"Therefore, if anyone is in Christ, he is a new creation; old things have passed away; behold, all things have become new."* 2 Corinthians 5:17.

In the *Kingdom Order*, we are AGENTS of Divine Transformation to become a LIGHT in a world that desperately needs love, hope, joy, peace, and another chance at becoming better, stronger, and wiser, *As It Pleases God*.

We are here to *Win the War and the Kingdom*, and if you are ready to become a *Rockable Diamond*, let us go deeper.

CHAPTER THREE
Rockable Diamonds

"You also, as living stones, are being built up a spiritual house, a holy priesthood, to offer up spiritual sacrifices acceptable to God through Jesus Christ." 1 Peter 2:5.

The Rockable Diamonds are hidden all around us in plain sight. Yet, if we dare to use *The Spiritual Middleman Approach* to unveil the veil, we will find the hidden Treasures of Greatness waiting for its Divine Moment.

Once we are trapped in time, *Rockable Diamonds* or not, we determine our value based on our perceptions. What is more, our perceptional value determines what we hear, see, think, and become when no one looks or pays attention to us. In addition, it develops our drive, perseverance, proactiveness, staying power, or the lack thereof.

What are the benefits associated with becoming *Rockable Diamonds*? In my opinion, it determines whether we pick up rocks to weigh us down or attract diamonds to build our internal and external value in or out of the Kingdom. Here is the Divine Perspective on this matter: "*Coming to Him as to a living stone, rejected indeed by men, but chosen by God and precious, you also, as living stones, are being built up a spiritual house, a holy priesthood, to offer up spiritual sacrifices acceptable to God through Jesus Christ.*" 1 Peter 2:4-5.

What do diamonds and rocks have to do with anything? They both contain dirt or some form of debris; however, picking up unproductive or unfruitful people, places, and things hindering or devaluing our progression decreases our productivity, especially without fully understanding it or them, *As It Pleases God*.

Amid all, keep in mind that deadweight, debris, or an uncanny appearance is a matter of perceptional value. Why? A rock or an uncut diamond may appear the same to the naked eye, especially if we do not know what we are looking for or do not have a clue about our Divine Blueprint. So, it is imperative to add God into the equation to better understand if our DIAMOND is hidden in the rock we are picking up or attempting to discard.

I commonly advise that we should leave no stone unturned. Still, in the turning process, *As It Pleases God*, if it does not fit into or distract us from our Divine Blueprint, it is okay to kindly keep it moving without offending, becoming arrogant, or demeaning anyone. What is the purpose of moving on? It prevents unwanted overloads, dealing with issues having nothing to do with us, wasting precious time, or risking exposure to avoidable contaminants. More importantly, if we are not well-versed in this area of determining stones or diamonds, it is best to examine ourselves first.

What is the purpose of examining ourselves, especially when we are examining others to determine if they fit into our Blueprinted Destiny? Suppose we do not examine our fruits and character with a Spiritual Mirror, *As It Pleases God*. In this case, we can quickly become deceived by the fruits of someone else due to conditioning, biases, traumas, perceptions, and so on. For example, when first meeting a potential mate, if we tell them all the fruits (qualities) that we are looking for, they will put on a mask to give us what we think we desire. Once we become comfortable with the person, the mask begins to slip off, giving us a red flag that we tend to ignore. The more we ignore the red flags, the more stones they leave behind until we become weighed down with rotten fruit that we did not ask for. Yet, clearly stated the type of mask to present to us without involving God in the equation at all.

With *The Spiritual Middleman Approach*, if we look within ourselves, *As It Pleases God*, while exhibiting the Fruits of the Spirit and Christlike Character, it will become clear if they are a stone or a diamond. How is this possible, especially when we have free will to choose whomever we like and whenever? We are indeed free, but it does not exempt us from examining ourselves accordingly, nor does it buffer us from making bad choices unless we include God. So, let us take this to the Scripture on how David examined himself: *"The LORD shall judge the peoples; Judge me, O LORD, according to my righteousness, and according to my integrity within me. Oh, let the wickedness of the wicked come to an end, but establish the just; For the righteous God tests the hearts and minds."* Psalm 7:8-9.

As a Word to the Wise, here is the Spiritual Decree to repeat, helping us with our stones and diamonds when examining ourselves accordingly, using the Fruits of the Spirit faithfully, and consistently exhibiting Christlike character. *"Vindicate me, O LORD, For I have walked in my integrity. I have also trusted in the LORD; I shall not slip. Examine me, O LORD, and prove me; Try my mind and my heart. For Your lovingkindness is before my eyes, And I have walked in Your truth."* Psalm 26:1-3. Why is it important to repeat these Scriptures? I consider it an EXAMINING CLEANSER for the human psyche to maximize *The Spiritual Middleman Approach.*

Examining Cleanser

The power hidden within the Word of God is often misunderstood and underestimated. Still, it is truly a Divinely Miraculous TOOL that can guide, cleanse, and restore us to live a more fulfilling life. In the Eye of God, this potent *Examining Cleanser* helps us to look deep within ourselves and examine our thoughts, actions, words, desires, behaviors, and intentions. It is through this examination that we can genuinely repent, forgive, and move forward in the Spirit of Excellence toward holiness and purity with a sense of peace, patience, and serenity, *As It Pleases God.*

What if we do not need an *Examining Cleanser*? I cannot determine what a person needs at their present state of being...that is between them and God Almighty. Then again, we can use a play on words such as: repenting, testing, confessing, understanding, surrendering, purging, pruning, and so on. The bottom line is that

"If we confess our sins, He is faithful and just to forgive us our sins and to cleanse us from all unrighteousness." 1 John 1:9.

As we say in the South, 'Even swap ain't no swindle.' We can change words around all we like; still, the Word and Mind of God does not change—He is ABSOLUTE. Here is what we must know: "*Examine yourselves as to whether you are in the faith. Test yourselves. Do you not know yourselves, that Jesus Christ is in you?—unless indeed you are disqualified.*" 2 Corinthians 13:5.

In the same way we cleanse our bodies, with or without the ego and attestation, we must do the same for the Mind, Soul, and Spirit. If not, our Spiritual Pores will become clogged by seen and unseen dirt, debris, germs, and fungus, making us toxic. "*For if anyone is a hearer of the word and not a doer, he is like a man observing his natural face in a mirror; for he observes himself, goes away, and immediately forgets what kind of man he was.*" James 1:23-24.

What does an *Examining Cleanser* have to do with our stones and diamonds? We all need a little dusting off from time to time, and if we are afraid to vindicate ourselves from the inside out, we will have issues in or out of the Kingdom and with our Spiritual Walk with God. As a result, we will seek retribution upon others without understanding our contributions to the matter. By not frequently conducting a checkup from the neck up and from within, we will create our very own cycle of déjà vu of unlearned lessons with a stiff neck and irresponsibility to follow.

The moment we choose not to walk in integrity or challenge it, we will have even more significant issues. How? If we continue to live a lie, it is common to lose track of the lies we tell as we become people pleasers and title seekers, causing us to miss the secret sparkles that clue us into the diamond potentiality or polarity. As a result, we will overlook our Blessings hidden in plain sight due to our known and unknown selfishness, competitiveness, jealousy, coveting, and so on, with negative character traits affecting our people skills while thinking or intending to be a good person. Really? Yes, really!

The truth of the matter is that not many people will walk up to us, admitting they are terrible, ruthless, rebellious, debauched, rude, vindictive, or lack integrity. But in all actuality, they somehow have a hidden ray of hope for their goodness. Still, they fail to know how to bring it forth due to some form of miscommunication, trauma, abuse, neglect, conditioning, biases, upbringing, mind control, deception, misdirection, and so on.

How is it possible not to know when we are operating with bad character traits, contradicting the Will of God? Believe it or not, I was one of those people who did not know about the Expectations of Excellence required in the Kingdom. No one formally advised or taught me. So, I confused my Spirituality with perfection, expecting Believers to be without blemish. Not realizing we are all a work-in-progress in need of continual repentance, forgiveness, and restoration. Thus, in the Rockable Diamonds collection, I bring forth the *Examining Cleanser* to clean us up, *As It Pleases God*, cutting through all of the fluff. Because *"Everyone who has this hope in Him purifies himself, just as He is pure."* 1 John 3:3.

What is the difference between Spiritual Excellence and perfection? Our MOTIVES! What do our motives have to do with anything? Perfection is a matter of perception, whereas when operating in the Spirit of Excellence, we add Spiritual Principles into the equation of what we are doing. For example, when embarking upon a task, listed below are two mindsets to compare regarding the circumstantial motives:

- ☐ We can half-heartedly or carelessly present shabby work, just to get it done with little or no desire to become better, wiser, or more creative.

- ☐ We can wholeheartedly or carefully do good work, giving it our best with an openness to become better, stronger, wiser, and creative.

Unbeknown to most, when doing all things in the Spirit of Righteousness or Excellence with clean hands and a pure heart, it changes the trajectory of what we are doing and our why, especially when we interject the Fruits of the Spirit and exhibit Christlike Character, even amid our flaws. Then again, if we are too busy being perfect or flawless, we may suffer multiple disappointments due to our thwarted perception, selfishness, lack of flexibility, or false expectations of our Heaven on Earth Experience or Divine Blueprint. Is this Biblical? Absolutely! *"For My thoughts are not your thoughts, Nor are your ways My ways, says the LORD. For as the heavens are higher than the earth, So are My ways higher than your ways, And My thoughts than your thoughts."* Isaiah 55:8-9.

The Drawing Board

In the Kingdom, we are designed to become trainable, extracting lessons to master what we excel in, around, or through, *As It Pleases God*. Frankly, I have had to go back to *The Drawing Board* so many times in the developmental phase that I have lost count. What was the purpose of going back to *The Drawing Board*? God had to build the Spiritual Astuteness needed for my Spiritual Journey for such a time as this. Once I mastered this understanding, against all odds, with a charactorial overhaul and regrafting, doing all things in the Spirit of Excellence, no one can discount my value unless they are lying to themselves.

Is not value a matter of perception? Absolutely. Then again, regardless of one's perception, a diamond is a diamond, whether it is in the rough or not. The value is hidden inside, irrespective of whether the onlookers recognize it. Still, the diamond must KNOW its worth without discounting, second-guessing, or proving its value or Divine Blueprint! Even when it becomes a little dull, it can get its shine back with a bit of cleansing.

How can I make such a comparison when we are not really diamonds? Unbeknownst to most, the carbon that makes up diamonds is also within us. Really? Yes, really! We are composed of approximately 18% carbon, which means the diamond principle is already within us.

All in all, regardless of the negative naysayers, dream killers, mockers, rock throwers, or distractions, I made a conscious choice to become Spirit-Led instead of self-led, unveiling the hidden diamond from within, *As It Pleases God*. Why for God and not for self? To maximize my Spiritual Anointing and avoid becoming lukewarm, dull, or stiff-necked in the Kingdom, I knew I could not tackle my Divine Blueprint independently. So, I could not settle for negativity, unrighteousness, mediocrity, or excuses while correcting the correctable according to the Biblical Principles set forth.

When going back to *The Drawing Board*, I needed Divine Intervention. For this reason, I had to Divinely Align myself with the Holy Trinity, examining and cleansing myself consistently, using the Fruits of the Spirit, and developing Christlike Character. And then, sharing with others how to do likewise, as my GIVE BACK to the Kingdom with outright integrity in Earthen Vessel.

According to the Heavenly of Heavens, if we are unwilling to trust God and put more trust in ourselves, we will find ourselves on a slippery slope in due season. Why? Since the Beginning of time, we have been prewired to trust God, making it a part of our DNA. The moment we omit trusting God, we inadvertently place our trust in something or someone else, contributing to idolatry, various lusts, pride, and greed.

Soon enough, without the Spiritual Bonding Agents of trust in Earthen Vessels, according to our Divine Design, it will begin breaking us down from the inside out as we create all types of illusions to cover ourselves with superficial facades. Meanwhile, we are in complete denial of our Spiritual Condition, as our DNA structure is backfiring and availing itself Mentally, Physically, and Emotionally.

Listen, the moment we speak, our trust, beliefs, thoughts, mindsets, fruits, and character are exposed to those who pay attention or are Spiritually Astute. How? Those who know who they are from the inside out will naturally invoke their instincts, similar to an animal, but a lot better. "*But the natural man does not receive the things of the Spirit of God, for they are foolishness to him; nor can he know them, because they are spiritually discerned.*" 1 Corinthians 2:14.

How are we above animals using our Spiritual Discernment? According to *The Divine Drawing Board*, we have DOMINION, and they do not. We are created a little lower than Angels, and they are not. We are created to worship, and they are not. Yet, in all actuality, they trust God and their Divine Nature more than we do, while doing what they are called to do. Or better yet, living their truth unless there is some form of human intervention.

Where is the proof of being Divinely Equipped? According to the Word of God, *"For we are His workmanship, created in Christ Jesus for good works, which God prepared beforehand that we should walk in them."* Ephesians 2:10.

Signs Of The Time

Unfortunately, as the Signs Of The Time are upon us, we are trying to prove ourselves worthy to people and not to God as we should. To add insult to injury, we omit testing the mind and heart, examining what comes forth, and letting it all hang out in the open without reeling ourselves in or exhibiting self-control.

According to the Heavenly of Heavens, behaving in such a manner is a high form of self-neglect and lack of stewardship of our Earthen Vessels.

Why do we overlook the contents of the mind and heart? We secretly fear what will come forth; therefore, we omit this self-cleansing agent of truth, opting to bury it until we are forced to confront ourselves. More importantly, without confronting ourselves from the inside out, we can become easily deceived and divided without realizing it, leaving a trail of traumatized victims.

What is more, we can also find ourselves playing the victim, granting the enemy access into our lives, opting out of the Divine Covering from the Holy of Holies. How is this possible? By neglecting our Spirit Man, doing our own thing without God, engaging in the wrong things contradicting His Divine Will, disregarding our Divine Blueprint, or hanging out in the enemy's den, it becomes easy to become influenced negatively. If it goes unrepented, uncorrected, or ungrafted, it can oppress us to the core through the lust of the eyes, the lust of the flesh, and the pride of life, even if we are Believers with good intentions.

When using *The Spiritual Middleman Approach*, we cannot play around, leaving the door open for the enemy to sift us as wheat. Why should we not leave an open door? Unfortunately, they will wait for the right moment of weakness to capitalize on where we fall short. With this in mind, we must gear up, putting on the Whole Armor of God, with the Holy Trinity at the forefront, and fully repented.

When we are backed by the Father, Son, and Holy Spirit, God will send us a ram in the bush to help us in our moments of weakness. Yet, we must do our part; if we require a Holy Trinity checklist, get it. If we need the Fruits of the Spirit or Christlike Character checklist, consider it done. When we are under pressure, or our buttons are pushed negatively, if we need to rely on some form of assistance to keep us Spiritually Grounded or Focused, we must do what we have to do to keep the enemy's schemes from penetrating. How can this help us? For example, here are a few questions to ask ourselves when being pressurized by negativity, but not limited to such:

- ☐ Have we involved God in the matter, *As It Pleases Him*?
- ☐ Have we invoked the Holy Spirit to assist or ask for guidance?
- ☐ Have we covered ourselves with the Blood of Jesus?
- ☐ Have we given thanks?
- ☐ Have we repented?
- ☐ Have we forgiven ourselves or others?
- ☐ Have we reversed the negative into a positive?
- ☐ Have we assumed responsibility for our role?
- ☐ Have we used the Fruits of the Spirit?
- ☐ Are we behaving Christlike?
- ☐ Have we examined ourselves Mentally, Physically, and Emotionally?
- ☐ Have we applied Biblical Scriptures to the matter?
- ☐ Have we prayed about it?
- ☐ Is the lesson, understanding, or experience documented?

Querying ourselves is of the utmost importance; therefore, it is not wise to lose our sense of reasoning when approaching anything or anyone, especially when needing deliverance from something or someone. In my opinion, it is always conducive to our well-being to involve God in every aspect of our lives.

Why should we involve God, especially if we want to live carefree and fancy? We do not know where the enemy wants to sucker-punch us, knocking the wind out of us, so our Divine

Rescuer should remain on RESERVE at all times, keeping the enemy from consuming us when we are caught slipping.

With God, regardless of how it appears to the naked eye, we have the bounce back needed to create a win-win. It does not matter if we get the VICTORY in the beginning or end, as long as we get it. So, if it takes us to ROCK with a Diamond Mentality, with *The Spiritual Middleman Approach*, it is a done deal! We are indeed CHAMPIONS in the Eye of God; we simply need to know, decree, and live it while developing a Kingdom Mindset geared to GREATNESS.

Winning in the Eye of God?

Unbeknown to most, we are genetically designed to WIN in our Heaven on Earth Experience; if not, we would not have been created in the first place. In *Winning in the Eye of God*, we simply need to KNOW this information without deviation or settling for defeat Mentally, Physically, Emotionally, or Spiritually. How do I know? According to Scripture, the very first Divine Commission is to "*Be fruitful and multiply; fill the earth and subdue it.*" Genesis 1:28. It is NOT to become fruitless, disruptive, manipulative, and destructive. What is more, this one Scripture sets apart the Dream Builders, the Destroyers, or the Pretenders.

Regardless of what we are going through or how we see life, we are already BLESSED beyond measure, despite what we see with our naked eyes. How is this possible, especially when life is complicated? We will all have this experience, but we must interject GRATEFULNESS because we do not have to hunt for our food; we can buy it. We do not have to go to the restroom outside; we have conveniences to accommodate. We do not live outside; we have a roof to shelter us from the elements of nature. We are not prey or have to sleep with our eyes open, protecting ourselves from the predators designed to consume us for dinner; we have 9-1-1 to call, alarm systems to alert us, Police Officers to protect, and a Judicial System to judge. We have the luxury of cleaning the dirt and debris off the body without having to walk around smelly. More importantly, we have CLEAN water to drink, and we dare to be ungrateful! In my opinion, this is *Winning in the Eye of God* at its best!

Now, let us get back on track; we are the ONLY ones who can reverse our Blessings. How is this possible, especially when we have a Promise? By not knowing we are Blessed, failing to understand our Blessings, becoming ungrateful amid them, or selling our Spiritual Covenant in exchange for seemingly greater, but lesser in the Eye of God. By knowing this information while standing our ground, the enemy must BLESS us or become our FOOTSTOOL, even if it appears as if they have the upper hand. Here is the Scripture, *"Behold, I have received a command to bless; He has blessed, and I cannot reverse it."* Numbers 23:20. The key is KNOWING it beyond a shadow of a doubt! Why? The enemy already knows this and is banking on our ignorance of the TRUTH.

Before we go any further, and to be clear, let me ask this question again: Who can reverse our Blessings? We are the only ones who can allow the reversal process to take place through the Spiritual Laws of the Kingdom. We instigate the reversal process when we allow our negative charactorial flaws to dominate with the lust of the eyes, the lust of the flesh, and the pride of life, casting a dark cloud from the inside out.

It is through the enemy's deception that causes us to stub our own toe, so to speak. For example, in the Garden of Eden, if the deceiver could reverse the Divine Blessings of man, he would NOT have to convince Eve to partake of the Forbidden Fruit. Nor would she convince Adam to do likewise. God would have dealt with Eve if Adam had not partaken of the Forbidden Fruit, and the Spiritual Covenant would have remained intact. However, we cannot change what happened back then. Still, we can pick up the Nuggets of Wisdom left behind by our Forefathers, moving forward in the Spirit of Excellence with the Blood of Jesus, who restored the Spiritual Covenant to its Rightful Owners.

As Believers, here is the deal: We need to expose ourselves to the Holy Trinity (Father, Son, and Holy Spirit), as well as the Promises of God. How do we pinpoint the Divine Promises? There are many Promises and Covenants written throughout the Bible, with Contingency Clauses we overlook. For this reason, we must get to know the Word of God for ourselves. Why? We must know what the Bible is saying to us through our *Spirit to Spirit* Connection. Unfortunately, if we are Spiritually Blind, Deaf, and Mute, we will inadvertently become reckless with the Promises due to the lack of UNDERSTANDING.

By all means, the *Spirit to Spirit* Connection we all secretly seek is an intimate relationship, making the Bible come alive for and through us in our daily living, as well as our walk with God. More importantly, when the Heavenly of Heavens notice we are wholeheartedly giving and doing our best, Divine Assistance is ushered in on our behalf, primarily if we are focused on being in Purpose on purpose for the Kingdom.

Listen, when it comes down to our Divine Blueprint, we do not need to focus on the *How-To* or *Know-How*. We must MASTER the *What* and *Why*, *As It Pleases God*. At the same time, polishing all of the Spiritual Tools associated, such as the Fruits of the Spirit, Christlike Character, Prayer, Repentance, Forgiveness, Fasting, Faith, Hope, Trust, Positivity, Obedience, and the use of the Word of God as Spiritual Weaponry, but not limited to such. Why must the Spiritual Tools come first? If we neglect them or take God out of the equation, we will sabotage the *How-To* and *Know-How* in due time by interjecting worldliness instead of Kingdomness, *As It Pleases Him*.

The 'as it pleases self' demeanor causes King Saul's Experience of oppression to come upon us. Hence, if we incorporate God in the equation, *As It Pleases Him*, anything we endure is training, testing, and molding for our Blueprinted Purpose. Once our *Spirit to Spirit* Communicable efforts are established, we must sharpen our earthly skills to properly align the Heaven on Earth experience we have been predestined to have.

We must do our due diligence; we cannot sit back and expect our Blessings to fall out of the sky...we must Spiritually Till our own ground. So, if we need to learn something from the world in which we live to build the Kingdom of God, then consider it done!

From the Ancient of Days, purposeful learning on behalf of the Kingdom carries serious weight in the Eye of God. For example, in the Bible, Joseph endured everything from being sold into slavery, being lied on, being thrown into prison, being purposefully used, and blatantly ignored. Yet, he never stopped learning on behalf of the Kingdom and the Promises of God. Amid all, he held true to his Godly Integrity, even when he had the opportunity to get revenge on his brothers. As a result of his heart and mind posture, his experiences TRAINED and EQUIPPED him to become Second in Command to save his people.

In my opinion, due to the different aspects of this elemental misinformation, we have put our earthly skills before our Spiritual Tools and Skills, which initiates backwardness in the Eye of God.

What is the big deal when we have everything we want and desire? It blocks our breakthroughs, instigating ungratefulness, competitiveness, and the lack of contentment, zapping our Peace. Without Peace or having a tainted perception, it blocks the Spiritual Downloads from the Heavenly Realms, causing us to become self-led or easily manipulated, and NOT Spirit-Led.

Why is our walk with God so important? As the Heavens concur, God has promised us LOVE amid all, regardless of whatever or whomever, primarily if we operate in a Repenting and Grateful Spirit. When we turn away from debauchery and disobedience to become a work-in-progress for the Kingdom, the Heavens will open up to train us, leading us toward the LIGHT; however, we must take the first step. When doing so, no one can do this for us; we must place one foot in front of the next while quoting this Scripture: "*Uphold my steps in Your paths, that my footsteps may not slip.*" Psalm 17:16. As "*Your word becomes a lamp to my feet and a light to my path.*" Psalm 119:105.

What can these Scriptures do for us? It will vary from person to person depending on our Divine Blueprint, soul ties, yokes, and so on. For this reason, regardless of one's condition or mindset, it is always best to have a Spiritually Illuminated path instead of a self-led dark one. Here is what we must know in two parts on how to work on ourselves from the inside out in *The Spiritual Middleman Approach*:

- ☐ "*Therefore God also has highly exalted Him and given Him the name which is above every name, that at the name of Jesus every knee should bow, of those in heaven, and of those on earth, and of those under the earth, and that every tongue should confess that Jesus Christ is Lord, to the glory of God the Father.*" Philippians 2:9-11.

> ☐ *"Therefore, my beloved, as you have always obeyed, not as in my presence only, but now much more in my absence, work out your own salvation with fear and trembling; for it is God who works in you both to will and to do for His good pleasure. Do all things without complaining and disputing, that you may become blameless and harmless, children of God without fault in the midst of a crooked and perverse generation, among whom you shine as lights in the world, holding fast the word of life, so that I may rejoice in the day of Christ that I have not run in vain or labored in vain."* Philippians 2:12-16.

How can we make life better for others when facing a tough situation? With all due respect, a challenging situation is a matter of opinion. Suppose one dares to change their cognitive power to glean lessons, get an understanding, learn how to become better, stronger, and wiser, find a way to give back to the Kingdom, or master ways to remain at peace. In this case, we will indeed create opportunities instead of obstacles, yokes, and more problems. More importantly, if we use Jesus as a drink offering as we approach ourselves and life, our self-examination efforts will become pristine in the Eye of God.

How do we use a drink offering with real-life issues? If we symbolically pour out a drink offering, *As It Pleases God*, we can instigate a positive flow in and out of our lives by using the Holy Spirit and the Blood of Jesus as our Mediator. Blasphemy, right? Wrong. The Bible asks us, *"How much more shall the blood of Christ, who through the eternal Spirit offered Himself without spot to God, cleanse your conscience from dead works to serve the living God?"* Hebrews 9:14. We must cleanse ourselves Mentally, Physically, and Emotionally if we want all God has to offer, especially with our Blueprinted Promises.

So, to begin *Winning in the Eye of God*, quote those Scriptures throughout the day, irrespective of what you see with the naked eye, while using the Fruits of the Spirit and Christlike Character. I PROMISE that you will begin to see a difference in how your steps are being ordered by the Heavenly of Heavens.

CHAPTER FOUR
The Four Corners

"To Jesus the Mediator of the new covenant, and to the blood of sprinkling that speaks better things than that of Abel." Hebrews 12:24.

With outstretched arms to embrace the seemingly unbraceable; we cannot deny the fact that God is real. Although there are many things we cannot explain. Yet, then again, there are many things we can explain. To do so, we must put on our thinking caps of Divine Wisdom buried within. With this untapped potential and *The Spiritual Middleman Approach*, we can move Heaven on Earth the way God intended without settling for the mediocrity of our self-induced or man-made limits.

Once we develop this Kingdom Mindset, the Spirit of Excellence can usher its way into our lives without reservation when doing our part. Is this Biblical? Absolutely! First, *"Whereas you have been forsaken and hated, So that no one went through you, I will make you an eternal excellence, A joy of many generations."* Isaiah 60:15. Secondly, *"For it is the God who commanded light to shine out of darkness, who has shone in our hearts to give the light of the knowledge of the glory of God in the face of Jesus Christ. But we have this treasure in earthen vessels, that the excellence of the power may be of God and not of us. We are hard-pressed on every side, yet not crushed; we are perplexed, but not in despair; persecuted, but not forsaken; struck down, but not destroyed—always carrying about in the body the dying of the Lord Jesus, that the life of Jesus also may be manifested in our body."* 2 Corinthians 4:6-10.

We as Believers often cringe when Divine Greatness or Order is introduced into our lives due to the lack of Spiritual Clarity. As a result, we become suspicious instead of embracing the authentic interjection of God's Mighty Hand. What does this mean? When wolves surround us in sheep's clothing, we tend to perceive the Vessel of God who is interceding on our behalf as a wolf when they are deflecting what we cannot see with our naked eyes. Whereas, if we properly sync ourselves with the Holy Spirit, He will grant us Divine Clarity to calm the human psyche, granting us peace. If not, we will begin to dig, looking for stuff to confirm our suspicions of God's Vessel while overlooking what has already penetrated our Four Corners.

What does the penetration of the Four Corners mean in layman's terms? It means that the enemy has penetrated the Four Corners of the Mind, Body, Soul, and Spirit, spreading outwardly, getting us to think with our senses or impulses instead of our Spiritual Receptors from the Heavenly of Heavens.

How can our Spirit become penetrated? If our Spirit is lying dormant, or better yet, sleeping...then how can it become One with the Holy Spirit? It cannot! As a result, it causes our instincts and conscience to become off-kilter, instigating an inner battle from within the human psyche, extending itself to the Four Corners of our home and abroad. *"Therefore thus says the Lord God: 'Behold, I lay in Zion a stone for a foundation, a tried stone, a precious cornerstone, a sure foundation; whoever believes will not act hastily.'"* Isaiah 28:16.

How can something or someone penetrate our Four Corners when we are Believers? Before the actual penetration, we must take a closer look at the distraction. If the distraction is enough to shake us to the core, causing us to second-guess or doubt ourselves, and then we are presented with something or someone appearing as what we desire from God, then BEWARE. What if it is really Heaven-Sent? Then my question is, 'What if it is not?'

We must Spiritually Check all systems, period! The Holy Spirit does not mind. Only the deceptive ones become offended! For this reason, they bombard us with accolades of distractions to keep us from interjecting the Holy Spirit and covering ourselves with the Blood of Jesus as we should. While, at the same time, causing Spiritual Blindness, Deafness, and Muteness to come upon us as they sit back and laugh about how we cannot discern properly. And then we run around saying, 'God told me this, or He told me that.' And yet, He did not forewarn us about the enemy lurking amongst us...the Devil is a liar! Henceforth, we must check the Spiritual System of whatever and whomever, not what appears to the naked eye.

For me, I do not engage in digging to approve or disapprove; I call forth the Divine System of the Heavenly of Heavens to UNVEIL that in which is veiled to others for the edification of the Kingdom. Simply put, I opt to extract the Lesson, Blessing, or Wisdom from whatever or whomever to Divinely Align to feed God's sheep, *As It Pleases Him*. In so many words, if I am on a Spiritual Assignment for the Kingdom, God is responsible for the Unveiling of Spiritual Information, Forewarnings, or whatever is needed for my Divine Mission.

Of course, with *The Spiritual Middleman Approach* I use, I must operate in the Spirit of Righteousness and Excellence with outright humility. I must also use the Fruits of the Spirit, exhibiting Christlike Character with the unified Oneness of the Holy Trinity at the Forefront, while staying in a constant state of repentance. All in all, it is well worth it.

As we move on, the Holy Spirit does not have to operate with distractions or mind games to break down, deceive, or create immoral breaches, getting us caught up, yoked, or oppressed. He operates with confirmations or alerts before the distraction, bringing AWARENESS to build, set free, and provide a way of escape. What is the purpose of knowing this information? The counterfeit will always avail itself before the Blessing, causing us to choose outside what is Divine, similar to how Jesus was tempted in the wilderness, in Luke 4:1-13. Is this fair? Absolutely! After all, we must be tested to avoid the shake-and-bake mentality or functionality.

As a whole, it is imperative to become One with the Holy Spirit and cover the DOORPOST of our Mind, Body, Soul, and Spirit with the Blood of Jesus. Why must we cover ourselves with the Blood of Jesus? Is this not a bit dated? Absolutely not! *"How much more, then, will the blood of Christ, who through the eternal Spirit offered himself* unblemished to God, cleanse our consciences from acts that lead to death, so that we may serve the living God!" Hebrews 9:14.

It ensures we do not go back to the Egyptian Formalities of what God has delivered us from. Nor do we want to wander around in our Desert Experience due to having a stiff neck or engaging in secret acts of idolatry when no one is looking. Therefore, we must pay attention to the Fruits of the Spirit, taking our focus off any form of worldliness designed to cloud our sense of good or rational judgment regarding deceptive measures, hidden motives, and situational manipulation.

Hint, hint, deceptive measures within others designed to trip us will always slip up, especially if we learn how to query, *As It Pleases God!* How can we query in such a manner? If we query with the Fruits of the Spirit, we can place ourselves on the leading edge of Divine Understanding of the System we are in question. Once we begin to approach life in such a manner, God will invariably send Divine Intervention to assist us in our moments of dire need for direction, correction, or quickening.

Regardless of who we are and why, we all have the same opportunity to protect the Four Corners of the Mind, Body, Soul, and Spirit. However, as a Believer, we must KNOW and UNDERSTAND they need to be protected. Blasphemy, right? Wrong.

Here is what we must know: "*After these things I saw four angels standing at the four corners of the earth, holding the four winds of the earth, that the wind should not blow on the earth, on the sea, or on any tree. Then I saw another angel ascending from the east, having the seal of the living God. And he cried with a loud voice to the four angels to whom it was granted to harm the earth and the sea, saying, 'Do not harm the earth, the sea, or the trees till we have sealed the servants of our God on their foreheads.'*" Revelation 7:1-3.

We can tiptoe around the value of the Tree of Life we possess from within, but if it involves a Spiritual Seal, then we must pay attention. Why should we pay attention to this? Unfortunately, the enemy is banking on our ignorance or the denial of the Divine Truth as the Vicissitudes of Life toss us to and fro, trying to wake us up from our Spiritual Slumber. What is the purpose of the Vicissitudes awakening us? Deception is among us, running rampant, devouring the weak, naive, and untrained. Really? Yes, really! According to Scripture, *"Now when the thousand years have expired, Satan will be released from his prison and will go out to deceive the nations which are in the four corners of the earth, Gog and Magog, to gather them together to battle, whose number is as the sand of the sea."* Revelations 20:7-8.

Once again, the target is the Mind, Body, Soul, and Spirit, making us dull, lukewarm, stiff-necked, disobedient, pompous, lethargic, and distracted, feeding into the lust of the eyes, the lusts of the flesh, and the pride of life. More importantly, no one, from the least to the greatest, is exempt from being tested in such a manner; therefore, we must become geared up with the Whole Armor of God, knowing how to use the Spiritual Tools and Arsenals available to us through the Word of God.

Simply put, we must know where to Divinely Access the information needed to Spiritually Align with what the Holy Spirit is saying. Why? To ensure that we are Spiritually Connecting and Downloading information from the Heavenly of Heavens properly. If not, we can become confused with who is speaking based on the condition of the Four Corners of the Mind, Body, Soul, and Spirit.

To be clear, even if we are full-fledged Believers used by God Almighty, it does not stop the enemy from interjecting or planting negative seeds. He will shoot his shots, and it is our responsibility to know the difference, casting it down or canceling it. How is it possible to know the difference? Once again, we must align it with the Word of God, Fruits of the Spirit, and Christlike Character, leading all things back to the edification and the building of the Kingdom, *As It Pleases God*.

Frankly, it does not matter how we complicate God; His Spiritual Demands and Decrees are always kept simple. The moment we attempt to complicate, rationalize, or justify God, it becomes an automatic sign of deception. Listen, everything we need for our Heaven on Earth Experience according to our Divine Blueprint is already written on the Tablet of the Heart, and we only need a reminder or an AWAKENING.

According to the Heavenly of Heavens, if we dare to allow Divine Reformation to occur with *The Spiritual Middleman Approach*, while, at the same time, wholeheartedly connecting the Four Corners of the Mind, Body, Soul, and Spirit to the Four Corners of the Holy Trinity, *As It Pleases God*, we will become Kingdomly Unstoppable.

Is this humanly possible? Of course, here is what we must know: "*Now I saw a new heaven and a new earth, for the first heaven and the first earth had passed away. Also there was no more sea. Then I, John, saw the holy city, New Jerusalem, coming down out of heaven from God, prepared as a bride adorned for her husband. And I heard a loud voice from heaven saying, 'Behold, the tabernacle of God is with men, and He will dwell with them, and they shall be His people. God Himself will be with them and be their God.'*" Revelations 21:1-3. With this in mind, if we embrace God in a *Spirit to Spirit* Connection, putting away our excuses or pointing the finger, He will indeed embrace us with open arms without reservation, breaking all types of limitations holding us back from Divine Greatness from the inside out.

The Change

Can God really change our lives for the better, even if we are caught up at the moment? Absolutely. He does not require us to be perfect; He only needs a WILLING Vessel to become a work-in-progress, *As It Pleases Him*. No one really knows who God will use until He uses them, which means *The Change* is within us all. I am not here to change anyone; I am here to PREPARE you for *The Change!* Through this AWARENESS, you can choose for yourself based on your own free will and according to your Predestined Blueprint or uniqueness.

In all actuality, I did not begin on this Spiritual Level. I ranked at the bottom, knowing nothing. And I really mean NOTHING! Yet, I was willing to become Spiritually Molded into what God needed me to become according to my Divine Blueprint.

After years of grueling preparation, refusing to give up on myself, allowing God to train me, *As It Pleased Him*, and pursuing my Spiritual Journey regardless, now here we are. More importantly, this is available to anyone willing to listen, learn, grow, and sow back into the Kingdom, putting away all malice while staying in a continual state of repentance.

What if we do not have any sin at all? Frankly, this is where we are deceived; sin is sin, big, small, or indifferent, regardless of whether we understand it or not. So, we must become careful about pointing the finger because we all have some form of residual residue lingering under a different label than what we are judging.

Unbeknown to most, sin may reside in seed form within the heart, through our thoughts, hidden in our emotions, or riddled in our words. Who knows, besides God, the Holy Spirit, or the heavy load bearer, right? *"For all have sinned and fall short of the glory of God."* Romans 3:23. What would cause this to happen? The reasons may vary from person to person, situation to situation, trauma to trauma, and so on; however, listed below are a few examples, but not limited to such:

- ☐ We are operating in self-righteousness.
- ☐ We are blinded by worldliness.
- ☐ Our conscience has become immune to ungodliness.
- ☐ We are outright lying to ourselves.
- ☐ We cannot recognize it due to the lack of humility.
- ☐ We are operating under a generational curse.
- ☐ We are suffering from Spiritual Blindness, Deafness, or Muteness.
- ☐ We are wallowing in self-denial.
- ☐ We are Spiritually Yoked, Oppressed, or Bound.
- ☐ We are clueless about our behaviors, thoughts, actions, words, or emotions.
- ☐ We are brainwashed, misled, or ungodly influenced.
- ☐ We are consumed with rotten fruits.

As we move through living our best lives, sin is introduced by lying to God, ourselves, and others, even if we pretend to be exempt from this practice. Then again, selfishly withholding or hiding the truth, causing someone to fall into a ditch, can become a Spiritual Vice or Weapon as well. By operating in such a manner, we create self-induced strongholds, preventing us from maximizing our greatest potential in or out of the Kingdom.

If we trust ourselves with a lie more than we trust ourselves with the truth, can we really say we trust God wholeheartedly? Allow me to present this question from another angle: 'If we are One with the Holy Trinity, and we wallow in a bed of lies, doubting ourselves or our potential, can we really say we trust God?' For this question, I will PLEAD the 5th on its answer. But I will say this: For these reasons, God requires Spiritual Transparency with Him through our *Spirit to Spirit* Relations.

The Facts

As we go deeper, repenting helps us trust ourselves to change for the better, even if it does not happen overnight. Having the courage to repent continually to become better, stronger, and wiser says a lot about someone who refuses to give up. Frankly, this is what God is looking for in those who are trustworthy with the Assets of the Kingdom or when Spiritually Capitalizing on Divine Wisdom from the Heavens Above. Plus, we are better able to look for the good in all things without negatively judging.

Why must we opt out of judging? Our perception has a way of circumventing the Will of God, especially if the sheep are not strong or wise enough to stand in or on the Word of God for themselves. Then again, if they do not have a clue about their Divine Blueprint or Mission, we can add fuel to the fire, getting them fired up for the wrong things with all sorts of unfruitful distractions, derailments, or traumatizations.

Then again, depending on the situation, we should KINDLY state the facts if necessary to get an understanding. To be crystal clear, getting an understanding in such a manner is not about our truth or their truth...it is about *The Facts*, taking our feelings out of the equation. If we cannot approach a situation in such a manner, it is best NOT to say anything until we take a time-out, a breather, or take it to God in prayer, filtering through the truth or falsity. Once done, we need to keep it moving in the Spirit of Excellence without losing our cool while giving THANKS to God in the highest for the experience.

The moment we give THANKS for the experience, it becomes our bulletproof vest, shielding us from the negative penetration designed to steal our joy and peace. In protecting our sanity the way God intended from the beginning, we must understand the truth versus the facts to avoid the enemy interjecting elements of deception or twisting words. Here is the deal: Our truth contains our perceptions, feelings, biases, conditioning, and so on...and this is what we must lay on the table with God in our transparent *Spirit to Spirit* Relations.

Now, on the other hand, when dealing with human relations, it is best to communicate with factual information, statements, and query questions unless we are speaking about ourselves only. If we have the desire to introduce truth from our eyes without facts regarding another, it is best to use a lead in such as, 'In my opinion,' 'This is how I feel or felt,' 'Based on my perception,' 'From my understanding,' 'This is my take on the situation,' and so on, but not limited to such. Prefacing our conversations with these types of statements creates an open invitation for dialogue of respect instead of disrespect, pointing the finger, or judging.

The key is to redirect back to oneself without projecting negativity upon another. Why is this so important, especially in our Walk with God? Unbeknownst to most, projecting negativity upon another is considered a form of witchcraft; therefore, we must be careful about our words. Unfortunately, this is where many Believers get in trouble in their Spiritual Relations with God, projecting unwarranted curses instead of Blessings. Or, we may find Believers who are Spiritually Decreeing what God has not Divinely Decreed!

For example, we have those condemning people to Hell without any form of compassion, mercy, understanding, or forgiveness. And, with all due respect, we DO NOT have such Spiritual Authority to cast someone into the PIT. Because as long as we have breath in our bodies, we all have a RAY OF HOPE. Whether it is big, small, or indifferent, it is enough in the Eye of God.

To be clear, we have the authority to speak to, bind, rebuke, and cast down the Spirit operating through whatever or whomever, NOT to curse someone. Picturesquely, this is similar to when Jesus said to Peter, *"Get behind Me, Satan! You are an offense to Me, for you are not mindful of the things of God, but the things of men."* Matthew 16:23.

God does not need our help to put people into a PIT. He needs us to exhibit the Fruits of the Spirit and behave Christlike, pulling people out, and everything else will take care of itself. When dealing with *The Facts*, we have two choices in *The Four Corners*:

- ☐ Operate where there is a Spiritual Law governing it. *"Put your sword in its place, for all who take the sword will perish by the sword."* Matthew 26:52.

- ☐ Operate where there is NO SPIRITUAL LAW governing. *"But the fruit of the Spirit is love, joy, peace, patience, kindness, goodness, faithfulness, gentleness and self-control. Against such things there is no law."* Galatians 5:22-23.

For example, Jesus' powerful and impactful dialogue with Peter in Matthew 18:18 was mind-boggling. He says, *"Assuredly, I say to you, whatever you bind on earth will be bound in heaven, and whatever you loose on earth will be loosed in heaven."* In all simplicity, Peter has been granted Spiritual Authority over both EARTHLY and HEAVENLY matters. In addition, his actions on Earth had sweeping, positive, or adverse consequences across the board, extending beyond what he could see physically. The case in point is transcending, and it applies to us as well. *"If my people, who are called by my name, will humble themselves and pray and seek my face and turn from their wicked ways, then I will hear from heaven, and I will forgive their sin and will heal their land."* 2 Chronicles 7:14.

The Chance

Some do not believe in chance, but I do. *"I returned and saw under the sun that—The race is not to the swift, Nor the battle to the strong, Nor bread to the wise, Nor riches to men of understanding, Nor favor to men of skill; But time and chance happen to them all."* Ecclesiastes 9:11.

Personally, I believe in second, third, fourth, fifth chances, and many more if needed to bring ourselves into Purpose on purpose, according to the Divine Blueprint set forth by the Heavenly of

Heavens. Amid multiple plunders for me, in and out of Kingdom Formality, and dropping the ball, I know what it is like to need mercy beyond measure. I am talking about REAL MERCY, the clinging-to-my-life kind of mercy.

In so many words, I needed God to grant me several opportunities to get it right with my Divine Mission, especially when the naysayers condemned me into the Abyss before my time. Had I given up on myself without pushing for another chance in my Relationship with God, *Spirit to Spirit*, I would not know the Power of Hope hidden within everyone, *As It Pleases Him*. Even if we cannot see the forest for the trees or they are blocking our view, just know that the trees blocking us have a mission, and so do we.

The Power of Exchange

When exchanging ideas, thoughts, and perceptions, they become beneficial once appropriately presented to the human psyche. What does the human psyche have to do with the power of exchange? We have an inner-born desire to respect and be respected hidden within each one of us, causing two things to happen:

- ☐ Lacking the interchange of respectfulness causes us to develop and feed our known or unknown insecurities and negativity.

- ☐ Receiving the interchange of respectfulness and humility, publically and privately, builds authentic confidence and courage amid insecurities or to overcome them altogether.

Unbeknown to most, the Kingdom of God does not compromise with those lacking respect and humility at the core. Why is the Kingdom so pristine in humility and respect? First and foremost, the lack of them instigates disobedience, dullness, stiff necks, and rebelliousness. Secondly, it determines our ability to usher in positivity instead of negativity, righteousness in the place of unrighteousness, good as opposed to bad, justice rather than injustice, and so on. Thirdly, without humility and respect, it creates Spiritual Blindness, Deafness, and Muteness, catering to the self-destructive characteristics of Saul, Jezebel, and Judas from the inside out.

As Believers, we often put on a good show, presenting our best side; however, God takes a look at our other side, which lacks proper illumination. He wants the 360-degree Internal View. Why? The human psyche tends to hide things from us, causing us to become blindsided by things we did not know we were dealing with or erecting roadblocks of insecurity. What if we are not insecure? We all have insecurities about something...this is one of the reasons we must trust and have faith in God.

Listen, the first man, Adam, showed us the first sign of insecurity in the Garden of Eden after he and Eve sought the power to know good and evil. Before this incident, partaking of the Forbidden Fruit, according to Scripture, *"They were both naked, the man and his wife, and were not ashamed."* Genesis 2:25.

How did he reveal the characteristics associated with insecurity? He opens his mouth, saying: *"I heard Your voice in the garden, and I was afraid because I was naked; and I hid myself."* Genesis 3:10. And soon after that, the second sign of insecurity appeared when he said: *"The woman whom You gave to be with me, she gave me of the tree, and I ate."* Genesis 3:12.

Regrettably, the natural tendency to be afraid in the commission of disobedience or playing the blame game is not a learned behavior; it is in our DNA. For example, we will notice this character flaw more readily with children because they have not yet learned how to mask it. We think it is cute for a child to behave in such a manner, but it has a severe stronghold attached, primarily if not rectified in its adolescent stages. Thus, we must unlearn or contain the desires associated with the Fruits of the Spirit and Christlike Character as a counteraction. If not, we can unawaringly become consumed by the grips of its hold, damaging the Mind, Body, and Soul.

When fear and blame are within us, we must understand that the insecurity stemming from disobedience linked to the Garden of Eden Experience is playing its rightful course. However, all is not lost; we have the Blood of Jesus to cover our nakedness, and we have the Holy Spirit to guide us amid whatever, with whomever, to avoid the blaming game. Unfortunately, if we choose not to take advantage of the Word of God and the Spiritual Edifices in our *Spirit to Spirit* Relations, *As It Pleases God*, we cannot blame deception for doing what it is designed to do.

Deception is intended to create strongholds, oppression, depression, and yokes. All these are designed to keep us in a power struggle, sorrow, discontentment, or rebellion, feeding what is tied into the lust of the eyes, the lust of the flesh, and the pride of life. If we are not extremely careful, we can turn on ourselves without knowing it, making us feel as if we do not know if we are coming or going. According to the Heavenly of Heavens, it behooves us to engage in the *Show Me* phase for clarity of the *Four Corners*.

Show Me

Have you ever needed someone to hold your hand and show you the way? In life, we often find ourselves at a crossroad or the *Four Corners* of life, unsure of whether we need to turn right, left, or continue straight. Then again, we may have tried everything in our power to make the right decisions but still feel lost, confused, uncertain, frustrated, or in between a rock and a hard place.

How do we rise out of our condition, *As It Pleases God*? We must yield to the 'Show Me' and 'Receiving' Phases in the *Spirit to Spirit* Connection for comfort and guidance. Needing God to show us the way is not new; it has been around since the Beginning of time, and it is not going anywhere. Admitting that we need help and support from our Heavenly Father is prewired in our DNA under the word called SURRENDERING.

For example, when a child is born, they do not know about the things of this world; they need someone to SHOW them, whether it is good, bad, or indifferent, as they mirror whatever is taught, seen, experienced, or heard. Meanwhile, with the Kingdom of Heaven, we have this Spiritual Initiation Phase as well. If we have a desire to Please God, simply and humbly ask Him to SHOW the way with a CLOUD by day (Covering) and a PILLAR of Smoke by night (Illumination) by reciting, "*Show me Your ways, O LORD; teach* me Your paths. Lead me in Your truth and teach me, for You are the God of my salvation; on You I wait all the day." Psalm 25:4-5. "You will show me the path of life; in Your presence is fullness of joy; at Your right hand are pleasures forevermore." Psalm 16:11.

Does quoting these Scriptures work? It works for those who are Willing to put their flesh under the subjection of the Holy Spirit, cover themselves with the Blood of Jesus, and put on the Whole Armor of God with His Word in hand. What about prayer and repentance? Anyone can pray and repent! Blasphemy, right? Wrong! "*You believe that there is one God. You do well. Even the demons believe—and tremble!*" James 2:19.

From experience, I have seen some of the best prayer warriors who could shake the roof off the house, but they lacked the Spiritual Anointing and Authority to cast out or down; plus, their fruits were all rotten and mangled. Then again, when the Vicissitudes of Life came knocking on their door, they crumbled or ran away with their tail in between their legs, turning on everyone or everything they knew to be true about the Heavenly of Heavens. Listen, "*God is not a man, that He should lie, nor a son of man, that He should repent. Has He said, and will He not do? Or has He spoken, and will He not make it good?*" Numbers 23:19.

As I take this a step further, I have seen the most persuasive prayers come from those who were royally on the DARK side, using the Bible to hurt others, but could NOT use the Blood of Jesus or the Holy Spirit in their wrongdoings. If I had not witnessed this with my own eyes, I would not believe it. But fortunately, I witnessed the truth we painstakingly overlook, thinking just because we know the Word of God, we are safe.

In the *Show Me* phase, God is looking for us to surrender to His Divine Will and Ways for the *Spiritual Nutrients* needed to go to the next level. "*Trust in the Lord with all your heart, and lean not on your own understanding; in all your ways acknowledge Him, and He shall direct your paths.*" Proverbs 3:5-6.

CHAPTER FIVE
Spiritual Nutrients

"My little children, these things I write to you, so that you may not sin. And if anyone sins, we have an Advocate with the Father, Jesus Christ the righteous."
1 John 2:1.

Noteworthiness in the Kingdom has a striking resemblance to what God is looking for in Earthen Vessel as opposed to notoriety, even if we appear torn up from the floor up to the naked eye. For example, a well-used Bible will suffer from ripped pages that we must sometimes tape, but regardless of the frailty of the pages, it does not make the Bible or the Word of God of no effect!

In my opinion, a worn or marked-up page says more than unused or untethered ones. Unbeknown to most, according to our DNA, consistent use releases power when used correctly, and *As It Pleases God*. More importantly, we are no different from the pages of our Bible. How is this humanly possible? Are we not a Living Testament or Testimony? Are we not on the same Spiritual Journey as the characters in the Bible? Are we not dealing with the same issues from back then to now? Are we not gleaning Divine Wisdom and Instructions from our Forefathers? Do we not have chapters in our lives serving a specific purpose? Does the Bible not have the answers to everything we are going through or will endure?

Regardless of how we look at the Bible or what we do with it, we are related. How is this possible? Through the Blood of our Forefathers, the Blood of Jesus, Spiritual Covenants, Divine

Promises, Unfulfilled Prophecies, Spiritual Seals, and Forthcoming Revelations. Unbeknown to most, the Blood Covenant runs really, really deep, connecting us to our *Spirit to Spirit* Relations through the Blood of Jesus, giving us Spiritual Access to the Holy Spirit, even if we are in denial of the onset.

For the Divine Unveiling of *The Spiritual Middleman Approach*, Jesus gives us the Lord's Prayer to help us with our Heaven on Earth Experience, separating us from man-made systems, techniques, and formulas regulating our salvation. It says, *"In this manner, therefore, pray: Our Father in heaven, Hallowed be Your name. Your kingdom come. Your will be done on earth as it is in heaven. Give us this day our daily bread. And forgive us our debts, As we forgive our debtors. And do not lead us into temptation, But deliver us from the evil one. For Yours is the kingdom and the power and the glory forever. Amen."* Matthew 6:9-13. Although we are all different with various wants, needs, and desires, this prayer provides a Heavenly Guideline of Kingdom Expectations.

What does using the Bible for our Daily Bread have to do with anything? It is a Spiritual Decree from God that we often overlook or forget about. When we lack sweating during our Spiritual Tilling process, eat freely without heavy toiling, refuse to get our hands dirty for the Kingdom, forget our ORIGIN, and take the easy way out without God, we set ourselves up for defeat. In so many words, we cannot become lazy regarding our Divine Blueprint and spiritual Gifts, or remove God from the equation of life. If we do, we will Spiritually Starve ourselves without realizing it, thinking someone else is the problem. When, in all actuality, the dust is calling our name because we cease to Spiritually Sweat, being in Purpose on purpose. Blasphemy, right? Wrong! I do not wish the dust upon anyone, but according to Scripture, once again, it says: *"In the sweat of your face you shall eat bread Till you return to the ground, For out of it you were taken; For dust you are, And to dust you shall return."* Genesis 3:19.

The sweat we put into the Word of God determines the type of BREAD we consume in or out of the Kingdom, regardless of how long it takes us to get it into our System of Conveyance. What does this mean for us in layman's terms? It does not matter if we are an early or late starter; the MILK to the MEAT of God's Word is required to understand what is required of us and why. With all due respect, the moment we omit them, we will tend to feast on the Word's Meat when we have not begun to suckle while missing the Bread of Life altogether. By doing so, we will begin to suffocate ourselves Mentally, Physically, Emotionally, and Spiritually because we have not learned how to digest the Milking Stages in our Spiritual Classroom. Still, we have the nerve to lead others with untilled ground as if we have it going on in the Eye of God. While, at the same time, knowing He is indeed giving us a side-eye as we continue in our folly on a cycle of déjà vu with little or no inner healing.

Why would God give us a side-eye when it is our choice to consume Milk, Meat, or Bread? According to the Heavenly of Heavens, as a part of our DNA in Earthen Vessels, we will need the Milk of the Word of God to draw us in to sustain us, particularly in the beginning, to understand who we are and why. For me, this is similar to a roadmap to developing discipline and getting our Spiritual Digestive juices flowing. The Meat of the Word is designed to align us with the Promises of God, our Divine Blueprint, and to lead God's sheep, in or out of the fold. The Bread of Life is the daily nutrients needed to sustain our human faculties in Earthen Vessels between the Milking and Meat stages for each level of our Spirituality.

All in all, Milk, Meat, and Bread are continuous cycles or stages, graduating us from one level to the next. The moment we stop drinking, eating, and receiving, *As It Pleases God*, we digress in status or regress levels. Why does regression or digression happen? We cannot eat, drink, and receive from the Kingdom's Table without putting in the work, Spiritually Tilling our own ground while becoming grateful, fruitful, and shareable.

We can quickly get the boot or wander in our Spiritual Desert like the Children of Israel if we begin to hoard, complain, or contend against the Will of God or His Vessels. Why would this happen, especially when we have grace and mercy working on our behalf? We cannot take grace and mercy for granted or misuse their intent. If we do, the System of the Kingdom will perceive us to be a lukewarm, stiff-necked, or dull robber or thief. Is this Biblical? *"Most assuredly, I say to you, he who does not enter the sheepfold by the door, but climbs up some other way, the same is a thief and a robber."* John 10:1.

For this reason, we must become careful about the alternative ways of beating the Spiritual Systems of God. They are ABSOLUTE, similar to the Law of Gravity, unless a HIGHER LAW supersedes it!

Now, on the other hand, we dare not tread out of our league or venture on untilled ground without the Holy Trinity. If we do, we become Spiritually Vulnerable, becoming susceptible to the enemy's wiles, especially when acting in total disobedience and self-induced piousness. More importantly, if we operate on a Spiritual Level we are not trained for, we can get hurt for opening doors we are not equipped to close, especially if we have unrepentant sin blocking our Divine Access.

How do we know if we are operating on untilled ground? It is revealed in our fruits, words, thoughts, and character. The moment we find ourselves out of control, envious, jealous, covetous, prideful, manipulative, hateful, cruel, and so on, with negative character traits, the bells and whistles of the conscience should alert us. In addition, a red flag of alarm also warns us when we are consumed with using others to do what we are not willing or capable of doing for ourselves. Unfortunately, this is where we can find the bullies and the control freaks hanging out, seeking the next victim to till their ground for them. Why? They often think Spiritually Tilling their ground is beneath them or their pedigree, similar to the Cain Experience.

Title Blockage Analogy

What is the Cain Experience? It is the *Title Blockage Analogy* where we become caught up in titles and not our Divine Blueprint, Spiritual Righteousness, or the Will of God. For example, Cain was given the Tiller of the Ground title, but he was unwilling to embrace it due to his secret envy and jealousy of his brother, Abel, the Keeper of Sheep.

In Genesis 4:2, it says, *"Then she bore again, this time his brother Abel. Now Abel was a keeper of sheep, but Cain was a tiller of the ground."* Cain continually allowed the negative manifestations of his unkempt feelings to consume him, waiting for the right moment to slay his brother. In my opinion, this was not a 'just happened' moment; it was a TIMING one. How can I say such a thing, right? Frankly, it was God who rejected his offering, not Abel. Yet, Cain became angry at his brother instead of God, which means he was looking for an excuse to play dirty. Why would he want to play dirty? He felt his brother had taken something from him or possessed what he deserved as being the elder brother.

All in all, Cain was waiting for a reasonable justification of his debauched conscience. He knew sin was lying at his door, but he chose not to overrule it. How do I know? God spoke directly to him, *Spirit to Spirit!*

Listen, God had a conversation with him about his inner struggles, feeding Him the Spiritual Meat he needed to overcome the temptation from within. If God took the time to query, point out his erring, and give him specific instructions in such a manner, it meant that Cain was out of the Milking Stages of his Spiritual Relationship with God. What does this mean? Cain knew better! Here is what Genesis 4:6-7 says: *"So the LORD said to Cain, 'Why are you angry? And why has your countenance fallen? If you do well, will you not be accepted? And if you do not do well, sin lies at the door. And its desire is for you, but you should rule over it.'"*

Yet, after this conversation with God and another with his brother, the Words from God fell upon deaf ears, causing Spiritual Blindness and some form of Spiritual Paralysis, blocking his sense of good or proper reasoning and judgment. As a result, Cain allowed sin to consume him, killing his brother without batting an eye. Here is what Genesis 4:8 says about this matter: *"Now Cain talked with Abel his brother; and it came to pass, when they were in the field, that Cain rose up against Abel his brother and killed him."*

What would cause Cain to want to silence his brother? He was hoping it would re-establish his relationship with God to what it was previously before the birth of Abel. The bottom line is that he had an underlying and unresolved issue with selfishness, which was reflected in his offerings to God.

In all actuality, when Cain ROSE against his brother, it is evident that he felt beneath him for some reason. Listen to me and listen well; there would be NO reason to RISE against his brother if he did not feel inferior somehow. Blasphemy, right? Wrong! Eve imparted to Cain early on, saying, *'I have acquired a man from the*

LORD.' Genesis 4:1. So, Cain subconsciously did not want anyone to take his place with Adam, Eve, and God, nor did he want to share his title, feel rejected, compared, or not meet up to God's Divine Standards because of another man.

From then to now, we will still see this selfish character trait in our children today, which must be corrected in the early or milking stages of development. Why? Unfortunately, it is a Seed of Deception of the 'Mine, Mine, Mine' systemic glitch designed for our children to assassinate each other without realizing what they are doing until the deed is done. More importantly, it is imperative to do a preservation title check to ensure we are not slaying our brothers and sisters who are above or beneath us. What is the reason for doing so? The identity crisis that Cain fell victim to is now running rampant among us today in plain sight. But hear this: Regardless of how we feel, we are accountable for our behaviors, actions, or reactions, positively or negatively, and we have authority over them as well. If we do not take authority, *As It Pleases God*, it can cause *Spiritual Tares*.

Spiritual Tares

What do Spiritual Tares have to do with our Spiritual Seeds? We must become cautious about sowing seeds of discord on good ground because the Spiritual Law of Multiplication or Duplication still applies accordingly. Here is what we must know: *"But he who received seed on the good ground is he who hears the word and understands it, who indeed bears fruit and produces: some a hundredfold, some sixty, some thirty."* Matthew 13:23.

According to the Heavenly of Heavens, even if we do not understand or willfully sow bad seeds, this Spiritual Law is still applicable, which can be Spiritually Enforced by those who UNDERSTAND this Divine Principle. What does this mean for the Spiritual Elites? This answer is in the next parable, *"The kingdom of heaven is like a man who sowed good seed in his field; but while men slept, his enemy came and sowed tares among the wheat and went his way."* Matthew 13:24-25. The enemy will blame God for orchestrating catastrophes or events that He only allowed to disrupt their hidden agenda or expose their seeds of corruption, allowing Believers to step up their game in the Kingdom.

When leaving a Trail of Tares or treading upon and disrespecting Spiritual Territories changes the Spiritual Rules to the GAME. How do we change the rules, especially when we are clueless? Whether we understand Spiritual Violations or not, *As It Pleases God*, the Spiritual Elites from the Ancient of Days gain Divine Leverage. How do they gain leverage? They can change the Spiritual Trajectory of the Four Winds for the GREATER GOOD due to profound Spiritual Error, Disrespect, Deception, or LIE. What does this mean for us? If one does not understand what I am saying here, IT IS NOT FOR YOU!

Now, for whom this is for, our Spiritual Forefathers demand RESPECT, regardless of whether or not we have taken the time to understand the Historical Edifices binding us to certain people, places, things, or Bloodlines. When we involve qualmish agendas into Spirituality to disrupt the lives of the innocent without doing our homework, we can involve Spiritual Principalities that we do not understand. For this reason, we should exercise extreme caution with all things Spiritual, primarily when operating in the Spirit of Error, Rebellion, or Disobedience.

Why is this such a big deal when we are free to do whatever, whenever, with whomever? Just because we are free does not mean we do not have consequences for our actions, reactions, words, or lack of respect. Nor does it negate the Spiritual Laws governing a particular person, place, thing, event, group, or culture.

Disrespecting another man's territory, who has sown the Spiritual Seeds in the ground, can create known or unknown Spiritual Taboos. Are Spiritual Taboos real? Or are they based on our beliefs, culture, or perception? They are real, containing our faith, beliefs, hopes, culture, perception, and a little bit of this and some of that, stemming back to the Book of Genesis, coming full circle to the present.

The first Spiritual Taboo was with the Tree of the Knowledge of Good and Evil. "*And the LORD God commanded the man, saying, 'Of every tree of the garden you may freely eat; but of the tree of the knowledge of good and evil you shall not eat, for in the day that you eat of it you shall surely die.'*" Genesis 2:16-17. And we all know what happened after that.

The second Spiritual Taboo was when Abel's Blood cried out from the ground. *"And He said, 'What have you done? The voice of your brother's blood cries out to Me from the ground. So now you are cursed from the earth, which has opened its mouth to receive your brother's blood from your hand.'"* Genesis 4:10-11. What does this have to do with us? According to Scripture, this Spiritual Taboo is still in effect. It says, *"By faith Abel offered to God a more excellent sacrifice than Cain, through which he obtained witness that he was righteous, God testifying of his gifts; and through it he being dead still speaks."* Hebrews 11:4.

The third Spiritual Taboo was when God placed a mark on Cain to prevent anyone from taking his life. *"And the LORD said to him, 'Therefore, whoever kills Cain, vengeance shall be taken on him sevenfold.' And the LORD set a mark on Cain, lest anyone finding him should kill him."* Genesis 4:15.

When dealing with God and His Divine Covenants binding us to Him, we may not get the full details of why He is doing what He does. We must RESPECT His decision, even when we do not understand it. Listen, a Spiritual Taboo is a Spiritual Restriction set forth by our faith and our *Spirit to Spirit* Connection to our Heavenly Father. Although it is available to all, only used by a few. And just because a person does not know how to develop a Spiritual Relationship that keeps on living, it does not give us the right to disrespect others or their Spiritual Mark or Testimony.

As a Word to the Wise, if one has a Spiritual Advisor or Seer who DID NOT warn of impending Spiritual DANGER when treading upon Spiritual Ground, a Spiritual Taboo, or a Trail of Tares, one should consider a Spiritual Replacement. Why do they need to be replaced? In or out of the Kingdom, they should KNOW better! How could they have known? Hear me, and hear me well; the Holy Spirit does not play around in this area, PERIOD! And, nor should you!

What if we are Highly Anointed, and the Holy Spirit does not reveal impending danger? It means we are severely Spiritually Blind, Deaf, Mute, or operating in the Spirit of Rebellion or Error. How can we operate in such a manner, especially when we are CHOSEN? Regardless of our Spiritual Status, our conscience, instincts, or Spiritual Compass should have kicked in, alerting us by default that something is not right or there is impending danger ahead. Even if we do not understand it, whether it is God-enabled or blocked, it is a misunderstanding, we have made an outright mistake, or we simply ignored the Spiritual Nudges, we should get something. If we get nothing whatsoever, it is an indication that our Spiritual Compass (instincts/conscience), our seeds are keeled, or there is a *Systemic Glitch*.

The Systemic Glitch

What is the big deal about sweat, systemic glitches, and our Spiritual Relationship with God? First and foremost, the enemy is busy recruiting those who let their guard down due to a lack of self-control or a victim mentality. Secondly, unbeknown to most, where there is no sweat involved, we will tend to fall asleep or become lazy Mentally, Physically, Emotionally, and Spiritually, leading us into all types of temptation. Unfortunately, this is why some people fall asleep on anything having to do with God. Or, they become a livewire with anything related to worldliness or selfishness. Really? Yes, really!

Even Jesus knew about the power of sweat and reminded us to watch and pray to avoid temptation. Here is the Scripture aligning: *"When He came to the place, He said to them, 'Pray that you may not enter into temptation.' And He was withdrawn from them about a stone's throw, and He knelt down and prayed, saying, 'Father, if it is Your will, take this cup away from Me; nevertheless not My will, but Yours, be done.' Then an angel appeared to Him from heaven, strengthening Him. And being in agony, He prayed more earnestly. Then His sweat became like great drops of blood falling down to the ground. When He rose up from prayer, and had come to His disciples, He found them sleeping from sorrow. Then He said to them, 'Why do you sleep? Rise and pray, lest you enter into temptation.'"* Luke 22:40-46.

Bread of Life

More importantly, Jesus promoted the Self-Contained Bread of Life as the Word of God, feeding and aligning us according to the Will of our Father in Heaven. Here is what we must know: *"For the bread of God is He who comes down from heaven and gives life to the world. Then they said to Him, 'Lord, give us this bread always.' And Jesus said to them, 'I am the bread of life. He who comes to Me shall never hunger, and he who believes in Me shall never thirst.'"* John 6:33-35.

The Breaking of Bread to open our Spiritual Eyes to see beyond the natural is at our fingertips. How is this possible? According to Scripture, *"Now it came to pass, as He sat at the table with them, that He took bread, blessed and broke it, and gave it to them. Then their eyes were opened and they knew Him; and He vanished from their sight."* Luke 24:30-31.

In my opinion, it is best to Break Bread with God first before doing it with anyone else. Why? There may be a Judas or Jezebel among us, so we need our Spiritual Eyes, Ears, and Voice open to Spiritually Discern, *As It Pleases God.*

Why can we not just excommunicate them? They may be a part of our Divine Plan or Blueprint; therefore, if we allow God to be God without playing Him, we can glean and extract the Spiritual Lessons, Blessings, and Wisdom from them as a stepping stone to our next. How is it possible to do so, or how do we know the difference? Simply put, keep the peace!

Just because God reveals information to us does not mean we must act upon it negatively, get out of character, or call someone out. Frankly, through the Grace of God, I would not be able to write on such a Spiritual Level without having the Judases and Jezebels provoking my Divine Training and Understanding, equipping me for such a time as this. What does this mean? God allowed my enemies to train and test me, building my Spiritual Fruits, Strength, and Astuteness. And all I did was step into the Spiritual Classroom to learn and document, learn and document, learn and document some more, leaving no stone unturned, allowing them to become my footstool.

Once we Break Bread with God, *As It Pleases Him,* using the Fruits of the Spirit, and behave Christlike, we can stand amongst whatever or whomever without flinching an inch or clueing them in that we are *'In The Know.'* Henceforth, with this same Spiritual Anointing in conjunction with *The Spiritual Middleman Approach,* we will also know when to move out, around, and about.

How do we recognize when to hold, fold, or walk away? When we have a *Spirit to Spirit* Connection, the nudging of the Spirit becomes undeniable, unquestionable, or unrelenting to a Divine Knowing. Similar to the Scripture, *"But he who enters by the door is the shepherd of the sheep. To him the doorkeeper opens, and the sheep hear his voice; and he calls his own sheep by name and leads them out. And when he brings out his own sheep, he goes before them; and the sheep follow him, for they know his voice. Yet they will by no means follow a stranger, but will flee from him, for they do not know the voice of strangers."* John 10:2-5. For *"My sheep hear My voice, and I know them, and they follow Me."* John 10:27.

What is the purpose of knowing all of this information? First, we need it! Secondly, according to Scripture, without pointing the finger, *"For the hearts of this people have grown dull. Their ears are hard of hearing, And their eyes they have closed, Lest they should see with their eyes and hear with their ears, Lest they should understand with their hearts and turn, So that I should heal them."* Acts 28:27.

As a part of our DNA, we all require healing or inspiration somehow from the Vicissitudes designed to train us in Earthen Vessels. Therefore, we should not omit the Bread of Life because it contains the Milk and Meat needed to sustain us Mentally, Physically, Emotionally, and Spiritually, taking us from the background into the forefront of Divine Greatness in due season.

Spiritual Benefits

The ambiguities in our ambitions determine the pleasantness or disgust in how we feel, think, or behave. Unbeknown to most, the way we perceive or process life is hidden in knowing the Benefits of God, the Kingdom, and worldliness. By understanding the differences, we can better put people, places, and things into their proper perspective. We cannot ignore God, the Kingdom, and worldliness as if it does not exist, or it will downplay our *Spiritual Benefits*.

Simply put, the *Spiritual Benefits*, or the lack thereof, are secretly GRAFTED in the way we truly feel. How would our feelings affect our *Spiritual Benefits*? If we are afraid of being ourselves, how can we maximize our Predestined Benefits or Blueprint, *As It Pleases God*? We cannot, and until we come to ourselves, God will not open the

Floodgates of the Kingdom to those hellbent on being a people-pleaser instead of a God-Pleaser.

Before we go any further, we should want to PLEASE God because it is the right thing to do, especially since we did not create ourselves. However, to receive the *Spiritual Benefits* of the Kingdom, have you taken the time to ask God Himself, *Spirit to Spirit*? Here is what Psalm 116:12-14 says about this matter: *"What shall I render to the LORD For all His benefits toward me? I will take up the cup of salvation, and call upon the name of the LORD. I will pay my vows to the LORD now in the presence of all His people."*

To take up our Spiritual Cup of Benefits, we must become a Servant of the Kingdom, feeding God's sheep and giving THANKS in all things, regardless of how it appears to the naked eye. Really? Yes, Really! So, let us align this accordingly, *"O LORD, truly I am Your servant; I am Your servant, the son of Your maidservant; You have loosed my bonds. I will offer to You the sacrifice of thanksgiving, and will call upon the name of the LORD. I will pay my vows to the LORD now in the presence of all His people, in the courts of the LORD's house, in the midst of you, O Jerusalem. Praise the LORD!"* Psalm 116:16-19.

In changing the trajectory of our lives, God PROMISED us the Holy Spirit, Who is indeed our Comforter in our time of need. The Holy Spirit is our personal assistant hidden in plain sight. For this reason, we must MASTER the ability to call upon Him before depending upon others to do what we may already have the *Know-How* to do. Or, better yet, relying on Him (The Holy Spirit) to answer questions, remind us of what we already have the answers to, or send confirmation to what He is relaying to us in our *Spirit to Spirit* Conversations is the right thing to do, especially in the Eye of God. According to Scripture, let us Spiritually Seal this Promise within the human psyche: *"But the Helper, the Holy Spirit, whom the Father will send in My name, He will teach you all things, and bring to your remembrance all things that I said to you."* John 14:26.

What is the purpose of having a Helper? If we do not receive Divine Help the way God has designed for us to receive it, we will become lonely, feeling like an orphan among the masses. While, at the same time, looking for love in all the wrong places, picking up habits catering to our longings, or developing character traits that take us away from the Will of God. But amid all, there is helpful hope for us. Here is the Divine Decree: *"And I will pray the Father, and He will give you another Helper, that He may abide with you forever—the Spirit of truth, whom the world cannot receive, because it neither sees Him nor knows Him; but you know Him, for He dwells with you and will be in you. I will not leave you orphans; I will come to you."* John 14:16-18.

As we all know, having ACCESS to God is essential. Yet, we do not often know that He has a way of hiding from us to see what we will do or how we will react. Really? Yes, really! What is the purpose of God going into hiding? It is designed to TEST us and our faith, determining the *Spiritual Benefits* or Repercussions. Here is what the Bible has to say about how He hides from us. *"And He said: 'I will hide My face from them, I will see what their end will be, For they are a perverse generation, Children in whom is no faith.' "* Deuteronomy 32:20.

How do we know if we are beginning to fail the God-Induced tests? It will vary from person to person, situation to situation, anointing to anointing, and so on. However, we must MASTER what He hates and what provokes Him. For example, Deuteronomy 32:21 says, *"They have provoked Me to jealousy by what is not God; They have moved Me to anger by their foolish idols. But I will provoke them to jealousy by those who are not a nation; I will move them to anger by a foolish nation."*

The bottom line is that by participating in what is NOT pleasing in the Eye of God and engaging in idolatry, they are both firestarters in the Kingdom. Why? They cause corruption and debauchery in everything we do, say, and become, without realizing what is happening until we are royally yoked or soul-tied. All of these will eventually result in some form of defeat or humiliation, as if we are the victim, forgetting the previous seeds sown in and out of season. Then again, it may place cracks in our foundation, initiating instabilities within the human psyche while appearing strong.

For this reason, we should keep in mind, when in a state of outright disobedience: *"The sword shall destroy outside; there shall be terror within for the young man and virgin, the nursing child with the man of gray hairs."* Deuteronomy 32:25. What does this have to do with us?

No one is exempt from inner trauma when the sword of deeds or destruction is involved.

Listen, we cannot approach God sideways and expect Him to accept what we are offering. From much experience, He will become SILENT on us. Why? Indulging in what He hates is an insult to the Kingdom and what it stands for. According to Proverbs 6:16-19, here is what God hates:

- ☐ Pride.
- ☐ A lying tongue.
- ☐ Hands that shed innocent blood.
- ☐ A heart that devises wicked plans.
- ☐ Feet that are swift in running to evil.
- ☐ A false witness who speaks lies.
- ☐ One who sows discord among brethren.

We cannot feed God what He does not like and then expect the *Spiritual Benefits* to flow in and out of our lives without fail.

As It Pleases God, if we give Him what He wants, He will give us the desires of the heart, benefiting us for the greater good. For the record, God is not complicated. We make Him appear as such because we like treading the fence, gratifying the lust of the eyes, the lust of the flesh, and indulging in the pride of life.

The superficial images of being Heaven Sent or superior over another exhaust us, complicating our lives beyond measure. In so many words, keeping up with the Joneses keeps us stressed out, confused, and frustrated with ourselves, others, and God.

When we expect outer benefits before the inner ones, we inadvertently set ourselves up to become wishy-washy, unpredictable, and self-made. Whereas, if we kept up with God, we would find our lives taking a whole new direction with an accurate filter and testing system from the Heavenly of Heavens. When our lives are appropriately aligned with the Will of God or our Divine Blueprint, it will attract those who are in the plan and purge those who are not. For this reason, when benefiting in the Eye of God, we cannot become too emotionally attached or refuse to let go of what or who is not a part of our Divine Mission.

To capitalize on the *Spiritual Benefits* of Pleasing God, we must know what moves Him to ACTION on our behalf. Listen to me and listen well: God loves the Fruits of the Spirit, which are Love, Joy, Peace, Patience, Kindness, Goodness, Faithfulness, Gentleness, and Self-Control. All of which cannot be bought, even if we attempt to do so. Plus, if we attempt to purchase something appearing as a Fruit of the Spirit, it is only temporary or conditional, and in due time, the wolf in sheep's clothing will reveal itself when provoked.

According to the Heavenly of Heavens, if we Master the Fruits of the Spirit, *As It Pleases God*, we will not have an issue with loving God, ourselves, and others with no strings attached. How can the MASTERING PROCESS work on our behalf? The ultimate bliss of Inner Joy will become surreal to the onlookers. Supernatural Peace brings a calmness within the human psyche that science has yet to tap into, making the issues of life become our driving force or footstool ALL THE WAY UP! Kindness can be exhibited amid the Vicissitudes designed to cause us to lash out or get out of character. Righteousness and Goodness Mentally, Physically, Emotionally, and Spiritually carry a Cloak of Favor, putting our enemies to boot. Trustworthy faith makes us a force to be reckoned with in or out of the kingdom. The Gentleness of the Kingdom helps us to speak the language of another, causing them to open up to us where they were previously closed. Most of all, the exhibition of Self-Control allows us to become disciplined in the areas that most would neglect correction.

What are the *Spiritual Benefits* associated with the Fruits of the Spirit and Christlike Character? It contains the Hidden Illumination of the Commandments already written on the Tablet of the Heart through the Blood of Jesus. Unbeknown to most, this is needed to keep our hands Blessed and Divinely Guided, allowing us to self-correct before God-Correction occurs. Here is what Proverbs 6:21-23 says, "Bind them continually upon your heart; tie them around your neck. When you roam, they will lead you; when you sleep, they will keep you; and when you awake, they will speak with you. For the commandment is a lamp, and the law a light; reproofs of instruction are the way of life."

When dealing with the *Spiritual Benefits* of God, the goal is to avoid the mindset of bargaining or begging Him for what rightly belongs to us. We must AWAKEN from our slumber; as iron sharpens iron, we have what it takes—we simply need to know it! Today, my friend, straighten your Spiritual Crown and step up to the plate to POSSESS the Promises and the *Spiritual Benefits* of the Kingdom.

Spiritual Strength

Why is it essential to develop and maintain our Spiritual Strength? It helps to avoid the secret annihilation from the inside out. We are designed to set and achieve goals. If we do not do so according to our Divine Blueprint, we will become subordinates to the Divine Blueprint of another, with or without our permission. Indeed, if this is what we desire, God does not have any qualms with us doing so. He is very patient because He knows the longing or emptiness from within is not going away. After all, it is embedded in our DNA.

Unbeknown to most, the Promises of God are also in our DNA as well, and the deficiencies in our blood are of our own making. For me, this concept is similar to NOT taking vitamins and causing our body to work against itself due to malnourishment or lack of nutrients needed to sustain a specific blood deficiency.

Whereas in the Kingdom, as it relates to our Divine Blueprint, the Spiritual Nutrients needed to nurture the Soil of our Blueprint involve becoming ONE with the Holy Trinity, using the Word of God, applying the Fruits of the Spirit, and exhibiting Christlike Character before attempting to seek the Promises. Why? We must approach God, *As It Pleases Him*, not how it pleases us or a list of wants or requests, without becoming GRATEFUL for what we already have.

If God desired for us to have a run-of-the-mill life, He would have given us a mill to think for us. Instead, He gave us Blessings, Birthrights, and Promises equipped with their own set of Divine Tools and Provisions to Spiritually Till our own ground while thinking for ourselves. More importantly, all of our Spiritual Means can transfer from one generation to the next, causing each generation to become better than the previous.

CHAPTER SIX
Kingdom Weights

"Therefore, having been justified by faith, we have peace with God through our Lord Jesus Christ, through whom also we have access by faith into this grace in which we stand, and rejoice in hope of the glory of God." Romans 5:1-2.

If one has ever been weighed down, we know what it is like to carry a heavy load Mentally, Physically, Emotionally, or Spiritually. Nor can we discount the experience because the Vicissitudes of Life were real and sometimes unrelenting, causing us to seek God like never before. However, when the Kingdom Weights are upon us, yoking us to the core, we have two options:

- ☐ We must step up to the Spiritual Plate, girding up our loins, walking in faith and not by sight, releasing our unlimited potentiality.

- ☐ We must step down, watching others pass us by, doing what we do not have the courage to do, or fear what we cannot, limiting ourselves.

Why do we only have two choices? Unfortunately, we cannot stay the same, even if we fool ourselves into thinking we can. Growth is inevitable! We grow up or grow down, positively or negatively. Even on the scale, we can visually see our weight fluctuate, depending on what we eat and drink, from the infant to the elderly stages of life. And so it is in the Realm of the Spirit. If we lack understanding in this area, negative growth will occur by default due to our worldly surroundings.

The elevated commitment factors are on a sliding scale, causing us to seek freedom outwardly when we are secretly yoked from within. To avoid having a weighted scale, we must place God on the rafter. Would God make it heavier? Absolutely not! He is weightless and all-knowing, yet He contains Absolute Power in and over all things as our burden bearer and heavy load carrier.

In my opinion, using The Spiritual Middleman Approach is like having a Bonus inside of a Pro-Bono Package, and all we have to do is AGREE and RECEIVE in Totality and Oneness. In doing so, As It Pleases God, we cannot become lukewarm, dull, or stiff-necked, especially when the Vicissitudes and Cycles of Life are designed to mature and train us to become better, wiser, and stronger for our Heaven on Earth Experience.

In seeking Divine Liberation, if we think of God, our Divine Blueprint, or our Spirit to Spirit Relations as a burden, it indicates a need for a Spiritual Overhaul. Regardless of what we require, please do not feel bad or guilty for feeling Spiritually Burdened; it is entirely normal. Even I, myself, had to go through a MASSIVE Spiritual Overhaul that I would not wish upon my worst enemy. As a part of my Spiritual Training Process, and under the Divine Authority of the Heavenly of Heavens, I know what I am talking about, especially when bringing others into Divine Alignment, As It Pleases God, and with The Spiritual Middleman Approach.

Unveiling The Pharisees' Spirit

In *Unveiling The Pharisees' Spirit* or Religious Sect of today, with their strict adherence to the law and their beliefs, it somehow leaves little wiggle room for being human. In reality, we are Spiritual Beings having a human experience. Even if we are corrupt and self-serving or have superiority and self-righteousness in public or private, life will happen to us all.

It does not matter if we believe that we are better than others because of our religious beliefs or practices; we are entitled to our opinions due to free will. Judging others harshly and looking down on those who do not share our beliefs or practices with a legalistic approach instead of *The Spiritual Middleman Approach* is the reason WHY Dr. Y. Bur, The WHY Doctor, exists. We do not focus on the Letter of the Law; we focus on the SPIRIT of the LAW and the SPIRIT behind the LAW, bringing the LETTER under it, *As It Pleases God*. Simply put, having the Spirit of God behind the Law and covering it with the Blood of Jesus is much more POWERFUL than having a man behind it.

Why not the Letter of the Law? Having the Letter without the Spirit can become tricky in the Eye of God. Why? It leads to all types of disobedience, pride, and a lack of humility or authenticity. Unfortunately, in this state of being, some may feel that they deserve God's favor more than others, and they may look down on those who struggle with sin or doubt. Then again, it can lead to a lack of empathy and compassion, as well as an unwillingness to help others, primarily if there are zero benefits in doing so.

Once again, we will all experience a heavy load of deprivation when transitioning from worldly to Spiritual. If someone DOES NOT experience withdrawal in the transitioning phase, I am immediately alerted with red flags. Is this not judging someone's journey? Simply put, the enemy fights for its territory, and if there is no battle, it means that it still has dominion. So, we should never become fooled by the hoopla, foolery, or masks; we must exercise WISDOM. We should stick to the Biblical Principles associated with Spiritual Protocols and Levels set forth by God Almighty, examining our Spiritual Fruits and Christlike Character while avoiding latching on to the Pharisees' Spirit. To avoid the Pharisees' Spirit, grab hold of the Holy Trinity and become ONE, *As It Pleases God*.

What does the Pharisees' Spirit have to do with anything? Respectfully speaking, first, the Pharisees are the ones who hit people over the head with the Bible without living by example or exhibiting love, compassion, and mercy for God's sheep. Secondly, this type of Spirit scatters the Flock of God or keeps them in chains, Mentally, Physically, Emotionally, and Spiritually, without teaching them the TRUTH. Thirdly, they are the ones who create the deadweight amongst God's sheep through vile manipulation, mind games, or pimping Him.

Is the Pharisees' Spirit Biblical? Of course, I would have it no other way. *"Woe to you, scribes and Pharisees, hypocrites! For you pay tithe of mint and anise and cummin, and have neglected the weightier matters of the law: justice and mercy and faith. These you ought to have done, without leaving the others undone. Blind guides, who strain out a gnat and swallow a camel! Woe to you, scribes and Pharisees, hypocrites! For you cleanse the outside of the cup and dish, but inside they are full of extortion and self-indulgence. Blind Pharisee, first cleanse the inside of the cup and dish, that the outside of them may be clean also."* Matthew 23:23-26.

We can pretend this whitewashing is not happening, but in all actuality, it is! This Pharisees' Spirit is hurting and destroying our own, causing them to look for another way or alternative means, especially when we KNOW the way, while leading God's sheep astray, Mentally, Physically, Emotionally, and Spiritually for selfish gain. Do we think God will sit on His hands without Divine Correction as if He does not possess the Spiritual Weights needed to bring Divine Change? Let us ponder this question deeply as we move on.

Nevertheless, in *Unveiling The Pharisees' Spirit*, whether it resides within us or someone else, here is what to look for, but not limited to such:

- ☐ Obsessing over rules and regulations.
- ☐ Violating the free will of another.
- ☐ Cannot show love, mercy, and compassion.
- ☐ Believing that one's religious practices are superior.
- ☐ Judging others harshly for their beliefs or practices.
- ☐ Putting on a show of righteousness in public while being corrupt in private.
- ☐ Believing that one is more deserving of God's favor than others.
- ☐ Believing that one's own knowledge and understanding of Scripture is superior to others.
- ☐ Being legalistic and inflexible in one's beliefs.
- ☐ Being quick to point out the faults of others while ignoring one's own faults.

- ☐ Looking down on those who struggle with sin or doubt.
- ☐ Lacking empathy and compassion for others.
- ☐ Believing that one is always right and others are always wrong.
- ☐ Refusing to listen to the opinions or perspectives of others.
- ☐ Being unwilling to help those in need.
- ☐ Using religion as a means of control or power over others.
- ☐ Being more concerned with outward appearances than inner character.
- ☐ Being critical and judgmental of those who do not share one's beliefs.
- ☐ Believing that one's own interpretation of Scripture is the only correct one.
- ☐ Refusing to acknowledge or admit one's faults or mistakes.
- ☐ Being hypocritical in one's actions and attitudes.
- ☐ Cannot exhibit the Fruits of the Spirit.
- ☐ Refuse to behave Christlike.
- ☐ Always pointing the finger, deflecting responsibility.
- ☐ Playing the blaming game.

Why do we need to know these characteristics? By not understanding the characteristics, we can fall victim. Then again, it can lead to a lack of trust, with a hidden fear of others not being genuine. Can this really happen? It is happening all around us, but we are NOT expressing our concerns openly, giving the psyche the power to yoke or fight against us. *"For where envy and self-seeking exist, confusion and every evil thing are there."* James 3:16. So, if we are a different person behind closed doors than when in public or have rotten fruits all over the place, we have work to do.

Why must we work on ourselves when in such a state? In *Unveiling The Pharisees' Spirit*, operating as such creates doubt and a double mind. Blasphemy, right? Wrong! *"But let him ask in faith, with no doubting, for he who doubts is like a wave of the sea driven and tossed by the wind. For let not that man suppose that he will receive anything from the Lord; he is a double-minded man, unstable in all his ways."* James 1:6-8.

If we are not sure where we stand in the Eye of God, then it is time to head into the Spiritual Classroom for *Spiritual Training* and updates, *As It Pleases Him*. What is the purpose of a *Spiritual Classroom*? *"Whoever has no rule over his own spirit is like a city broken down, without walls."* Proverbs 25:28.

Spiritual Training

We are in the Season of Shifting. *"The eyes of the LORD are on the righteous, and His ears are open to their cry."* Psalm 34:15. What does this mean for us in layman's terms? Well, the corrective measures are in full bloom, bringing our Spiritual Burdens to the forefront for open training. God is bringing our *Spiritual Training* to the limelight instead of training us in the back office. More importantly, we must become okay with the open rebuke, especially if we desire the STAYED HANDS of God, and we must open our hands, releasing our Spiritual Burdens, *As It Pleases Him*.

What is the purpose of this sort of *Spiritual Training*? God is weighing our motives. According to Scripture, *"Even so you also outwardly appear righteous to men, but inside you are full of hypocrisy and lawlessness."* Matthew 23:28.

Why would we become Spiritually Burdened? The human psyche wants to remain in control, doing whatever it wants to do without Divine Intervention, Supervision, Repentance, or Remission. The only reason it feels like a burden is that the worldly toxins remaining in the Mind, Body, and Soul are causing withdrawals. Thus, they will often never appear as such because they are covered up by something else. For instance, this is similar to being addicted to food, drugs, alcohol, sugar, sex, and so on, while not appearing as what it is or exposing the ROOT.

Regardless of where we are or who we are, we must bring the Holy Trinity into the matters at hand, *As It Pleases God* and on His Divine Terms. Blasphemy, right? Wrong. According to Scripture from the Ancient of Days, here is what we need to know: *"Assuredly, I say to you, all these things will come upon this generation. 'O Jerusalem, Jerusalem, the one who kills the prophets and stones those who are sent to her! How often I wanted to gather your children together, as a hen gathers her chicks under her wings, but you were not willing! See! Your house is left to you* desolate; for I say to you, you shall see Me no more till you say, 'Blessed is He who comes in the name of the LORD!' " Matthew 23:36-39.* By no means should this cause us to become unsettled; once again, all we have to do is AGREE and RECEIVE in Totality and Oneness, *As It Pleases God.*

How can we remain calm when we are weighed down Mentally, Physically, Emotionally, and Spiritually? Remaining calm is a choice, and so is fear. From experience, if we place God at the forefront of our lives without trying to take the wheel and control everything, we will find God doing a better job in our lives than we could ever do. Plus, we have the Holy Spirit to help us in *The Spiritual Middleman Approach*, so we can quickly request the help needed at the drop of a dime.

Then again, if we find ourselves straying, we can also cover ourselves with the Blood of Jesus or plead the Blood when tempted. Does it work? Absolutely, especially when the heart is right, or we are wholeheartedly trying! Without a doubt, it will kick our conscience into high gear so fast it will make our heads spin or cause a complete halt in midair, even when we use our inaudible inside voice in such a manner. Really? Yes, really! In addition, we can also repeat this Scripture: *"Plead my cause, O LORD, with those who strive with me; Fight against those who fight against me. Take hold of shield and buckler, And stand up for my help."* Psalm 35:1-2. *"Plead my cause and redeem me; Revive me according to Your word."* Psalm 119:154.

What is the benefit of using the Holy Spirit and the Blood of Jesus as *The Spiritual Middleman Approach*? If we desire Divine Foreknowledge, the multiplication of Divine Grace and Mercy, we must ELECT to follow Spiritual Protocol, *As It Pleases God.* Here is what we need to know, *'Elect according to the foreknowledge of God the Father, in sanctification of the Spirit, for obedience and sprinkling of the blood of Jesus Christ: Grace to you and peace be multiplied."* 1 Peter 1:2. Most would think this Scripture does not apply to them, but I am here to Divinely Decree that it does! But we must keep the peace, become patient, and remain calm to maximize the benefits of using the Holy Spirit and pleading the Blood. Why is this so important? Attempting to use the Holy Spirit or the Blood of Jesus in our debaucherous acts changes the trajectory of our intents while nullifying *The Spiritual Middleman Approach.*

As a rule of thumb, especially when desiring to live our best lives, we must become cautious about the contents of the heart, especially when anger, disobedience, ungratefulness, hatefulness, and chaos are involved. Of course, we are all subjected to error. Still, it is imperative to cast down the Spirit of Error, seeking Divine Light in all things, becoming true to thyself about the ROOT of whatever and with whomever. Using this Spiritual Filtering process helps us better understand ourselves and get rid of the willful contaminants we invite into our lives.

Here is what we must know: *"This is the message which we have heard from Him and declare to you, that God is light and in Him is no darkness at all. If we say that we have fellowship with Him, and walk in darkness, we lie and do not practice the truth. But if we walk in the light as He is in the light, we have fellowship with one another, and the blood of Jesus Christ His Son cleanses us from all sin. If we say that we have no sin, we deceive ourselves, and the truth is not in us. If we confess our sins, He is faithful and just to forgive us our sins and to cleanse us from all unrighteousness. If we say that we have not sinned, we make Him a liar, and His word is not in us."* 1 John 1:5-10.

Once we obey the Holy Trinity with outright humility and become a work-in-progress to the molding of Kingdom Standards, the Heavenly of Heavens will send Spiritual Servants to assist us on our Spiritual Journey according to our Blueprinted Destiny. In addition, they are designed to help develop our Spiritual Eyes, Ears, and Language, our Spiritual Fruits, how to operate with Christlike Character, and how to use our Spiritual Armor to contend with the enemy's wiles, leading toward the Kingdom, NOT away from it.

The Handiwork of God, engrafted in *The Spiritual Middleman Approach,* works better when we are at peace with ourselves and others, regardless of what is taking place around us. For example, when we remain calm in a lightning storm, it symbolically means we trust God to do His handiwork, even though the bolts of lightning and vicious sounds of thunder can stir up a scare. Then after the storm, we continue with our lives as if nothing ever happened, right? Frankly, this is how God wants our lives to pan out as Believers. Why would God operate in such a manner? He will ruffle our feathers from time to time, getting our attention to train, nurture, move, position, or speak to us. If we are stuck, yoked, easily provoked, or chaotic internally or externally, it can add kryptonite into the equation.

As Believers or non-believers, we all have a desire embedded in our DNA to possess Divine Favor, making us sweet mush to those who convey it. What is the purpose of this DNA strand? Simply put, we are created as emotional beings with the innate ability to love and be loved. The moment we turn our ability to love God, ourselves, and others into hate, we infect or mutate our DNA strand by default, invoking a great divide.

As a whole, it is imperative to reel ourselves in, doing what we are PREDESTINED to do in Earthen Vessels with Divine Unity. We cannot play around with God, thinking He does not have a WATCHFUL EYE. *"The eyes of the LORD are in every place, Keeping watch on the evil and the good."* Proverbs 15:3. The moment we think we have the upper hand on God, His Mighty Hand has already swept the earth, doing what needs to be done, getting us to the Appointed End of Victory.

Regardless of where we are on our Spiritual Journey, it is our responsibility to step up to the plate, do what needs to be done for the sake of the Kingdom, and get rid of any form of Spiritual Blindness, Deafness, and Muteness. Why? Misappropriated or misdirected attention has placed us between a rock and a hard place with God, without realizing we are there. How is it possible to become stuck in such a manner, especially when we are Believers, trusting God? If we are not on a daily regimen of repentance and forgiveness, we must question ourselves accordingly.

Why must we question ourselves when operating in the Spirit of Righteousness, doing no wrong? If we have nothing to become sorry or apologetic about, to God be the Glory. Yet, at the same time, make sure there is no internal glitch within the human psyche hidden within the conscience, placing us in a state of denial.

In Earthen Vessels, we are all on a learning curve, mainly with the condition of the heart and its motives; therefore, if we fail to exhibit compassion for ourselves and others, it is crucial to examine ourselves. Here is what we need to know to avoid internal glitches: *"For even if I made you sorry with my letter, I do not regret it; though I did regret* it. *For I perceive that the same epistle made you sorry, though only for a while. Now I rejoice, not that you were made sorry, but that your sorrow led to repentance. For you were made sorry in a godly manner, that you might suffer loss from us in nothing. For godly sorrow produces repentance leading to salvation, not to be regretted; but the sorrow of the world produces death. For observe this very thing, that you sorrowed in a godly manner: What diligence it produced in you, what clearing of yourselves, what indignation, what fear, what vehement desire, what zeal, what vindication! In all things you proved yourselves to be clear in this matter."* 2 Corinthians 7:8-11.

Clearly, I do not discount anyone's walk with God or Spiritual Level, and I wish the best for all. Yet, when we are stepping on others for elevation, it is imperative to do a check-up from the neck up without covering up. What is the purpose of doing so, primarily when we have worked to become better, wiser, and stronger? Becoming better, wiser, and stronger is a matter of perception, and if we have not learned the value encased in trusting God, *As It Pleases Him*, we will find ourselves secretly gleaning for a mask to cover up.

Spiritual Refreshers

The ultimate goal is to receive Heavenly Downloads of Divine Wisdom with staying power, instead of gleaned information with zero know-how on ways to apply it to real-life situations, circumstances, thoughts, behaviors, and so on. Even if we cannot tangibly see, feel, or touch our experiences, the comforts and the lack thereof are real beyond human understanding. Hence, if we simply engage wholeheartedly in our Heaven on Earth Experiences, *As It Pleases God*, it allows the Holy Spirit to *Spiritually Refresh* from the inside out when wronged, rejected, ostracized, and so on.

On the other hand, the moment we try to refresh ourselves on our own, outside of *The Spiritual Middleman Approach*, we will find ourselves giving in to various lusts and pride derived from our ungoverned thoughts, senses, and emotions. With this in mind, it is not wise to eradicate the Holy Trinity from the equation of our daily lives. Nor should we avoid covering ourselves with the Blood of Jesus as Spiritual Atonement.

How do we receive *Spiritual Refreshers* or Divine Comfort? We must redirect everything back to God, extract the Spiritual Lessons, Blessings, or Tests associated, and give THANKS. By approaching life in such a manner, we become open to understanding what the Word of God is saying amid whatever or whomever. Now, if we take things into our own hands, leaving God out, refusing to learn, or becoming ungrateful, we inadvertently douse ourselves with heavy burdens and unrest from within.

Why would God not grant a *Spiritual Refresher* or Comfort automatically? God's Divine Grace and Mercy will vary from person to person, situation to situation, trauma to trauma, and so on. For the most part, a *Spiritual Refresher* or Comfort is a choice, and He will not violate free will.

For the Promises of God, we must do our due diligence in examining ourselves thoroughly, getting rid of any form of corruptibility. Here are the Spiritual Expectations of Oneness we must know: *"Therefore, having these promises, beloved, let us cleanse ourselves from all filthiness of the flesh and spirit, perfecting holiness in the fear of God. Open your hearts to us. We have wronged no one, we have corrupted no one, we have cheated no one. I do not say this to condemn; for I have said before that you are in our hearts, to die together and to live together."* 2 Corinthians 7:1-3.

As we go a little deeper, regardless of how people, places, and things appear to the naked eye, our Spiritual Journey is real, relevant, and commissionable. For this reason, we need the presence of the Holy Trinity as *The Spiritual Middleman Approach* to guide us along the way, helping us contend with the enemy's wiles.

Whether we use *The Spiritual Middleman Approach* or not, we will face the Vicissitudes and Cycles of Life without fail. Actually, some are unavoidable in building us up in Earthen Vessels, training the trainable, testing the tested, and positioning the positionable. Amid all, do not be deceived; we must know the Word of God is here to assist us along the way, even if we opt out of *The Spiritual Middleman Approach.*

Here is the Heavenly Mindset expected from us, written by Paul: *"Remember that Jesus Christ, of the seed of David, was raised from the dead according to my gospel, for which I suffer trouble as an evildoer, even to the point* of chains; but the word of God is not chained. Therefore, I endure all things for the sake of the elect, that they also may obtain the salvation which is in Christ Jesus with eternal glory." 2 Timothy 2:8-10.

What do we need to do to ensure we do not become self-entangled or self-chained? What is required will vary from person to person, depending upon their Divine Blueprint and Spiritual Level. However, listed below are a few basic Spiritual Principles, *As It Pleases God*, getting the ball rolling in our favor, but not limited to such:

- ☐ We must die to ourselves and live for God, *As It Pleases Him*. "This is a faithful saying: For if we died with Him, We shall also live with Him." 2 Timothy 2:11.

- ☐ We must be willing to endure without taking the easy way out or denying our faith in Jesus, our Lord and Savior, *As It Pleases God*. "If we endure, We shall also reign with Him. If we deny Him, He also will deny us." 2 Timothy 2:12.

- ☐ We must have faith in the reason Jesus died on the cross for us, *As It Pleases God*. "If we are faithless, He remains faithful; He cannot deny Himself." 2 Timothy 2:13.

- ☐ We must remind ourselves daily of the Word of God, meditating on it *As It Pleases Him*, ensuring we do not misrepresent or deceive others through it. "Remind them of these things, charging them before the Lord not to strive about words to no profit, to the ruin of the hearers." 2 Timothy 2:14.

- ☐ We must rightly divide the Word of Truth, *As It Pleases God*. "Be diligent to present yourself approved to God, a worker who does not need to be ashamed, rightly dividing the word of truth." 2 Timothy 2:15.

- ☐ We must learn how to kindly cast down negativity or redirect conversations with positive means, such as the Fruits of the Spirit and Christlike Character, *As It Pleases*

God. *"But shun profane and idle babblings, for they will increase to more ungodliness."* 2 Timothy 2:16.

- We must become cautious about what we set in motion, Mentally, Physically, Emotionally, and Spiritually, without straying or distracting, displeasing God. *"And their message will spread like cancer. Hymenaeus and Philetus are of this sort, who have strayed concerning the truth, saying that the resurrection is already past; and they overthrow the faith of some."* 2 Timothy 2:17-18.

What can these Spiritual Principles do for us? They will help build our foundation and workmanship, *As It Pleases God*. Why must we *Please God*? My question is, 'Why should we not *Please Him*?' He has our Divine Blueprint with our best interests at heart, keeping us from straying into webs of deceit or debauchery. In my opinion, what better person to trust than the ONE who designed us, knowing our inner faculties better than anyone else, right? But, let us interject Scripture: *"Nevertheless the solid foundation of God stands, having this seal: 'The Lord knows those who are His,' and, 'Let everyone who names the name of Christ depart from iniquity.'"* 2 Timothy 2:19.

How do we depart from iniquity? We must understand the surface and underlying issues we are dealing with or will face, while repenting, cleansing, and aligning ourselves with the Word of God consistently. Some do this once or twice a week, but for the Kingdom of God, we must do this daily, getting rid of the chaff accrued.

What if we do not accrue chaff? Unfortunately, we all will experience the chaff of deception that we may not recognize as such. For example, after taking a bath, we cannot see the dirt granules attaching to the body, and denying dirt or debris does not make it of no effect. With or without our opinions or perceptions of chaff, it will do what it is designed to do, regardless of how much we deny its impact or the lack thereof. Yet, if we use an outside source, such as an alcohol swab, to wipe the skin, we will see the impact the dirt is making without the appearance of the impact, stench, or what lies beneath, hidden in our pores.

So, enough about the outer grunge, let us apply Scripture to the inner grunge, having the potential to corrupt us in Earthen Vessels. *"But in a great house there are not only vessels of gold and silver, but also of wood and clay, some for honor and some for dishonor. Therefore if anyone cleanses himself from the latter, he will be a vessel for honor, sanctified and useful for the Master, prepared for every good work. Flee also youthful lusts; but pursue righteousness, faith, love, peace with those who call on the Lord out of a pure heart. But avoid foolish and ignorant disputes, knowing that they generate strife.* 2 Timothy 2:20-23.

How can we become better people, especially when we have issues? In becoming a better person, we cannot put down another for their issues, but offer them help, while offering a few other items, but not limited to such:

- ☐ We must offer Divine Servanthood.
- ☐ We must offer Divine Peace.
- ☐ We must offer Divine Gentleness.
- ☐ We must offer Divine Shareability and Teachability.
- ☐ We must offer Divine Patience.
- ☐ We must offer Divine Humility.
- ☐ We must offer Divine Forgiveness.
- ☐ We must offer Divine Agreement of Understanding.
- ☐ We must offer Divine Encouragement.
- ☐ We must offer Divine Freedom.
- ☐ We must offer Divine Transparency.
- ☐ We must offer Divine Communication, *As It Pleases God*.

How can we offer this to someone who is using, abusing, mistreating, or deceiving us? We offer this to them with a long-handled spoon, but we dare not mistreat others, making them feel less than a Child of God. Why must we become the bigger person? We are all God's sheep in need of something, regardless of whether it is apparent or not. For this reason, *As It Pleases God*, we must lead by example, knowing how to effectively communicate with those in or out of the Kingdom.

What is the purpose of being nice to someone nasty, rude, obnoxious, or hits below the belt? Here is my question: 'How can we win someone to the Kingdom, particularly if we are behaving like them without any form of self-control?'

To be clear, this does not mean to remain in the situation, but it does mean that we must maintain our composure while removing ourselves from a Spiritual Infraction. Is this Biblical? I would have it no other way! *"And a servant of the Lord must not quarrel but be gentle to all, able to teach, patient, in humility correcting those who are in opposition, if God perhaps will grant them repentance, so that they may know the truth, and that they may come to their senses and escape the snare of the devil, having been taken captive by him to do his will."* 2 Timothy 2:24-26.

In so many words, if the devil is using someone in the commission to sift us, we do not have to surrender to the snare. We just have to keep it moving in the Spirit of Excellence, use the Fruits of the Spirit, behave Christlike, and take all things to God in prayer, forgiving, and covering it with the Blood of Jesus while allowing the Holy Spirit to do what He does best.

Spiritual Snares

As we journey through life, we are faced with many challenges that can test our faith, loyalty, heart posture, and character. One of the most insidious challenges we will face when 'life is lifing' is a *Spiritual Snare*. In my opinion, this is like getting a run in our stockings during a pristine event.

A *Spiritual Snare* is a trap set by the enemy to ensnare us to impose their own agenda and lead us away from God or our Predestined Blueprint. These snares can be subtle and are sometimes difficult to detect without Spiritual Discernment, which is why it is essential to view them through the Eye of God.

The most common *Spiritual Snare* is the LOVE of money, fame, power, sex, and affirmational prestige. Although money answers everything, according to Ecclesiastes 10:19, on the other hand, with a *Spiritual Snare*, it can cost us everything. Why would it cost us, especially if money answereth? A *Spiritual Snare* is NOT a thing; it is an OCCURRENCE or FORCE that uses THINGS (like power, money, sex, lust, fame, and status) as BAIT. Suppose we do not have them in their proper perspective, *As It Pleases God*. In this case, we can 'get got' in various ways that we did not see coming, stemming from underlying envy, jealousy, pride, greed, selfishness, coveting, competitiveness, or disobedience. All of these contribute to known and unknown triggers and foolery in the Eye of God. Plus, it can also cause us to become blind to our own faults and weaknesses or invoke fears that traumatize or paralyze us with anxiety, worry, despair, paranoia, and depression. Unfortunately, in this condition, we may miss out on the blessings and opportunities that God has for us or outright self-sabotage ourselves.

To avoid *Spiritual Snares* designed to entrap us, what do we need to look for? First and foremost, we must search within ourselves for the inward snares before probing outwardly. Secondly, repent and forgive, drawing closer to God in a *Spirit to Spirit* Relationship. Thirdly, we must cover ourselves with the Blood of Jesus as Spiritual Atonement. Fourthly, invoke the Holy Spirit by becoming ONE with Him. Fifthly, make a conscious effort to use the Fruits of the Spirit to the best of one's ability with a work-in-progress mentality. Lastly, behave Christlike while moving in the Spirit of Excellence, staying vigilant and alert at all times, and guarding ourselves against the traps by TESTING the Spirit, *As It Pleases God*.

What is the purpose of taking heed of how to avoid *Spiritual Snares*? It keeps us from pointing our fingers at others before taking a bird's eye view of our fruits. Meanwhile, it also assists in building our faith and trust in God for our Divine Provisions according to our Predestined Blueprint. Then again, it keeps us humble and teachable, willing to listen to the wisdom and guidance of others that lead us to victory, peace, and freedom. More importantly, approaching *Spiritual Snares* in such a manner keeps us from giving the enemy any justifiable ammunition to use against us.

Justifiable Ammunition

Justifiable ammunition, in the Eye of God, may be seen as the use of force in self-defense or to protect ourselves and others from harm in the Realm of the Spirit. Clearly, this is not violence…it is understanding if something will be God-Allowed, God-Invoked,

God-Used, or God-Blocked based on whether something is justified or unjustified.

Unfortunately, with justifiable ammunition, this is how a lot of Spiritual Elites turn on themselves without knowing it. In the same way that we are allowed to defend ourselves in the physical world, we also have more profound Spiritual Rights to do so in the Spiritual Realm. What does this mean in layman's terms? We have a right to defend ourselves, whether we are justified or unjustified. Now, with unjustification of any kind, REPENTANCE and FORGIVENESS are required. Without it, offense can occur with instances of trauma, especially when the Fruits of the Spirit are not used, *As It Pleases God*.

For example, this is when our inside circle cringes when we walk into the room because we are dulling the light in their eyes instead of providing authentic illumination, Mentally, Physically, Emotionally, or Spiritually.

As a result of the dimness, they give us a secret side-eye as they question our character, but do not have the guts to tell us the truth. The truth about what? The truth is that our character sucks. The truth that we are mean, rude, and hateful, all in the name of the Lord. The truth is that we lack compassion, mercy, and forgiveness. The truth is that we are wrong in our approach. The truth that they are afraid to speak the truth in love.

So, instead of telling the truth that would hurt our feelings, they absorb the charactorial trauma on themselves. As a result, they allow it to fester, contributing to an informal breakdown of the human psyche to repeat the same cycle with another instead of breaking it altogether. Then again, it may cause insecurities within oneself, contributing to other negative characteristics associated with jealousy, envy, greed, pride, coveting, control, revenge, spitefulness, and so on.

For me, I check the character traits within myself to get an understanding, and then I can apply the necessary Spiritual Counteraction needed to reverse it, *As It Pleases God*. Doing so helps me to apologize or self-correct amid whatever or with whomever, breaking the negative cycle. Then again, when exercising tough love or decreeing a Divine Message from the Heavenly of Heavens or when I must remain neutral, I may withhold the reversal until I get all the FACTS.

When conveying factual truths associated with self-correction, I must unapologetically state the facts, period. However, we need to involve the Holy Spirit in the equation to know when to exercise Spiritual Authority or Humility and the need for both simultaneously. What is the purpose of doing so? When dealing with certain types of Spiritual Oppression, we cannot show any signs of weakness, or they will hang us out to dry.

Why would deception or oppression occur? Please allow me to align this with the Word of God. *"But evil men and impostors will grow worse and worse, deceiving and being deceived."* 2 Timothy 3:13. Thus, we must make sure we are not on the WORSE or EVIL side of this matter. If we are...deception is at the door!

Here are a few red flags on who the enemy will often use as *Justifiable Ammunition* against us to dim our lights in the Eye of God, but not limited to such:

- ☐ Those who are unapologetically selfish, abusive, and reckless, while not caring about how their behaviors affect the innocent.

- ☐ Those who place money over integrity and are willing to compromise their values for financial gain, selling their souls at the drop of a dime.

- ☐ Those who constantly boast about themselves and belittle others without self-correction, self-reflection, or self-control.

- ☐ Those who speak ill will, debauchery, negativity, and curses over the life of another, without any form of restraint and lack the basic principles of respect and empathy.

- ☐ Those who are rebellious, rude, disruptive, or disobedient, particularly towards their parents or elders.

- ☐ Those who tend to be unappreciative, belittling, complaining, and scrutinizing everything and everyone around them, without ever acknowledging their own shortcomings. Meanwhile, they pretend as if they are faultless, untouchable, and flawless.

- ☐ Those who are unforgiving, crucifying others without any form of mercy, compassion, understanding, or grace.

- ☐ Those who have a critical attitude and are comfortable creating an atmosphere of negativity with a long list of detrimental and toxic relationships.

- ☐ Those who slander others, talking down to them without taking a moment to build, inspire, or motivate.

- ☐ Those who limit their personal growth and operate without any form of self-control whatsoever, while giving in to all types of unhealthy lusts or perversions.

- ☐ Those who exhibit extreme brutality in their behavior, whether it be Mentally, Physically, or Emotionally, particularly when they are denied what they desire or fail to have the final say.

- ☐ Those who disregard doing good or what is deemed right in the Eye of God, and will betray anyone without giving it a second thought.

- ☐ Those who give in to worldliness as a wolf in sheep's clothing, playing pretend, or selfishly using people to get what they want.

The above characteristics are not designed to point the finger; they are used for AWARENESS and self-correction, protecting ourselves from the enemy's wiles. Here is the Scripture to align: "*But know this, that in the last days perilous times will come: For men will be* lovers of themselves, lovers of money, boasters, proud, blasphemers, disobedient to parents, unthankful, unholy, unloving, unforgiving, slanderers, without self-control, brutal, despisers of good, traitors, headstrong, haughty, lovers of pleasure rather than lovers of God, having a form of godliness but denying its power. And from such people turn away!" 2 Timothy 3:1-5.

Suppose we do not want to fall prey or become the next victim. In this case, we must get rid of these negative character traits, reversing them into positive ones to ensure we do not unawaringly infect or affect ourselves, our families, or others. Really? Yes, really. Unbeknown to most, if we are a Believer, attempting to walk the walk and talk the talk, we will become a target for sifting; so, we must stay on READY! If not, our gullibility can cost us.

How is it possible to become gullible when we are faithfully serving God? If we do not seek the TRUTH from the inside out, correcting the correctable, *As It Pleases Him*, we can very well please something or someone else in our known and unknown acts of idolatry. Am I pulling for straws here? Of course not! According to Scripture, *"For of this sort are those who creep into households and make captives of gullible women loaded down with sins, led away by various lusts, always learning and never able to come to the knowledge of the truth."* 2 Timothy 3:6-7. All in all, we must make a conscious attempt to come into Divine Alignment with ourselves, our lives, and our Divine Blueprint using *The Spiritual Middleman Approach*.

According to the Heavenly of Heavens, to ensure our truth, the Truth, and the facts permeating through us align, *As It Pleases God*, it is imperative to use the Word of God as a Spiritual Compass. Why do we need the Word of God when we know our Divine Mission? In the Illumination of our Spiritual Journey of Greatness, the Bible says, *"All Scripture is given by inspiration of God, and is profitable for doctrine, for reproof, for correction, for instruction in righteousness, that the man of God may be complete, thoroughly equipped for every good work."* 2 Timothy 3:16-17. With this in mind, we cannot eliminate the Word of God from our lives, nor are we exempt from its use; we need it for Spiritual Alignment.

For the record, anything or anyone outside of the Holy Trinity, the Divine Alignment of the Bible, and without leading all things back to the Kingdom, we are destined to please another on their terms, NOT God's. What does this mean in layman's terms? We can inadvertently put a kink in our DNA according to our Divine Blueprint by doing our own thing with worldly tools and systems, especially when we are Spiritual Beings having a human experience.

How can we possibly disrupt our Genetic Design, especially when we are Believers? By functioning outside of the Will of God, contradicting our Divine Blueprint, or not aligning with the Word of God, we can cause a mix-up regarding who we are and why.

For example, animals are designed to reproduce after their kind; however, if we tamper with mating animals outside of their natural design, we can cause a mutation or genetic yoke. From my perspective, this is similar to mating a horse with a donkey. As a result of the tampering outside of God's original design for mating a horse or donkey, we get a mule as an offspring that can NEVER reproduce after its own kind due to the genetically mutated reproductive yoke.

So, when it comes down to our Divine Blueprint, it may be non-transferable to the next in line, depending upon the stipulations set forth by God Almighty. Nor should we want to take such a risk, but to each his own—I am just the Messenger!

Spiritually Sharp

In the Eye of God, we are on the decline due to the lack of understanding, contributing to our Spiritual Dullness according to Kingdom Standards. However, if we were to operate in our Spiritual Gifts according to our Divine Blueprint, they would make us *Spiritually Sharp* by default. Plus, we would have a Winning Personality with outright humility, regardless of what others think.

According to the Heavenly of Heavens, being *Spiritually Sharp* is what makes Kingdom Champions out of those rejected by society or written off as a lost cause. From experience, I am so GRATEFUL that God does not see as man sees!

Besides, when dealing with the Promises of God, we all have likes and dislikes for a reason, be it known or unknown, but we do not need to pressure or trick others to concede, especially when it takes the same amount of energy to own our truth. Amid all, we should care about what God thinks of us and what we think about ourselves, *As It Pleases Him*. Once we become laser-focused in such a manner, it will change the trajectory of the iron that sharpens us or what irons we sharpen. Does it make a difference as long as we are sharp? Of course, it makes a difference.

If we are sharpened away from our Divine Blueprint, we lose the associated Spiritual Benefits, Provisions, and Perks. But if we become sharpened to possess our Birthrights, Blessings, Promises, and Divine Blueprint, our Spiritual Irons will become so sharp that they will cut through all the hogwash, blocking what or who is not a part of it! Therefore, we should stay spot-on, looking for the positive LIGHT.

Remember that when we are in Purpose on purpose, God comes through without fail, especially when integrity, self-control, respect, humility, and confidence are involved! On the other hand, if we do not know and understand this fact, we can easily be swayed to compromise.

Life is designed to pose objections to TEST or CHALLENGE our staying power; if we are quick to give up, settling for defeat, the Vicissitudes are indeed doing their job. Suppose we dare to become ambitious, enthusiastic, teachable, and respectful regarding our Spiritual Gifts, doing what it takes in the Spirit of Righteousness and completing the Mission set before us. In this case, Divine Overflow and the Cloak of Favor will overtake us.

With God's Promises, never give up...our Divine Blueprint is here to serve us with Supernatural Provisions, containing a Gravitational Pull beyond human comprehension. In due time, as a Tilling Self-Starter, it will yield. Thus, we must LISTEN to the Voice of God, making it imperative to develop a *Spirit to Spirit* Connection. We do not want to become like Moses, who struck the rock when God told him to speak to it.

Keep in mind that simple acts of disobedience may seem small in our eyes, yet paramount in the Eye of God. So, it is always best to obey to avoid suffering dismay! We must tap into what is already, while Divinely Aligning ourselves to become diligently proactive in *The Way*, NOT reactive.

CHAPTER SEVEN
The Way

"Jesus said to him, 'I am the way, the truth, and the life. No one comes to the Father except through Me.' " John 14:6.

Resilient Brilliance is our Spiritual Portion if we dare to take advantage of it, *As It Pleases God*. Just think about someone who has it going on without God; how much more could they do with God in their corner? The relevance of this question is positioned on a level to get us to think about our lives in two ways, proactively:

☐ Would our lives become better with God?
☐ Would our lives become better without God?

The moment we agree with our answer, publicly or privately, our lives will begin to serve us the portion of our decision. Even if we do not understand the impact of our subconscious decisions, life is designed to serve as the heart's desires. By not understanding our position in Christ Jesus, the Kingdom, or with God, we will find ourselves trying to fit in with others, appearing superior in some way.

Negating the Spiritual Impact of choosing NOT to involve God or *The Spiritual Middleman Approach* in our lives consistently, we will find ourselves unawaringly creating our self-induced yokes, chains, bondages, and enslavements. At the same time, we try to lay the blame elsewhere, make excuses, or point the finger without realizing we are doing so.

According to the Heavenly of Heavens, if we dare to interject the Holy Trinity hidden in *The Spiritual Middleman Approach* into our lives, *As It Pleases God*, we will find the Spiritual Lessons, Tools, and Ammunition needed for our Spiritual Journey according to our Divine Blueprint at our beck and call. But...yes, there is a but in this matter! We need to know this information without wavering while claiming our Spiritual Birthrights and Promises. By not laying claim to our Spiritual Rights or becoming stuck in the muck of complaining, fussing, and fighting, we can get trapped in our Egypt, wandering in our Desert Experience, or fearing the Fruits of the Promises, Mentally, Physically, Emotionally, or Spiritually. More importantly, if we wait for someone to lay claim for us, we will find ourselves forfeiting our full portion of our Birthrights, Promises, or whatever, similar to a lawyer taking a portion of a settlement in a case.

How can we compare our Birthrights or Promises with a case settlement? Simply put, if we cannot state our case, there cannot be a settlement. If we do not use the Word of God to plead our case in the Heavens, with man, and life, we cannot effectively place legitimate demands. By not stating our case in our *Spirit to Spirit* Relations, we cannot decree the necessary evidence to stake our claim. More importantly, if we do not know we have a case, we cannot demand justifiable restitution, nor can we invoke the Holy Spirit in a place of negligence without demanding illumination or wholehearted repentance.

In receiving the entire portion of what belongs to us, we must Spiritually Till our own ground according to our Divine Blueprint. What is the purpose of doing so? It causes us to engage in a *Spirit to Spirit* Relationship to receive detailed instructions and keep us from using or begging others, especially when the Promises of God have Divine Provisions attached. Hence, here is what the Bible says about this matter: *"The lazy man will not plow because of winter; He will beg during harvest and have nothing."* Proverbs 20:4.

Although God sends His Servants out to help His sheep, we cannot do the work for them—they must WILLINGLY put their hands to the plow. Really? Yes, really! God does not like us depending upon man; He wants us to depend upon Him to send what we need, when we need it, the know-how needed, and whom we need to assist. Using God in such a manner helps avoid making unwise choices or pandering to the wolves in sheep's clothing.

On the other hand, if we do the seeking, searching, and knocking without Him, then whatever we want to do is up for grabs. What does this mean? We are on our own, creating a seemingly self-made miracle without staying power. As a result, it causes us to bounce all over the place, getting bored, outright losing interest, moving on to the next quick fix, dream-killing, or dream-stealing. We can whitewash this behavior, but it is real!

How can we pinpoint this behavior? It is found in our excuses. The moment we do not want to do something, we naturally tend to make an excuse to fit our situation. Unbeknown to most, no one is exempt from this internal glitch. For this reason, we need truth, transparency, and discipline to contend with our human nature.

When it comes to Spiritually Tilling, we cannot take this portion of our lives for granted. Why is this so important in Kingdom Formality? According to the Word of God, here is why it is essential for us to Spiritually Till our own ground, *As It Pleases Him.* "*But Jesus said to him, 'No one, having put his hand to the plow, and looking back, is fit for the Kingdom of God.*'" Luke 9:62. The bottom line is that we must focus on the Kingdom, doing what we are called to do.

Is it not cruel to focus on the Kingdom and no one else? In my opinion, cruelty is NOT leading ourselves and others with God at the forefront. Why is this cruelty? Allow me to counteract this question with another, "If God is not leading us, then who is?' "If the Word of God does not govern our thoughts, then what or who is governing them?'

Better yet, cruelty is when we selfishly block or mistreat others by using God as a guise to do underhanded activities to victimize, oppress, and yoke. Frankly, Luke 9:62 from the above Scripture is designed to keep us focused on moving ahead without focusing on the past, delivering us from the judgments and opinions of people designed to detour, distract, and disrupt.

Listen, if we are so worried about pleasing, impressing, or catering to others, putting God on the back burner, we can indeed be a Believer and NOT fit for the Kingdom. There is a big difference between the two, which is why we have a lot of backbiting and division in Religion.

In so many words, just because we are Religious or Believers, it does not make us usable in the Kingdom by default. We still must be Spiritually Trained to Kingdom Standards, similar to how Jesus trained the Disciples in 'The Way.' What does this mean for us? 'A Way' is often confused with 'The Way' in and out of our daily lives. Here is the difference, but not limited to such:

- ☐ '*A Way*' seems fitting, catering to the senses, impulses, and emotions with a twist of worldliness, with the hidden lust of the eyes, the lust of the flesh, and the pride of life, leading us into self-destructive behaviors, thoughts, actions, and beliefs. "*There is a way that seems right to a man, but its end is the way of death.*" Proverbs 14:12.

- ☐ '*The Way*' is The *Spiritual Middleman Approach* built upon Spiritual Righteousness with the Fruits of the Spirit and Christlike Character. While at the same time, having the Holy Spirit leading the way with the Divine Covering of the Blood of Jesus. Here is the Spiritual Seal to The Way: "*Thomas said to Him, 'Lord, we do not know where You are going, and how can we know the way?' Jesus said to him, 'I am the way, the truth, and the life. No one comes to the Father except through Me.'*" John 14:5-6.

What is the purpose of knowing the difference between the two? Knowing the difference helps us self-correct by self-analysis and repenting, instead of self-destructing through self-paralysis due to Spiritual Blindness, Deafness, or Muteness. Here is what we must know: "*The backslider in heart will be filled with his own ways, but a good man will be satisfied from above.*" Proverbs 14:14.

When we are not satisfied, it will always come with a little twist...a little twist of this and a little twist of that. What is *The Twist*? It depends on what you like or your type!

The Twist

The Twist has become a thing of the norm in today's time; however, in the Eye of God, it takes on a whole new light, tainting The Way. How do we make The Twist make sense, especially when dealing with the Kingdom of God? *"You shall not pervert justice; you shall not show partiality, nor take a bribe, for a bribe blinds the eyes of the wise and twists the words of the righteous. You shall follow what is altogether just, that you may live and inherit the land which the LORD your God is giving you."* Deuteronomy 16:19-20.

What if this does not apply to us because it is a part of the Old Testament? Then my question would be, 'What if it does apply to us in real-time?' Unfortunately, this is how we 'get got' in the Eye of God and the eyes of man. *"The foolishness of a man twists his way, And his heart frets against the LORD."* Proverbs 19:3.

What is the big deal, primarily when we have free will to believe what we so desire? We pick and choose what is right or wrong, when we already know this is written on the Tablet of the Heart of everyone, called BEFOREHAND KNOWLEDGE. For the record, nothing can be twisted if we do not have FOREKNOWLEDGE.

Is any of this Biblical? I would have it no other way! *"As also in all his epistles, speaking in them of these things, in which are some things hard to understand, which untaught and unstable people twist to their own destruction, as they do also the rest of the Scriptures. You therefore, beloved, since you know this beforehand, beware lest you also fall from your own steadfastness, being led away with the error of the wicked; but grow in the grace and knowledge of our Lord and Savior Jesus Christ. To Him be the glory both now and forever. Amen."* 2 Peter 3:16-18.

Here is what King David had to say about this matter. *"In God (I will praise His word), In God I have put my trust; I will not fear. What can flesh do to me? All day they twist my words; All their thoughts are against me for evil. They gather together, They hide, they mark my steps, When they lie in wait for my life."* Psalm 56:4-6.

By ignoring Kingdom Factors or not using *The Spiritual Middleman Approach* the way God intended, we can become twisted and mocked, publicly and privately. If one does not believe this, just remember how a twisted crown was placed upon the head of Jesus as a state of mockery. *"When they had twisted a crown of thorns, they put it on His head, and a reed in His right hand. And they bowed the knee before Him and mocked Him, saying, 'Hail, King of the Jews!' Then they spat on Him, and took the reed and struck Him on the head. And when they had mocked Him, they took the robe off Him, put His own clothes on Him, and led Him away to be crucified."* Matthew 27:29-31.

In light of our faithfulness, we must know what to do proactively, while getting an understanding of the twang of the twist. What does this mean? A twist of mockery may present itself in several ways, with a twang of something else masking it. Listed below are a few examples, but not limited to such:

- ☐ Twisted Faith.
- ☐ Twisted Thoughts.
- ☐ Twisted Attitudes.
- ☐ Twisted Emotions.
- ☐ Twisted Mindsets.
- ☐ Twisted Ideas.
- ☐ Twisted Beliefs.
- ☐ Twisted Conditioning.
- ☐ Twisted Relations.
- ☐ Twisted Agreements.
- ☐ Twisted Communication.
- ☐ Twisted Love.
- ☐ Twisted Trauams.
- ☐ Twisted Biases.
- ☐ Twisted Understandings.
- ☐ Twisted Character.
- ☐ Twisted Fruits.

With every twist we consciously choose not to untie, we may suffer public or private mockery or undue pressure in this area. In The Spiritual Middleman Approach, know this: *"From Jesus Christ, the faithful witness, the firstborn from the dead, and the ruler over the kings of the earth. To Him who loved us and washed us from our sins in His own blood."* Revelation 1:5. With every twist or twang, we must cover it with the Blood of Jesus to contain it, *As It Pleases God*.

Why does God allow us to become twisted internally, externally, or both? God often targets our acts of disobedience, idolatry, rebellion, negativity, unrighteous judgment, debauchery toward the innocent, rotten fruits, and so on, even if we are playing pretend with a twanged mask.

In the same way that every fruit has a twang before becoming ripe or consumable, so do we. Therefore, NO ONE is exempt from *The Twist* or Twang! We simply need to grow, develop, learn, and share when the time is right, *As It Pleases God*.

Straight Way Faith

To unravel ourselves Mentally, Physically, Emotionally, and Spiritually, we must invoke our *Straightway Faith*. Is this Biblical? Absolutely! *"Now there was a certain disciple at Damascus named Ananias; and to him the Lord said in a vision, 'Ananias.' And he said, 'Here I am, Lord.' So the Lord said to him, 'Arise and go to the street called Straight, and inquire at the house of Judas for one called Saul of Tarsus, for behold, he is praying.'"* Acts 9:10-11.

Acting in obedience, *As It Pleases God*, brings the Divine Revelation of what is needed to usher us into Spiritual Alignment with our Divine Blueprint, guiding us to our next step. But if we are not willing to listen, learn, and obey, we may find ourselves lost, confused, and frustrated with the Vicissitudes of Life designed to remove or seal the scales on our eyes.

Had Ananias refused to apply his *Straightway Faith* or *The Spiritual Middleman Approach*, Saul of Tarsus, soon turning Paul, would not have been set STRAIGHT. Here is what we need to know: *"And Ananias went his way and entered the house; and laying his hands on him he said, 'Brother Saul, the Lord Jesus, who appeared to you on the road as you came, has sent me that you may receive your sight and be filled with the Holy Spirit.' Immediately there fell from his eyes something like scales, and he received his sight at once; and he arose and was baptized. So when he had received food, he was strengthened. Then Saul spent some days with the disciples at Damascus. Immediately he preached the Christ in the synagogues, that He is the Son of God."* Acts 9:17-20.

When operating in the Spirit of Righteousness with repentive *Straightway Faith* with *The Spiritual Middleman Approach*, God can and will untangle any twist residing from the inside out, then use us for His Divine Glory to set another on a STRAIGHT path. Here is a Testament of Saul turned Paul experience, "*Then Saul, who also is called Paul, filled with the Holy Spirit, looked intently at him and said, 'O full of all deceit and all fraud, you son of the devil, you enemy of all righteousness, will you not cease perverting the STRAIGHT WAYS of the Lord? And now, indeed, the hand of the Lord is upon you, and you shall be blind, not seeing the sun for a time.' And immediately a dark mist fell on him, and he went around seeking someone to lead him by the hand. Then the proconsul believed, when he saw what had been done, being astonished at the teaching of the Lord.*" Acts 13:9-12.

For the record, it does not matter where we are in life or what we are going through; *Straightway Faith* is available to untwist the twisted and un-twang the deceptive twanged. Hence, we must want it for ourselves, taking the necessary steps to walk toward whatever or whomever. It does not matter if we were born with a weakness or inherited one; our path can become Straight when our faith becomes narrowly weaved, *As It Pleases God*.

Here is another Testimony on Saul that turned Paul's watch. "*And in Lystra a certain man without strength in his feet was sitting, a cripple from his mother's womb, who had never walked. This man heard Paul speaking. Paul, observing him intently and seeing that he had faith to be healed, said with a loud voice, 'Stand up straight on your feet!' And he leaped and walked.*" Acts 14:8-10. What did Paul see? Paul discerned this man's faith through the Holy Spirit and connected to and through him, using *Straightway Faith* with *The Spiritual Middleman Approach*.

How can we work on ourselves to untwist a self-induced one? Listed below are a few questions to ask ourselves, but not limited to such:

- ☐ First, we must acknowledge **WHAT** type of twist we are dealing with.
- ☐ Secondly, we must consider **WHY** we became twisted in the first place.
- ☐ Thirdly, we must pinpoint **HOW** the twist is affecting us or others.

- ☐ Fourthly, we must identify **WHEN** the twist presents itself in our lives.
- ☐ Fifthly, we must recognize **WHERE** the twist takes place.
- ☐ Sixthly, we must know **WHO** is involved in the twist.

We can dissect our queries as much as we like; however, in doing so, make sure they are documented to ensure we do not forget. We can also use the information to build ourselves up or dig a little deeper, especially when dealing with deep-rooted and sensitive issues. What is more, regardless of how tempted we are to run away, the desire to hide, the constant thoughts of burying our issues or twisting and twanging them (the bitter-sweet mask), we must face them for what they are.

What is the purpose of dealing with a twist and twang in such a manner? They are not going away until it is resolved or the lessons are learned. *"Therefore strengthen the hands which hang down, and the feeble knees, and make straight paths for your feet, so that what is lame may not be dislocated, but rather be healed."* Hebrews 12:12-13. Once we become humble in such a manner, it is imperative to seek a few other items, but not limited to such:

- ☐ Get rid of hostility or negative aggression. *"For consider Him who endured such hostility from sinners against Himself, lest you become weary and discouraged in your souls."* Hebrews 12:3.

- ☐ Avoid spilling the blood of another, Mentally, Physically, Emotionally, and Spiritually. *"You have not yet resisted to bloodshed, striving against sin."* Hebrews 12:4.

- ☐ Refrain from extorting God, ourselves, and others for selfish gain or exhortation of self. *"And you have forgotten the exhortation which speaks to you as to sons."* Hebrews 12:5a.

- ☐ Accept Spiritual Correction to become better, stronger, and wiser. *"My son, do not despise the chastening of the LORD, Nor be discouraged when you are rebuked by Him."* Hebrews 12:5b.

- ☐ Understand that Spiritual Chastening is an Act of Love from God. *"For whom the LORD loves He chastens, And scourges every son whom He receives."* Hebrews 12:6.

- ☐ We must exhibit RESPECT, period! From the least to the greatest, this is a must. *"Furthermore, we have had human fathers who corrected us, and we paid them respect. Shall we not much more readily be in subjection to the Father of Spirits and live?"* Hebrews 12:9.

- ☐ We must become partakers of Holiness. *"For they indeed for a few days chastened us as seemed best to them, but He for our profit, that we may be partakers of His Holiness."* Hebrews 12:10.

- ☐ Accept the joyfulness and peaceable fruits of righteousness from our Spiritual Training. *"Now no chastening seems to be joyful for the present, but painful; nevertheless, afterward it yields the peaceable fruit of righteousness to those who have been trained by it."* Hebrews 12:11.

- ☐ Seek peace. *"Pursue peace with all people, and holiness, without which no one will see the Lord."* Hebrews 12:14.

- ☐ Uproot all forms of bitterness to avoid defiling ourselves. *"Looking carefully lest anyone fall short of the grace of God; lest any root of bitterness springing up cause trouble, and by this many become defiled."* Hebrews 12:15.

- ☐ Avoid selling out or selling ourselves short for temporary fixes. *"Lest there be any fornicator or profane person like Esau, who for one morsel of food sold his birthright."* Hebrews 12:16.

- ☐ We must position ourselves in a *Spirit to Spirit* Relationship to hear what the Spirit of the Lord is saying. *"See that you do not refuse Him who speaks. For if they did not escape who refused Him who spoke on earth, much more shall we not escape if we turn away from Him who speaks from Heaven, whose voice then shook the earth; but now He has promised, saying, 'Yet once more I shake not only the earth, but also Heaven.'"* Hebrews 12:25-26.

With all of the twists and turns taking place, it does not mean we should be shaken to the core or turned upside down, especially in our Walk with God. Using *The Spiritual Middleman Approach*, it is time to put on the Whole Armor of God, doing what it takes to secure our Spiritual Portion.

Doing all things, *As It Pleases God*, is our STRAIGHTWAY ticket out of whatever, with whomever, straight into the Spiritual Classroom for Kingdom Preparation. It does not matter if we are enslaved in our Egypt; our Pharaoh will not let us go; we are at the Red Sea waiting for the parting of water; we are wandering in our Wilderness Experience, or we have our marching orders for the Promise, 'The Way Out', or our Exodus is already! We only need to Spiritually Align ourselves according to our Divine Blueprint or become a Servant Workman of the Kingdom.

Whether we had a rough or smooth start in life, in the end, Greatness and Glory are ours for the taking. So, it behooves us to twist our way STRAIGHT, *As it Pleases God.*

Here is a Scripture to repeat daily: *'Lead me, O LORD, in Your righteousness because of my enemies; Make Your way STRAIGHT before my face."* Psalm 5:8. *"The voice of one crying in the wilderness: Prepare the way of the LORD; Make straight in the desert A highway for our God. Every valley shall be exalted And every mountain and hill brought low; The crooked places shall be made straight And the rough places smooth; The glory of the LORD shall be revealed, And all flesh shall see it together; For the mouth of the LORD has spoken."* Isaiah 40:3-5.

Think of it like this: It is either our way or God's way. Whichever one we choose, we are free to do so; however, we also must consider the best plan for us in the long run. In my opinion, with all due respect, we can barely see twenty or so feet in front of us clearly, and zero feet behind us, without turning around. And then, we have God, who sees and knows all things in Heaven and on Earth. So, for the Promises of God, we are going to trust whom? Are we trusting ourselves for this? Seriously, the Devil is a liar, and the truth is nowhere in sight!

As we live in the LIGHT, *As It Pleases God*, the ultimate goal from the Heavenly of Heavens is to give us the Spiritual Opportunity to LOVE the Divine Potential we already possess. We do not need to look to the right or left; whatever we need is already there, so look within. The outer manifestations will take care of themselves if we BELIEVE. In today's day and age, we will find ourselves investing in everything else while forgetting to invest in ourselves, contributing to stagnation within the human psyche.

If a betting man does not bet on himself, he becomes lost in the shuffle of life without knowing he has been sifted in Earthen Vessel, falling prey to a worldly system of conveyance. The TRUTH is that Heaven's System of Conveyance outweighs anything we see with the natural eye. Why? We are Spiritual Beings having a human experience. If we do not add God, our Creator, into the equation, we miss our full potential without maximizing the time to manifest the Genius from Within. Only to find ourselves attempting to take down or destroy what we should build in the Eye of God, Spiritually Sealing our Oneness in the Kingdom.

As It Pleases God, we cannot go wrong using the Fruits of the Spirit, behaving Christlike, and maximizing every opportunity, redirecting it back to the Kingdom of Heaven using the Word of God. By maintaining this Positive, yet Spiritual Mindset for the building up of the SAINTS in Christ Jesus, ushering in the LIGHT in the Spirit of Righteousness, Humility, and Obedience, God will move Heaven and Earth for us, GUARANTEED!

CHAPTER EIGHT
The Spiritual Middleman Approach

"Now, therefore, you are no longer strangers and foreigners, but fellow citizens with the saints and members of the household of God, having been built on the foundation of the apostles and prophets, Jesus Christ Himself being the chief cornerstone." Ephesians 2:19-20.

Our Spiritual Fourth Man Approach to God, ourselves, others, and life ultimately determines their response to us. We can say it does not matter, but in all reality, it does! Spiritual Blindness, Deafness, or Muteness is not an uncommon commodity to have, primarily when responding contrary to the expectations set forth by our Heavenly Father, or when downplaying the Greatness or Genius from within. *"Yet for us there is one God, the Father, of whom are all things, and we for Him; and one Lord Jesus Christ, through whom are all things, and through whom we live."* 1 Corinthians 8:6.

The story of the *Fourth Man* in the Fire originates from Daniel 3:16-30, recounting the experience of the three young Hebrew men, Shadrach, Meshach, and Abednego. Who defied the orders of King Nebuchadnezzar, who decreed that they were to worship a golden statue. In a move to shatter their faith in God, the King of Babylon made bold moves to secure his reign for absolute power. Nevertheless, Shadrach, Meshach, and Abednego were not having it, nor were they going to play his game. So they opted to remain faithful to God Almighty, their source of real hope, courage, love, and protection. Due to their refusal to partake in idolatry, they were thrown into a fiery furnace seven times hotter than normal to be burnt to a crisp, suffering a grueling death. But God said, 'NOT SO'...Sending the Fourth Man to save them from utter demise. They emerged from the fiery furnace unharmed, without any signs of burns or singed hair. Some say it was the pre-incarnate appearance of Jesus Christ, and others say that it was an Angel sent from God. What do I say, 'It was Divine Intervention!'

God will use anything or anyone to save His precious sheep. Just remember, Jesus is already within us if we allow Him to be present to come FORTH like Lazarus, as the *Fourth Man*. Regardless of how insignificant we think we are, God can use us. Here is what Micah 5:2 says: *"But you, Bethlehem Ephrathah, though you are little among the thousands of Judah, yet out of you shall come forth to Me the One to be ruler in Israel, whose goings forth are from of old, from everlasting."*

In this chapter, we will learn how to harness our next move of Divine Creativity, *As It Pleases God*, with the *Fourth Man Approach* or *Middleman Approach* according to the Divine Blueprint already set forth from within. Knowing how to Spiritually Approach God and using these strategic and timely Powerhouse Principles the way He intended, we will find ourselves on the cutting edge of Greatness with no sorrow attached. If we think we have it going on now, with the use of *The Spiritual Middleman Approach*, I promise it will change the trajectory of what we think we know to a Divine Level of WISDOM, putting our enemies to boot.

The Spiritual Middleman Approach is a Spiritual System from the Heavenly of Heavens using the Holy Trinity (The Father, Son, and Holy Spirit) as our go-between in a *Spirit to Spirit* Divine Union of ONENESS. In the Kingdom, using our Spiritual Mediator in such a manner gives us Divine Leverage in knowing, understanding, learning, and conveying the Wisdom of the Ancients according to our Predestined Blueprint.

In addition, this *Heavenly Fourth Man or Middleman Approach* provides the resources needed to assist with using our Spiritual Tools, *As It Pleases God*, for the Divine Unveiling and Discipline needed to DOWNLOAD or CONNECT. Listed below are a few benefits *The Approach* provides, but are not limited to such:

- ☐ *The Approach* aids us in WALKING according to the Spirit, *As It Pleases God*, not ourselves. "*That the righteous requirement of the law might be fulfilled in us who do not walk according to the flesh but according to the Spirit.*" Romans 8:4.

- ☐ *The Approach* assists us in Mindfully Living, *As It Pleases God*. "*For those who live according to the flesh set their minds on the things of the flesh, but those who live according to the Spirit, the things of the Spirit.*" Romans 8:5.

- ☐ *The Approach* weeds out carnality by interjecting Mental Peace, *As It Pleases God*. "*For to be carnally minded is death, but to be spiritually minded is life and peace.*" Romans 8:6.

- ☐ *The Approach* nudges us in the areas that need repentance by convicting us in our wrongdoings, *As It Pleases God*. "*For as many as are led by the Spirit of God, these are sons of God. For you did not receive the spirit of bondage again to fear, but you received the Spirit of adoption by whom we cry out, 'Abba, Father.'* " Romans 8:14-15.

- ☐ *The Approach* purifies the conscience by releasing the contaminants to provide freedom from the inside out, *As It Pleases God*. "*For the creation was subjected to futility, not willingly, but because of Him who subjected it in hope; because the creation itself also will be delivered from the bondage of corruption into the glorious liberty of the children of God.*" Romans 8:20-21.

- ☐ *The Approach* heightens our Spiritual Instincts beyond our senses, reasonings, or impulses, knowing what to do, when to, how to, where to, why, and with whom to receive a glorified outcome, *As It Pleases God*. "*The Spirit Himself bears witness with our spirit that we are children of God and if children, then heirs—heirs of God and joint heirs with Christ, if indeed we suffer with Him, that we may also be glorified together.*" Romans 8:16-17.

- ☐ *The Approach* monitors the intents of the heart consistently, bringing awareness to our motives to Spiritually Align us to Kingdom Standards, *As It Pleases God*. "Now He who searches the hearts knows what the mind of the Spirit is, because He makes intercession for the saints according to the will of God." Romans 8:27.

- ☐ *The Approach* assists with our known and unknown intercession process, *As It Pleases God*. "Likewise the Spirit also helps in our weaknesses. For we do not know what we should pray for as we ought, but the Spirit Himself makes intercession for us with groanings which cannot be uttered." Romans 8:26.

- ☐ *The Approach* rearranges our failed lessons and tests by placing us back into the Spiritual Classroom to preserve our Blessings, Birthrights, and Promises, *As It Pleases God*. "And we know that all things work together for good to those who love God, to those who are the called according to His purpose." Romans 8:28.

- ☐ *The Approach* keeps us from comparing ourselves as God does a NEW THING within us, *As It Pleases God*. "For I consider that the sufferings of this present time are not worthy to be compared with the glory which shall be revealed in us. For the earnest expectation of the creation eagerly waits for the revealing of the sons of God." Romans 8:18-19.

- ☐ *The Approach* gives us hope to endure and persevere through the Vicissitudes, Cycles, and Seasons of Life, *As It Pleases God*. "For we were saved in this hope, but hope that is seen is not hope; for why does one still hope for what he sees? But if we hope for what we do not see, we eagerly wait for it with perseverance." Romans 8:24-25.

- ☐ *The Approach* nurses us through the labor pains when giving birth to our Divine Blueprinted Mission of Redemption, *As It Pleases God*. "For we know that the whole creation groans and *labors with birth pangs together until now. Not only that, but we also who have the firstfruits of the Spirit, even we ourselves groan within ourselves, eagerly waiting for the adoption, the redemption of our body."* Romans 8:22-23.

The Spiritual Middleman Approach will not do all the work for us; we still need to pray, repent, forgive, fast, and meditate to Spiritually Till our own ground. We must also keep the negative cobwebs from consuming the mind by Spiritually Aligning ourselves and our lives with the Word of God with positive affirmations.

As we go DEEPER, *The Spiritual Middleman Approach* is predicated on this Scripture: *"And Moses said to the children of Israel, See, the LORD has called by name Bezalel the son of Uri, the son of Hur, of the tribe of Judah; and He has filled him with the Spirit of God, in wisdom and understanding, in knowledge and all manner of workmanship, to design artistic works, to work in gold and silver and bronze, in cutting jewels for setting, in carving wood, and to work in all manner of artistic workmanship."* Exodus 35:30-33. Simply put, using the *As It Pleases God Program* with *The Spiritual Middleman Approach* will provide the illumination needed to guide us into our Destiny Enriched Provisions, guaranteed.

How can I make such a guarantee? In conjunction with the use of *The Spiritual Middleman Approach* and based upon these Scriptures, I can stake my claim without reservation. *"For whom He foreknew, He also predestined to be conformed to the image of His Son, that He might be the firstborn among many brethren. Moreover whom He predestined, these He also called; whom He called, these He also justified; and whom He justified, these He also glorified. What then shall we say to these things? If God is for us, who can be against us?"* Romans 8:29-31.

In fact, I am living proof of *The Spiritual Middleman Approach* beyond a shadow of a doubt, so I do not take this Spiritual System of Conveyance lightly. In activating the Law of Reciprocity as a Spiritual Testament, I am now sharing this Divine Informative Wisdom as my Give-Back to the Kingdom, helping others to do likewise.

Specific Instructions

When we are in Purpose on purpose, God gives *Specific Instructions* To those who heed to a *Spirit to Spirit* Relationship, *As It Pleases Him*. Biblically, this is similar to how God gave *Specific Instructions* and resources to Noah to build the Ark in Genesis 6.

In addition, He also gave *Specific Instructions* and Covenants to Abraham, Isaac, Jacob, Moses, and many more documented accounts throughout the Bible. Now, my question is, 'Do we think we are any different?' For the record, we are no different—our *Specific Instructions* are waiting for us. Really? Yes, really! I would not know this information if I were not given *Specific Instructions* on WHAT to document, WHEN to document, WHY to document, HOW to document, WHERE to document, and with WHOM to listen. If this book has found you...,you are no different from me. All you need to do is follow the instructions and document, *Spirit to Spirit*.

Our Spiritual Forefathers left us a Supernatural Trail of Sacred Information to glean. We only need to learn how to tap into the Divine Access readily available. If not, we will find ourselves sleeping on the people, places, and things needing our attention.

Sleeping at the wheel of life is not a conducive position to find ourselves in, especially in the Eye of God. Still, it happens all too often. According to the Heavenly of Heavens, Spiritually Sleeping individuals most often do not know they are in such a condition. Why would this happen to us when we are wide awake? Our physical awakeness is not the same as our Spiritual Awakeness in the Eye of God.

Awakening Effect

Spiritually Speaking, through our Spiritual Relationship with our Heavenly Father, we become AWAKENED, *As It Pleases Him*. By coming into ONENESS with the Holy Spirit and accepting the Blood of Jesus as our FORMAL SACRIFICE, we open ourselves to its Spiritual Probabilities. What does this mean for us? Our Spiritual Awakening or *Awakening Effect* has Heavenly Conditions we must meet, regardless of the man-made insinuations that do not align with the Bible. Failing to do so according to the Word of God, our Spirit disconnects, reverting to a state of sleepiness. For sure, this is similar to flipping the light switch on to bring illumination and turning it off to revert the room back into a state of darkness.

As a forewarning, when using *The Spiritual Middleman Approach* for our *Awakening Effect*, the last thing we want to do is awaken ourselves to a Spirit of Darkness. Therefore, we must exercise extreme caution when exposing ourselves to ungodliness and pleasing ourselves without any form of restraints.

What happens to the *Awakening Effect* if we do? I am not here to pass judgment upon anyone. However, it will negatively impact the lust of the eyes, the lust of the flesh, and the pride of life, playing out in our habits, thoughts, beliefs, attitudes, words, and areas in which we have little or no self-control, even if we exhibit good fruits and character. Really? Yes, really!

Remember, fruits and charactorial skills are trainable, but the consistency of the heart or the heart posture is not, especially when pressured without Divine Illumination or Intervention. In all simplicity, what is in us will come out when placed under pressure. Why? The heart must be cleansed and renewed, *As It Pleases God*. Here is what we must know about the *Awakening Effect*: *"For I will sprinkle clean water on you, and you shall be clean; I will cleanse you from all your filthiness and from all your idols. I will give you a new heart and put a new spirit within you; I will take the heart of stone out of your flesh and give you a heart of flesh. I will put My Spirit within you and cause you to walk in My statutes, and you will keep My judgments and do them."* Ezekiel 36:25-27.

Listen, many elements form the psyche that produce our character. Due to these multiple elements, the psyche is very fickle and fights for control, like a kid having a temper tantrum. Even if we adjust our thoughts, the warring from within may remain; we must choose righteousness over the temptation of unrighteousness on a moment-by-moment basis. *"And do not be conformed to this world, but be transformed by the renewing of your mind, that you may prove what is that good and acceptable and perfect will of God."* Romans 12:2.

What is the purpose of continuously renewing the mind and choosing good over evil? We can be triggered easily, and this is the reason for self-control, self-mirroring, self-correction, and the Fruits of the Spirit. Frankly, this is why King David said: *"Create in me a clean heart, O God, And renew a steadfast spirit within me."* Psalm 51:10.

We cannot get caught up in the self-aggrandizing hype; we must pay attention and TEST the Spirit to understand what or who we are dealing with and why. We must become Spiritually AWAKENED, *As It Pleases God*, to do so properly. If not, we will call what is good bad and what is evil good; so beware! Here is what we must know: *"Either make the tree good and its fruit good, or else make the tree bad and its fruit bad; for a tree is known by its fruit. Brood of vipers! How can you, being evil, speak good things? For out of the abundance of the heart the mouth speaks. A good man out of the good treasure of his heart brings forth good things, and an evil man out of the evil treasure brings forth evil things."* Matthew 12:33-35.

In *The Spiritual Middleman Approach*, regardless of how the package is presented to us, in due time, the intents of the heart will find their way out of the mouth; so, we must pay attention, work on ourselves, *As It Pleases God*, and stay on READY at all times. This strategic Spiritual Approach is predicated on this one Scripture: *"Therefore He says: 'Awake, you who sleep, Arise from the dead, And Christ will give you light.' See then that you walk circumspectly, not as fools but as wise."* Ephesians 5:14-15.

When dealing with the *Awakening Effect*, we must protect it. In facing the hills of life, particularly when we do not know what or who is on the other side waiting to ambush us, we must protect our Spiritual Awakening to avoid being put to sleep by some form of known or unknown kryptonite.

For the *Awakening Effect*, it is best to recite these Scriptures daily: *"I will lift up my eyes to the hills—From whence comes my help? My help comes from the LORD, Who made heaven and earth. He will not allow your foot to be moved; He who keeps you will not slumber. Behold, He who keeps Israel Shall neither slumber nor sleep. The LORD is your keeper; The LORD is your shade at your right hand. The sun shall not strike you by day, Nor the moon by night. The LORD shall preserve you from all evil; He shall preserve your soul. The LORD shall preserve your going out and your coming in From this time forth, and even forevermore."* Psalm 121:1-8.

Spiritual Walk

The Spiritual Approach we take determines our staying power and willingness to walk in our Blueprinted Destiny at all costs. Suppose we do not know what the Will of God is for our lives. In this case, it will cause our *Spiritual Walk* to waver due to our questions regarding whether we are making the right or wrong moves. Do not worry too much about this; it happens to us all.

The Spiritual Middleman Approach to our *Spiritual Walk* is of the utmost importance because it determines our actions, reactions, and thoughts on a moment-by-moment basis. The concept of having a Spiritual Intermediary between us and God has been around for centuries and has been a CORNERSTONE of our Forefathers' Greatness. And now, we are required to perfect our *Spiritual Walk* in the FAITH, *As It Pleases God*. Not just to talk the talk but walk the walk, as *The Spiritual Middleman Approach* helps to guard against the pitfalls associated with lies, arrogance, selfishness, and self-righteousness.

In our *Spiritual Walk*, we can directly communicate with our Heavenly Father, *Spirit to Spirit*, by using *The Spiritual Middleman Approach*. The key to unlocking our Spiritual Potential and Blueprint is readily available for us to glean. As we move on with our *Spiritual Walk*, here is what the Heavenly of Heavens wants us to know: "Therefore we do not lose heart. Even though our outward man is perishing, yet the inward man is being renewed day by day. For our light affliction, which is but for a moment, is working for us a far more exceeding and eternal weight of glory, while we do not look at the things which are seen, but at the things which are not seen. For the things which are seen are temporary, but the things which are not seen are eternal." 2 Corinthians 4:16-18.

As a word of warning, when using *The Spiritual Middleman Approach*, we cannot mock another, period. Why should we steer clear of mockery? Unbeknown to most, mockery is a negative seed associated with ungodly behavior. *As It Pleases God*, the goal is to remain on the positive side of the spectrum, and if we are mocking another, we will find the seeds sown will bring fruit in due season, while making known and unknown enemies.

In or out of the Kingdom, mockery is a form of disrespect regardless of our beliefs, desires, intents, or biases. For the record, there is a thin line between helping someone with advice and making fun of them, especially when they lack understanding or Divine Revelation about something or someone. When engaging in such negative behavior on our *Spiritual Walk*, we must ask ourselves, 'Who really lacks understanding of the matter according to the Word of God?'

Why must we query ourselves? According to Proverbs 17:5, "*He who mocks the poor reproaches his Maker; He who is glad at calamity will not go unpunished.*" Therefore, we must tread with extreme caution for ourselves and when hanging out with those who engage in such behavior.

Why must we exercise caution with those in Purpose on purpose? In or out of Divine Purpose, we do not know who or what God is using to accomplish a specific task for the Kingdom without having the Holy Spirit on high alert or Spiritual Discernment. And, if the person is genuinely in Purpose on purpose, using *The Spiritual Middleman Approach*, the Fruits of the Spirit, and exhibiting Christlike Character in the Spirit of Righteousness, we can heap coals on our heads. Really? Yes, really!

What are the differences to look out for, especially if we struggle in our *Spirit to Spirit* Relationship? First, we must look for the Fruits of the Spirit. Secondly, we must look for their charactorial behaviors because anyone is subjected to having a bad day. For example, according to Scripture, here are a few simple personality types to watch out for on our *Spiritual Walk*, but not limited to such:

- ☐ **Personality Type One**: A person who will give or deprive someone of basic necessities. "*Like one who takes away a garment in cold weather, and like vinegar on soda, is one who sings songs to a heavy heart.*" Proverbs 25:20.

- ☐ **Personality Type Two**: If a person would deprive a person of food or drink who is truly hungry or thirsty, beware! "*If your enemy is hungry, give him bread to eat; and if he is thirsty, give him water to drink.*" Proverbs 25:21.

☐ **Personality Type Three**: If a person brags about what they do for others, it is an indication that they hold grudges and set false expectations based upon the lies they feed themselves and others, so beware. *"Whoever falsely boasts of giving is like clouds and wind without rain."* Proverbs 25:14.

☐ **Personality Type Four**: If a person is greedy, never satisfied, finds fault with everything, and is always on the take, beware. *"Have you found honey? Eat only as much as you need, lest you be filled with it and vomit."* Proverbs 25:16.

☐ **Personality Type Five**: If a person lies just to be lying, beware. *"A man who bears false witness against his neighbor is like a club, a sword, and a sharp arrow."* Proverbs 25:18.

☐ **Personality Type Six**: If a person is so arrogant as if they rule the world and are without fault, beware. *"It is not good to eat much honey; So to seek one's own glory is not glory."* Proverbs 25:27.

☐ **Personality Type Seven**: If a person lacks essential self-control and exhibits recklessness with themselves and others, beware. *"Whoever has no rule over his own spirit is like a city broken down, without walls."* Proverbs 25:28.

☐ **Personality Type Eight**: If a person entertains foolery without withdrawing themselves quickly, beware. *"Do not answer a fool according to his folly, lest you also be like him. Answer a fool according to his folly, lest he be wise in his own eyes."* Proverbs 26:4-5.

☐ **Personality Type Nine**: If a person is a know-it-all, giving no THANKSGIVING to God, beware. *"Do you see a man wise in his own eyes? There is more hope for a fool than for him."* Proverbs 26:12.

- **Personality Type Ten**: If a person meddles in everyone's business, especially spreading rumors without getting the facts or stirring the pot, beware. *"He who passes by and meddles in a quarrel not his own is like one who takes a dog by the ears."* Proverbs 26:17.

- **Personality Type Eleven**: If a person would secretly destroy someone, their brand, or their business for laughs, beware. *"Like a madman who throws firebrands, arrows, and death, is the man who deceives his neighbor, and says, 'I was only joking!'"* Proverbs 26:18-19.

- **Personality Type Twelve**: If a person is hateful, jealous, envious, rude, or covetous, beware. *"Fervent lips with a wicked heart are like earthenware covered with silver dross. He who hates, disguises it with his lips, and lays up deceit within himself."* Proverbs 26:23-24.

Although there are many more, these twelve can determine who we are dealing with quickly, even if they are faking their fruits or trained to play possum. If some of these character traits reside within us, we must correct the correctable, *As It Pleases God*.

What is the purpose of making the corrections in our charactorial behaviors? For a Spiritual Elite, we are trained to pump the brakes on someone behaving in such a manner, while keeping them at arm's length. Is this not judging? No, it is protecting our Spiritual Anointing by being in the KNOW about what and who we are dealing with, safeguarding ourselves from becoming accountable for someone else's folly.

The guilt by association applies to Kingdomly Commission individuals as well, especially if we condone this behavior without bringing Divine Illumination to shed light on a particular area of concern. Please allow me to align what happens when we become reckless in or out of Kingdom Formality, primarily if left unrepented. According to Scripture, *"When he speaks kindly, do not believe him, For there are seven abominations in his heart; Though his hatred is covered by deceit, His wickedness will be revealed before the assembly. Whoever* digs a pit will fall into it, and he who rolls a stone will have it roll back on him. A lying tongue hates those who are crushed by it, and a flattering mouth works ruin." Proverbs 26:25-28.

When motivating positive change in or out of the Kingdom, we must MASTER our Spiritual Approach in doing so, similar to how Jesus presented His case among Believers and non-believers alike without condemning. How do we discuss sensitive issues without pointing the finger? Jesus approached individuals with questions or told a story. He elaborated on the answer or solution without pointing the finger or mocking anyone while leading the way by EXAMPLE.

Condescendingly speaking to others, derogatory slander, making a joke for giggles at the expense of the innocent, or laughing at others for what they believe can create a slippery slope for us, especially when we are called to speak life into another. Frankly, the enemy uses mockery as a secret uppercut for the Spiritually Righteous. What does this mean? Untactfully condemning or unwitting remarks can become a quick way to contaminate our fruits. Please allow me to align: *"Brethren, if a man is overtaken in any trespass, you who are spiritual restore such a one in a spirit of gentleness, considering yourself lest you also be tempted."* Galatians 6:1.

Do we not have the right to say or behave how we so desire? Absolutely. We have free will to do whatever, with whomever. Nevertheless, when it comes down to Kingdom Standards, *The Spiritual Middleman Approach*, and the Promises of God, we have a different set of Spiritual Rules, especially when it pertains to mockery.

In our *Spiritual Walk*, we cannot discount someone's experiences, nor should we make them feel bad or dysfunctional. The goal is to help them get an understanding through the Lenses of God on how to become better, stronger, and wiser from the inside out.

Spiritual Lenses

How do we develop *Spiritual Lenses*, seeing people, places, and things, *As It Pleases God*? First, we must develop a *Spirit to Spirit* Relationship with our Heavenly Father. Secondly, we must

AWAKEN our Spirit to become ONE with the Holy Spirit. Thirdly, we must COVER ourselves with the Blood of Jesus, accepting Him as a Formal Sacrifice. Fourthly, we must consistently pray, repent, forgive, fast, and meditate on the Word of God.

In *The Spiritual Middleman Approach*, listed below are a few pointers on how to develop our *Spiritual Lenses*, but not limited to such:

- ☐ We must examine ourselves thoroughly to ensure that what we are mocking is not represented as another form, label, or mask in our own house. *"For if anyone thinks himself to be something, when he is nothing, he deceives himself. But let each one examine his own work, and then he will have rejoicing in himself alone, and not in another."* Galatians 6:2-4.

- ☐ We must take responsibility for our actions, reactions, thoughts, and beliefs, redirecting all things back to God, *As It Pleases Him*, without shifting blame. *"For each one shall bear his own load."* Galatians 6:5.

- ☐ We must sow seeds of goodness, making our communication palatable to everyone. *"Let him who is taught the word share in all good things with him who teaches."* Galatians 6:6.

- ☐ We never know what God allowed into someone's life to train them; therefore, we should not judge, misrepresent, mock, or mistreat another. Simply put, we do not know what a person is going through; thus, we should stay in the non-judgmental zone to avoid bringing Divine Judgment or Reaping upon ourselves. *"Do not be deceived, God is not mocked; for whatever a man sows, that he will also reap."* Galatians 6:7.

- ☐ We must know why we do what we do and for whom, eliminating the 'just because' or selfish mentality. *"For he who sows to his flesh will of the flesh reap corruption, but he who sows to the Spirit will of the Spirit reap everlasting life."* Galatians 6:8.

- ☐ We must stay focused on doing the right things, even if we do not appear to be getting ahead. *"And let us not grow weary while doing good, for in due season we shall reap if we do not lose heart."* Galatians 6:9.

- ☐ We must be willing to help others, as God BLESSES us to be a BLESSING. *"Therefore, as we have opportunity, let us do good to all, especially to those who are of the household of faith."* Galatians 6:10.

- ☐ We must exhibit peace and mercy in our daily endeavors without boasting or excluding anyone from the Spiritual Newness in Christ Jesus. Doing so ensures peace, mercy, and newness will remain with us and in our Bloodline. *"But God forbid that I should boast except in the cross of our Lord Jesus Christ, by whom the world has been crucified to me, and I to the world. For in Christ Jesus neither circumcision nor uncircumcision avails anything, but a new creation. And as many as walk according to this rule, peace and mercy be upon them, and upon the Israel of God."* Galatians 6:14-16.

- ☐ We must stand firm with our Divine Blueprinted Mission in hand, as our Testimony witnesses to the Spiritual Refinement of the Spirit Man of another for Kingdom Purposes. *"From now on let no one trouble me, for I bear in my body the marks of the Lord Jesus. Brethren, the grace of our Lord Jesus Christ be with your Spirit. Amen."* Galatians 6:17-18.

- ☐ We must focus on becoming Spirit-Led in all things, casting down the lust of the eyes, the lust of the flesh, and the pride of life, and developing our *Spiritual Lenses*. *"I say then: Walk in the Spirit, and you shall not fulfill the lust of the flesh. For the flesh lusts against the Spirit, and the Spirit against the flesh; and these are contrary to one another, so that you do not do the things that you wish. But if you are led by the Spirit, you are not under the law."* Galatians 5:16-18.

- [ ] We must love each other to receive Spiritual Freedom from the inside out, *As It Pleases God*. *"For you, brethren, have been called to liberty; only do not use liberty as an opportunity for the flesh, but through love serve one another. For all the law is fulfilled in one word, even in this: 'You shall love your neighbor as yourself.' But if you bite and devour one another, beware lest you be consumed by one another!"* Galatians 5:13-15.

- [ ] We must use the Fruits of the Spirit to crucify our ungodly behaviors, thoughts, and emotions, helping us develop Christlike Character to avoid the negative desires to mock others. *"But the fruit of the Spirit is love, joy, peace, patience, kindness, goodness, faithfulness, gentleness, self-control. Against such there is no law. And those who are Christ's have crucified the flesh with its passions and desires."* Galatians 5:22-24.

What is the purpose of knowing this information when developing our *Spiritual Lenses*? As Believers, we will be mocked. If we become a mocker ourselves, we deplete our Spiritual Reservoir of Power, diminishing our Kingdom Authority unawaringly. Doing so causes us to Mentally, Physically, Emotionally, or Spiritually fold when contending with the enemy's wiles instead of STANDING TALL with the Kingdom of Heaven backing us. As a result, we become doubters of the Word of God, not knowing how to benefit from our Spiritual Tools or Masonry, putting us at a disadvantage.

Voice of Mockery

A mocker is nothing more than a bully in disguise, using some form of leverage to oppress another. Usually, the leveraging points include power, money, sex, or Religion. If it is all four, we have a master manipulator at work, most often under the guise of the 'wolf in sheep's clothing.' When we do not know what we are working with or how to use it, we become easily afflicted, passing on our secret afflictions to others through the *Voice of Mockery*.

Does mockery really have a voice? Absolutely. The Voice of Deceit is the *Voice of Mockery*, hidden under layers of something else. Most often, the something else is misrepresentation and the misunderstanding of those appearing weak, underprivileged, or beneath the status quo.

The best example, according to Scripture, is in the life of Joseph in Genesis 39 when Potiphar's wife was swirling accusations of him mocking and primitively assaulting her, which landed him in prison. In all actuality, she was the culprit of deceptive measures due to her unresolved feelings of rejection from Joseph, and her underlying hidden dissatisfaction with her husband. Still, it was easier for her to blame Joseph!

By Joseph refusing to feed into the lust of the eyes, the lust of the flesh, and the pride of life, ruining his integrity and reputation with God, Potiphar's wife sought revenge to ruin his life instead. Although in the end, all things work together for Joseph's good. Unfortunately, this is how the *Voice of Mockery* attempts to silence us, zapping our Blessings and Birthrights, especially if we play dirty like the ones trying to bury us.

In the Eye of God, the *Voice of Mockery* and the behaviors associated have continued to permeate our culture from generation to generation, leaving a trail of victims placed in some form of Mental, Physical, Emotional, and Spiritual Prison as a form of spite. Nor do they know how to use the Word of God in their favor, *As It Pleases Him.*

Why would someone ruin the life of an innocent person? The reason may vary from person to person, situation to situation, trauma to trauma, and so on. Still, it is linked to the inability to handle or understand rejection, a form of conditioning, refusal to acknowledge wrongness, to cover their tracks, or masking willful acts of debauchery, leading to all other negative character traits and behaviors, contradicting the Word of God.

The *Voice of Mockery* speaks louder than we think, causing us to feel insecure, unlovable, unworthy, deprived, and so on, full of doubt instead of hope. Unbeknownst to most, mockery causes a level of trauma to the human psyche, placing a dent of rejection, and making us feel as if we are missing out on something or someone.

What does mockery have to do with rejection? They are negative character traits that are intertwined, piggybacking on each other to oppress or place a yoke. For example, when mocked, we feel the sting of rejection, and when we are rejected, we become a mocker, mainly if Spiritual Intervention does not occur to counteract. In short, this unresolved feeling causes us to second-guess ourselves or indulge in acts of disobedience, similar to the Adam and Eve Experience in the Garden of Eden.

The seeds of doubtful mockery are nothing to joke around with! They are designed to take root wherever and whenever the opportune moment presents itself. Why is this such an issue, especially when we are Believers? We do not know where the seeds will land; they go from generation to generation, sorting their oats among the weak, fragile, and naive. Unfortunately, this seed has been around since *"The serpent said to the woman, 'You will not surely die.' For God knows that in the day you eat of it your eyes will be opened, and you will be like God, knowing good and evil."* Genesis 3:4-5.

Due to our hidden desire for superiority, God will TEST our ability to handle rejection before Kingdomly Commissioning us according to our Divine Blueprint. Why would He do this to us? The enemy will attack us in our places of weakness or areas of mockery, and if we are not strong enough to withstand the enemy's wiles, it is back to the Spiritual Classroom for another round or dose until we get it right.

What do we need to get right, especially in *The Spiritual Middleman Approach*? Being that we have a different Soul Print, Mind Print, Spirit Print, and Blueprint, it will vary from person to person. In addition, it will also depend on our areas of trauma, rejection, weaknesses, disobedience, biases, fears, lusts, pompousness, insecurities, or whatever is feeding our hidden desire to be more than we are, especially in the Eye of God or when it is contradicting His Word. For this reason, in the Kingdom, humility is required!

According to the Ancient of Days, this Mocking Spirit is an old wound that needs healing because we keep going around the mulberry bush, receiving the same results, *Unpleasing To God*. What does a mulberry have to do with our wounded areas or mockery? It is a matter of uprooting the traumatized plague of whatever, with whomever. According to Scripture, *"So the Lord said, 'If you have faith* as a mustard seed, you can say to this mulberry tree, Be pulled up by the roots and be planted in the sea,' and it would obey you.' " Luke 17:6.

It is now time for us to take Spiritual Authority over whatever is designed to beset us. In the same way David received his marching orders in front of the mulberry tree on how to defeat the Philistines, we now have ours with *The Spiritual Middleman Approach*. Here is the Scripture: "*Therefore David inquired again of God, and God said to him, 'You shall not go up after them; circle around them, and come upon them in front of the mulberry trees. And it shall be, when you hear a sound of marching in the tops of the mulberry trees, then you shall go out to battle, for God has gone out before you to strike the camp of the Philistines.' So David did as God commanded him, and they drove back the army of the Philistines from Gibeon as far as Gezer. Then the fame of David went out into all lands, and the LORD brought the fear of him upon all nations.*" 1 Chronicles 14:14-17.

In *The Spiritual Middleman Approach*, God is looking for the upright Mentally, Physically, Emotionally, and Spiritually, who will listen and obey without complaint. He is also seeking those who flee from any form of folly or recklessness in or out of the Kingdom as well. Here is what we must know: "*The wisdom of the prudent is to understand his way, But the folly of fools is deceit. Fools mock at sin, But among the upright there is favor.*" Proverbs 14:8-9.

As Believers, once we become Spiritually Trained and Developed, *As It Pleases God*, His Divine Favor is for the taking. Our responsibility is to change the trajectory of mocking, causing others to feel secure, loved, worthy, confident, hopeful, certain, and welcomed. Meanwhile, perfecting our *Spiritual Language* from the Heavenly of Heavens.

Spiritual Language

When it comes to Spirituality, *As It Pleases God*, there is no one-and-done approach to Him due to our varying differences, backgrounds, and needs. Actually, there are many different approaches to CONNECTING to Him *Spirit to Spirit*, so we must find what works for us according to our Predestined Blueprint. *The Spiritual Middleman Approach* emphasizes developing our *Spiritual Language* that is PLEASING to Him, bridging the gap between our Heaven on Earth Experience. Meanwhile, connecting with our innermost being and listening to the silent whispers from our Heavenly Father.

Can we really develop our *Spiritual Language*? Absolutely. We must pay close attention to our thoughts, feelings, senses, conscience, nudges, and actions. Why? The *Spiritual Language* from our Heavenly Father may not speak; it may be a feeling, sensation, nudge, dream, or whatever. Thus, we must notice when anything is out of alignment to perfect the conscience, developing our instincts, Spiritual Compass, and Spiritual Discernment, *As It Pleases God*. How do we know the difference? We must perfect the art of asking fact-finding questions.

Our *Spiritual Language* from the Heavenly of Heavens is a powerful Spiritual Tool that is misunderstood by most, and is only used by a few in the way God rightfully intended. Our unique Spiritual Dialogue with God, *Spirit to Spirit*, can help us navigate through challenges and protect us from harm by using our conscience to set rules, boundaries, or guidelines for us. However, we must use it *As It Pleases Him* without becoming blinded by our emotions and unable to see the bigger picture.

Listen, the affairs of the heart can become tricky because they can become powerful and all-consuming. Whether it is the excitement of a new relationship, heartbreak from a breakup, or complex emotions of a long-term relationship, matters of the heart can leave us feeling vulnerable and exposed. However, it is essential not to let these affairs block out the *Spiritual Language* designed to protect us.

In spite of everything life presents us, it helps us to fine-tune the *Spiritual Language* needed to ALIGN ourselves *Spirit to Spirit* with the Will of God, gleaning the Divine Wisdom needed to think on our feet. Along with the ability to know beyond a shadow of a doubt who is speaking. For example, listed below are a few Voices that we will encounter daily, but not limited to such:

- ☐ We have the Voice of God.
- ☐ We have the Voice of the Holy Spirit.
- ☐ We have the Voice of the Conscience or Instincts.

- ☐ We have the Voice of Man (opinions).
- ☐ We have the Inside Voice (peacemaker, baby talk, or sweet mouth).
- ☐ We have the Voice of the Critic.
- ☐ We have the Voice of Reasoning or Justification.
- ☐ We have the Voice of Common Sense.
- ☐ We have the Voice of Experience.
- ☐ We have the Voice of our Past.
- ☐ We have the Voice of Trauma.
- ☐ We have the Voice of Deception or the Hellion.

As a whole, we have a lot of Mental, Physical, Emotional, and Spiritual Balancing going on simultaneously. So, we can easily become confused about who is speaking because the human psyche (the flesh) aims for control, setting the pace for all else. With this being said, we are often in denial about these back-and-forth conversations we have with ourselves, as if they will not become evident in our actions, reactions, words, or demeanor.

Having unrestrained, unqueried, misaligned, ungoverned, and unpleasing conversations or negative chatter will cause problems for us. Why? Dialogue contradicting the Word of God or the Fruits of the Spirit leaves room for deceitful matters of the heart or ulterior motives to fester.

Even when having adult conversations, we must know when to draw the line to redirect the conversation or set the appropriate boundaries of comfort. As a Vessel of God, we must be willing to have those hard conversations to interject the Word of God, or that 'aha moment,' getting others to think about what they are doing, saying, or becoming, and the reasons why.

For example, as one can see, I think and speak differently than the average person by Divine Design. Amid entertaining a conversation with someone to build them positively, they claimed I said something negative, degrading them. To add insult to injury, what they claimed I said was out of character for me, nor do I speak rudely or derogatively to people in such a manner. And here I am asking myself, 'How did they extract that out of what I said?'

Therefore, I responded, 'I did not say that!' And their response was, 'Well, that is what I heard.'

Regardless of what they heard or their internal dialog, whether fact or fiction, they did not seek clarity before falsely accusing me of a mental playback they constructed on their own, based upon the voice of deception they entertained without correction. For this reason, we must become ever so cautious about what we are hearing and the inner chatter we are entertaining, slandering others without just cause.

With this Spiritual Approach in determining the different voices speaking, here is what we must know: *"Therefore do not be unwise, but understand what the will of the Lord is. And do not be drunk with wine, in which is dissipation; but be filled with the Spirit, speaking to one another in psalms and hymns and spiritual songs, singing and making melody in your heart to the Lord, giving thanks always for all things to God the Father in the name of our Lord Jesus Christ, submitting to one another in the fear of God.* Ephesians 5:17-21.

People will hear what they want to hear and say what they desire. By aligning what we are saying with the pleasantness of the Scriptures, with the fear of God inside of us, and the Holy Spirit at the forefront, we can better govern the voices from within and interpret what is conveyed without offense.

When we are in Purpose on purpose, it comes with many fringe benefits from the Kingdom, but we must know how to treat others, especially when no one is looking. Yet, we must also become cautious about how we allow others to treat us in public and private.

According to the Heavenly of Heavens, God did not create us as doormats; He created us as Vessels of the Kingdom for His use. So, not only do we need to respect others, but we must also respect ourselves. How do we go about doing so? First, we must UNDERSTAND who we are in and out of the Kingdom of God. Secondly, we must KNOW how His System works on our behalf. Thirdly, we must MASTER how to approach Him and keep from boiling over when we are misunderstood, misused, mistreated, misquoted, or considered a mistake, especially when we all have an innate desire to be accepted. Plus, the worldly approach is not going to get it. Here are a few pointers, *As It Pleases God*, but not limited to such:

- ☐ He desires a *Spirit to Spirit* Relationship with us. "*Exalt the LORD our God, And worship at His footstool—He is holy.*" Psalm 99:5.

- ☐ He wants us to recognize He is the Creator, and we are the sheep in need of nurturing, *As It Pleases Him*. "*Know that the LORD, He is God; It is He who has made us, and not we ourselves; We are His people and the sheep of His pasture.*" Psalm 100:3.

- ☐ He wants us to happily and willingly serve Him. "*Serve the LORD with gladness; Come before His presence with singing.*" Psalm 100:2.

- ☐ He wants us to exhibit festive illumination when we speak about Him. "*Make a joyful shout to the LORD, all you lands!*" Psalm 100:1.

- ☐ He wants us to give THANKS in all things, regardless of how it appears. "*Enter into His gates with thanksgiving, And into His courts with praise. Be thankful to Him, and bless His name.*" Psalm 100:4.

- ☐ He wants us to recognize His mercifulness, extending it outwardly to others for His Name's Sake. "*For the LORD is good; His mercy is everlasting, And His truth endures to all generations.*" Psalm 100:5.

- ☐ He does not want us to become deceived through our acts of disobedience. "*Let no one deceive you with empty words, for because of these things the wrath of God comes upon the sons of disobedience. Therefore do not be partakers with them.*" Ephesians 5:6-7.

- ☐ He wants us to remain in the LIGHT, *As It Pleases Him*, once we are removed from the darkness. *"For you were once darkness, but now you are light in the Lord. Walk as children of light (for the fruit of the Spirit is in all goodness, righteousness, and truth), finding out what is acceptable to the Lord."* Ephesians 5:8-10.

- ☐ He wants us to walk in love in the pleasantness of the Kingdom. *"And walk in love, as Christ also has loved us and given Himself for us, an offering and a sacrifice to God for a sweet-smelling aroma."* Ephesians 5:2.

- ☐ He wants us to remove ourselves or quickly repent of negative, destructive, or debauched character traits to protect our Kingdomly Treasures. *"But fornication and all uncleanness or covetousness, let it not even be named among you, as is fitting for saints; neither filthiness, nor foolish talking, nor coarse jesting, which are not fitting, but rather giving of thanks. For this you know, that no fornicator, unclean person, nor covetous man, who is an idolater, has any inheritance in the kingdom of Christ and God."* Ephesians 5:3-5.

- ☐ He wants us to put on the Whole Armor of God, knowing what to do when our Mind, Body, or Soul has seemingly jumped the track. *"Put on the whole armor of God, that you may be able to stand against the wiles of the devil."* Ephesians 6:11.

- ☐ He wants us to become Spiritual Ambassadors for the Kingdom of Heaven. *"For which I am an ambassador in chains; that in it I may speak boldly, as I ought to speak."* Ephesians 6:20.

When using this Divine Approach, the Spiritual Seals for our *Spiritual Language* will reside in our ability to remain in a State of Peace, helping us think on our feet, *As It Pleases God*.

CHAPTER NINE
Divine Agreement

"Again I say to you that if two of you agree on earth concerning anything that they ask, it will be done for them by My Father in heaven." Matthew 18:19.

As we come into Divine Agreement with God and the Heavenly of Heavens with *The Spiritual Middleman Approach*, we must ask ourselves, *"Can two walk together, unless they are agreed?"* Amos 3:3. With this Divine Union with the Holy Trinity, *Spirit to Spirit*, there is no limit on what we can achieve if we BELIEVE. Once we get to this point in our Spiritual Journey, *"Endeavoring to keep the unity of the Spirit in the bond of peace."* Ephesians 4:3. We do not have to depend upon others to agree or support our endeavors, especially when God is on our side, regardless of the worldly hype.

Yet, the moment we become secret or open people pleasers or users, we redirect our attention back to outside sources or some form of idolatry instead of focusing on our Divine Source of Heavenly Provisions.

As we look toward Heaven from whence our strength cometh, God will take a second look at our righteousness and integrity consistently. What is the purpose of doing so, especially when we have the guidance of the Holy Spirit? Fortunately, we are all subjected to erring, trials, defeats, persecutions, and challenges on occasion, even if we think we are perfect, have the upper hand, or are a Vessel of God. Therefore, for the proper edification of the

Kingdom, these two items determine our Spiritual Bounce Back or Credibility regarding our fruits and character.

Unbeknown to most, God will withhold the Divine Secrets of the Heavenly of Heavens if our Spiritual Fruits and Character are NOT being worked on consistently. Based upon my careful observations, we often play ourselves short when neglecting the Spiritual Aspects hidden in our fruits and character. While at the same time, bypassing Divine Order to get to the Secrets of the Kingdom, primarily when the Fruits of the Spirit provide the Spiritual Lifeline we need for this Heaven on Earth Experience.

The moment we ignore our fruits, they will prevent us from receiving or working on what is already there. As we all know, rotten fruits spoil the whole bunch. Not realizing they have a job to do with or without our permission. More importantly, our responsibility is to remove the negative, rotten, debauched, immature, yoking, or unyielding fruits from within, spreading outwardly.

Suppose we deal with the outward manifestations of our fruits without dealing with the inner? It is a recipe for disaster, placing us on a cycle of déjà vu until we examine ourselves according to Kingdom Standards.

We can tiptoe around, deciding to help ourselves from the inside out, but our pangs of hunger and thirst are relentless. For this reason, rest assured that the outward manifestations will rat us out in due time. Why? We can only mask who we are for a short time, and when the right buttons are pushed, what is in us will come forth. In so many words, what is breeding life or keeping us bound in graveclothes must avail itself similar to how Jesus called Lazarus forth in John 11:43-44.

What does Lazarus have to do with our fruitful or fruitless manifestations? Frankly, we are all dealing with or healing from some sort of sickness, disability, weakness, or shortcoming that we must surrender to the deliverance of or from. Yet, we will often find it hidden or bandaged, full of stink, ungodliness, or whatever, keeping us from moving forward with clean hands and a pure heart.

What is the big deal about having secrets? There is nothing wrong with keeping things to ourselves based upon Godly or moral discipline. Still, if we are battling with the lack of self-control, zero humility, or ungodly immorality, our secrets are not secrets; they are a maskful cover-up or unresolved yokes. Unfortunately, in the Kingdom, they are considered hindrances or kryptonite, preventing the unveiling of our Divine Blueprint or circumventing our efforts of being in Purpose on purpose, *As It Pleases God*.

How can the outward manifestations reveal our secrets, especially when we are closed-lipped? According to our Divine Design, positively or negatively, our aura says what we are unwilling to speak. If we take this a step further, listed below are a few pointers, but not limited to such:

- ☐ Our actions unveil our hidden or open motives.
- ☐ Our thoughts determine our reactions or behaviors.
- ☐ Our body language speaks to those who pay attention.
- ☐ Our fruits expose our sweetness or tartness.
- ☐ Our character determines our personability, reclusiveness, or repulsiveness.
- ☐ Our transparency exposes the heart's contents, helping us deal with shamefulness or shaming others.
- ☐ Our honesty keeps us veering ourselves away from lies and deceitfulness.
- ☐ Our words reveal our self-control, respect, or the lack thereof.
- ☐ Our Mind, Body, and Soul become what we feed them.
- ☐ Our discipline determines whether we are teachable, shareable, or stiff-necked.
- ☐ Our repenting hearts keep our conscience Spiritually Lubricated.
- ☐ Our gratefulness gives us the ability to see the BIG PICTURE when others are settling for defeat.

Amid living our best lives, we are all a work-in-progress with the potential to become better, wiser, and stronger daily. Listen, it is okay to glean from another man's Spiritual Reservoir temporarily to learn, grow, and sow back into the Kingdom when called upon. Thus, the ultimate goal is to jumpstart the Divine Flow of WISDOM to and through us, sustaining our Spiritual Reservoir and standing on our own two feet to avoid being swept away by the Vicissitudes or Wiles.

Direct Connect

Everyone has a *Direct Connect* to the Heavenly of Heavens, but NOT everyone knows how to gain Spiritual Access, *As It Pleases God*, without showboating. The moment we begin to showboat, it indicates the absence of humility and more of a need to use the Fruits of the Spirit as a Spiritual Guideline to redirect, revamp, or regraft our lives, ushering in the LIGHT or ILLUMINATION.

Humility is one of the keys to God's heart, written throughout the Bible in plain sight. And still, it is one of the biggest VICES, yoking us to the core until this very day.

How do we know when our fruits are working on our behalf, *As It Pleases God* to establish a *Direct Connect*? To fairly answer this question, allow me to counteract it with a few other questions, but not limited to such:

- ☐ When we are wronged, do we have the courage to do the right thing without seeking revenge?
- ☐ When we are rejected, do we have the tenacity to be kind and compassionate anyway?
- ☐ When we are falsely accused, do we have the courage to walk with our truth confidently?
- ☐ When we are mocked, do we have the esteem to understand who we are in the Eye of God?
- ☐ When we are used, do we have the know-how to unselfishly lend a helping hand?
- ☐ When we suffer a setback or setup, do we know how to look for a win-win?
- ☐ When we make a mistake, do we understand how to take responsibility and self-correct simultaneously?
- ☐ When we are victims, do we understand how to seek victory in seeming defeat?
- ☐ When we are faced with the negative, do we know how to convert it into a positive?

- When we are behind closed doors, do we have the willpower to do the right thing regardless?
- When we are unloved, do we have the heart to love others unconditionally?
- When we are treated like a junkyard dog, do we have enough self-control and discipline to flip the script, extending kindness and goodness?

In or out of the Kingdom of God, we must have the maturity to look for the Big Picture without pointing the finger, becoming emotionally mushy, losing our common sense, or outright getting out of character with profound, ungodly foolery. Listen, whenever we are close to our breakthrough, God will allow our enemies to push our weak buttons or dig into our wounds to test us or provoke us to err. Why? Once again, God keeps a close eye on our integrity and righteousness.

Even if we think or it appears as if we are getting ahead, the setback of the human psyche is no joke. When we become unrighteous or lack integrity amid whatever or whomever, it is back to the Spiritual Classroom or Drawing Board for us. Then again, we can lose our Spiritual Crowns depending on the severity of the victims left on the ground as we become an inner vagabond.

How do we become a vagabond for doing what is right in our own eyes? In my opinion, this is similar to Abel's blood crying out to God in Genesis 4:10-16 when Cain unrepentingly slew him, doing what he wanted to do without considering his well-being. Had Cain placed God into the equation while understanding and dealing with his issues from the inside out, he would not have become overcome with negative emotions or become a vagabond with unresolved issues.

Listen, King David slew more men than we care to imagine in war, yet he was after God's own heart. Why? It was due to his repenting and humble heart, placing God first amid whatever and whomever, even when he erred. However, he knew the value hidden in humility that we overlook repeatedly. Here is the Wisdom of David on a Silver Platter, *"And those who know Your name will put their trust in You; For You, LORD, have not forsaken those who seek*

You. Sing praises to the LORD, who dwells in Zion! Declare His deeds among the people. When He avenges blood, He remembers them; He does not forget the cry of the humble." Psalm 9:10-12. What does this mean? It will vary from person to person; however, based upon what we are discussing, here is what I extracted to make a *Direct Connect*, but not limited to such:

- ☐ We must place our TRUST in God.
- ☐ We must DEVELOP an intimate *Spirit to Spirit* Relationship with Him.
- ☐ We must SEEK and involve Him in all we do, say, and become.
- ☐ We must PRAISE Him.
- ☐ We must openly DECLARE His good deeds through the power of our Testimony or Testament.
- ☐ We must SURRENDER all things to Him, placing Him at the forefront of our lives.
- ☐ We must EXPECT Him to work all things together for our good, regardless of how it appears to the naked eye.

Does this work in making a *Direct Connect*? Absolutely! "But now in Christ Jesus you who once were far off have been brought near by the blood of Christ." Ephesians 2:13. Yet, we must repentantly stay on the righteous side of the spectrum. What is the purpose of doing so? In all actuality, if we are serving up unrighteousness, the seeds of unrighteousness are justified.

On the other hand, if we are humbly serving righteousness with good motives, then the seeds of unrighteousness are unjustified. More importantly, they are also recompensable. What does this mean? We can Spiritually Declare restitution, whereas when we behave unrighteously, we cannot demand compensation. Why? Unfortunately, if we demand good when serving debauchery, we may reap coals instead; therefore, it is best to repent, asking for grace and mercy instead. Blasphemy, right? Wrong!

Here is what David says in the Book of Psalms about this matter. "The LORD shall judge the peoples; Judge me, O LORD, according to my righteousness, And according to my integrity within me. Oh, let the wickedness of the wicked come to an end, But establish the just; For the righteous God tests the hearts and minds. My defense is of God, Who saves the upright in heart. God is a just judge, And God is angry with the wicked every day. If he does not turn back, He will sharpen His sword; He bends His bow and makes it ready. He also prepares for Himself instruments of death; He makes His arrows into fiery shafts. Behold, the wicked brings forth iniquity; Yes, he conceives trouble and brings forth falsehood. He made a pit and dug it out, And has fallen into the ditch which he made. His trouble shall return upon his own head, And his violent dealing shall come down on his own crown. I will praise the LORD according to His righteousness, And will sing praise to the name of the LORD Most High." Psalm 7:8-17.

Spiritual Crown

Our *Spiritual Crown* is a powerful representation of coming into *Divine Agreement* with the Heavenly of Heavens. *"As iron sharpens iron, so a man sharpens the countenance of his friend."* Proverbs 27:17. How much more do we think our *Spiritual Crowns* can do for us and through us if we allow God to sharpen us, *As It Pleases Him*? Wait, wait, wait, do not answer this yet. Let us go deeper...

"And when the Chief Shepherd appears, you will receive the crown of glory that does not fade away." 1 Peter 5:4. By getting to this point in the Eye of God, we will experience a sense of ONENESS with a Divine Presence that will penetrate the core of our being. This deep sense of purposeful knowing is like the ultimate Spiritual Bliss. Nevertheless, it takes work to get to this point in our *Spirit to Spirit Relations*.

Furthermore, this is not a bunch of hype...I am laying out the Spiritual Blueprint for those who desire their *Spiritual Crown*. Here is the deal: If someone says we cannot lose our *Spiritual Crowns*, we do not have to do anything to become better in our walk with God, or we do not need to Spiritually Till our own ground, know that we are being deceived. We must work on ourselves and our fruits daily to keep the soulish psyche from dominating our lives with foolery, debauchery, or selfishness.

Just because we do not see man's psyche, we tend to overlook it based on our understanding, omitting the Creator of it all. Listen, the way into ourselves or others is through God, period! Without God, everything is temporary. Any other way, we can only deal with the surface issues, not the real ROOT. Why can we not do so, especially if we have trained or gone to school to resolve human issues? God has the Divine Blueprint, knowing everything about them and us, even if we are deceived or in denial.

By neglecting God and leaving Him out of the equation, we inadvertently neglect ourselves or others, especially when no value is involved, or we are not getting paid to help another. What does this mean in layman's terms? We are created in HIS IMAGE, according to His LIKENESS in Genesis 1:26-31.

In short, we are Spiritual Beings with Divine Expectations for our Heaven on Earth Experience. If we attempt to help others without an underlying Spiritual Preface, we can misguide based on our experiences, expectations, perceptions, motives, biases, traumas, and so on. So, instead of fixing the issue, we become susceptible to it, absorb it, or transfer it to a weaker vessel, which is most often our children. Really? Yes, really!

How can we avoid misleading others? Avoid negatively judging, extend mercy and compassion, speak the truth in love, involve the Holy Spirit in the equation to guide us, and cover ourselves with the Blood of Jesus, *As It Pleases God*.

God is clear about His intentions. For the record, He is NOT created in our image, even if we develop the mindset of bringing Him to our level or becoming an idolistic god to others. The moment we behave in such a manner, we secretly or openly turn on ourselves while justifying what we do and why. And then again, we may outright cover up our behaviors with superficial excuses without taking the time to work on ourselves daily. To add insult to injury regarding this matter, if someone dares to point out our point of erring, we turn on them as if we are possessed.

For example, we have a married couple vowing before God to love each other for better or worse. Yet, when the worst avails itself, they head to divorce court, turning on each other like archenemies while their children are watching.

Then again, we may find some using their children as leverage or pawns, sometimes in the name of God. For others, outside of His

Name, to get what they want or to spitefully hurt the other person for deciding to move on with their life without them.

If we cannot see this happening all around us, it is best to take a second look to avoid this from happening on our behalf or becoming a victim. Regardless of what type of picture is painted before us, just know that God did not design us to behave or treat each other in such a manner, nor should we use our children as scapegoats.

How is it possible to use our children as scapegoats? We can easily sacrifice the well-being of our children if we fail to take care of ourselves, Mentally, Physically, Emotionally, or Spiritually. When our behaviors, attitudes, thoughts, words, or character traits negatively affect them, we put them at risk of doing likewise, becoming traumatized, falling prey to predators, or repeating the same cycle as a victim.

How is this a sacrifice, especially when we care for our children, and they lack nothing? First and foremost, in all things, we are allowed to indulge in righteousness or unrighteousness, period. Secondly, in doing what we do, we are accountable if we intentionally place our children at a disadvantage by choosing NOT to do the right thing out of selfishness or lack of self-control. Thirdly, we are required to *"Train up a child in the way he should go, And when he is old he will not depart from it."* Proverbs 22:6. For this reason, we must pay attention to what we are doing, saying, becoming, and spreading. Why? We never know who is watching or what our children are picking up; therefore, it is best to keep all things positive, productive, and fruitful, *As It Pleases God*.

What if our children do not listen to us? With all due respect, no one is perfect. Kids will be kids, doing what kids do. More importantly, listening or developing a deaf ear is a trained behavior. For this reason, before judging their listening abilities, we must make sure ours are up to par, exercise patience, and not abuse them Mentally, Physically, Emotionally, or Spiritually. So, it is always best to add God into the equation while communicating effectively, allowing the Holy Spirit to work to guide and the Blood of Jesus to cover all involved.

This chapter is not about parenting skills, so let us go deeper into how we scapegoat our children without realizing it. Here is the deal...we are the prime example our children glean from, even if we hide our truths. Believe it or not, children are the little geniuses we fail to give credit to. In my opinion, they are the best at playing mind games and using psychology on their parents without being formally educated in the field. They can learn any language or multiple languages simultaneously without setting foot into a classroom. Not to mention the ability to master today's technologies by being exposed to them.

Failing to acknowledge this genius at a young age, they inadvertently bury it to pick up mediocrity, pleasing their parents instead of God, even when becoming educated. For this reason, we have more educated individuals working for others or building an empire for those who are not formally educated by the system. What does this mean? Most businesses are owned by those who DO NOT have degrees. While at the same time, they are genius enough to hire those who have degrees to do the work from top to bottom, getting the job done or plugging and playing others on the level of their perceived capacity or mindset to accomplish the Company's Vision.

God has given us TALENTS and CREATIVITY, and if we do not uncover them, we subject ourselves to doing it for another in exchange for power, money, or sex. In the Bible, this is referred to as the lust of the eyes, the lust of the flesh, and the pride of life. Due to our lack of understanding, *As It Pleases God*, we teach this to our children out of custom without teaching them how to avoid such snares, especially when it takes the same amount of energy to humbly build, grow, and nurture their genius from within.

I am not saying that we should never work for someone else to develop experience or become educated. All I am saying is we must work with a PLAN to develop or establish our OWN in due time, according to our Spiritual Gifts or Divine Blueprint. If we train our children young, building their CREATIVITY and follow-through, by the time they are done with schooling, they are ready to apply their skills earlier than those who get a late start. Nor do we want to deprive them of the opportunity to have a positive entrepreneurial mindset early in the game, giving them more staying power than those stuck on negative.

Remember, all of these traits are trainable, and the earlier we start, the less we have to force our genius abilities to work on our behalf. For example, it is similar to learning how to ride a bike. Once we learn how to do so, if we get a little rusty...the skills are designed to come back once we take action, setting our skills in motion without becoming a victim of time past. With this analogy, our Spirit Man works the same way once it is AWAKENED to become ONE with the Holy Spirit. What does this have to do with riding a bike? Once we connect with the Holy Spirit in such a manner, our little genius becomes a capital G, working in our favor 24/7!

What is a capital G? We have to put a little respect on the Genius from within when involving the Holy Spirit. Why? Anything Spiritual in nature, we must RESPECT, period! *"Therefore, since we are receiving a kingdom which cannot be shaken, let us have grace, by which we may serve God acceptably with reverence and godly fear."* Hebrews 12:28. Am I pulling for straws on this one? Absolutely not! I write with RESPECT, and guess what? The Divine Well of Wisdom overflows! *"If any of you lacks wisdom, let him ask of God, who gives to all liberally and without reproach, and it will be given to him."* James 1:5.

Doing so ensures our humility stays intact to glean on a Spiritual Level, *As It Pleases God*. The moment we lack respect, the Holy Spirit has to lie dormant or bring the Rod of Correction, especially if repentance or self-correction does not take place. If we refuse, we will begin to operate from self and not under Divine Wisdom, making us accident-prone Mentally, Physically, Emotionally, and Spiritually.

Age of Faith

When we need what money cannot buy, it changes the most challenging person into a humble servant in the Kingdom of God. In short, it behooves us to become Spiritually Proactive, including God in the equation of all things. Why must we proactively include God, especially when we do not have it all together? No one has it together 100% of the time because we are all a work-in-progress with strengths and weaknesses, learning and growing daily. For this reason, we need the Holy Spirit to guide us continually. And, we need the Blood of Jesus to cover our known and unknown atrocities, keeping us Spiritually Synced in ONENESS with God. So, if we think we can approach the Vicissitudes and Seasons of life on our own without Spiritual Guidance from the Heavenly Realms, then have at it!

Why Must We Please God? When the Kingdom of God is backing us, no man can contend or stop His Promises; they cannot circumvent the Gospels from unveiling what is veiled or prevent our Divinely Blueprinted Purpose from doing what it is Spiritually Designed to do, *As It Pleases Him*. Yet and still, if we do not KNOW or UNDERSTAND this Factual Truth for our Heaven on Earth Experience, we can indeed miss our Spiritual Mark or Cue due to self or worldly deception, blindness, deafness, or muteness, causing us to second-guess what we ALREADY know. Still, we may have forgotten due to the Vicissitudes of Life.

According to the Heavenly of Heavens, the '*Age of Faith*' or Spiritual Evolution is upon us, Building, Pruning, and Regrafting; therefore, we must step up our game, *As It Pleases God*. Why must the things of God be a game? For example, if we play by the rules, we have a better chance of winning than cheating, right? Game or not, obeying or disobeying, this same concept applies in the Kingdom, and if we want Divine Grace to reside and abide within the human psyche, we must position ourselves to RECEIVE. What is the purpose of doing so? To ensure Divine Grace does not pass over whatever, with whomever, because the Heavenly Consummation is upon us, regardless of what we understand or believe.

In the past, God used the Prophets to speak to the masses, then He used His Son, Jesus Christ, and now He is speaking directly to us, *Spirit to Spirit*. What does all of this mean? Simply put, He will speak directly to you, in SPIRIT and TRUTH! So, if you are ready, let us go deeper in the next chapter.

CHAPTER TEN
Heavenly Perception

"Nor is there salvation in any other, for there is no other name under heaven given among men by which we must be saved." Acts 4:12.

The *Heavenly Perception* has prominence in the lives of those who are ready to have a *Spirit to Spirit* Connection with God, the Divine Creator of all things. Unbeknown to most, our perception is tested right along with our trustworthiness, faith, motives, character, obedience, and so on. Unfortunately, by not knowing we are being tested in this area, we tend to fail by default based on our thoughts alone, overlooking this one Scripture: *"And why do you look at the speck in your brother's eye, but do not perceive the plank in your own eye?"* Matthew 7:3. How we secretly or openly perceive ourselves determines how we perceive others, especially when we do not need them or cannot benefit from them.

In my opinion, our planks should provide a seat of mercy and forgiveness for others; if it is not, it is best to take a seat in the Spiritual Classroom for a refresher course on Kingdom Etiquette. The problem we are dealing with today is determining the difference between our Heavenly Perceptions and personal ones. In the same way we pride ourselves on communicating with others, we must also make a conscious effort to do likewise in Earthen Vessels for our Heaven on Earth Experiences, perfecting our perceptions, *As It Pleases God*.

According to the Heavenly of Heavens, ignoring this highly sensitive matter is causing us to bump heads with the Kingdom, live a double life, or scatter God's flock. Jesus warned the Disciples about safeguarding their perception in Mark 8:15-18. It says, *"Then He charged them, saying, 'Take heed, beware of the leaven of the Pharisees and the leaven of Herod.' And they reasoned among themselves, saying, 'It is because we have no bread.' But Jesus, being aware of it, said to them, 'Why do you reason because you have no bread? Do you not yet perceive nor understand? Is your heart still hardened? Having eyes, do you not see? And having ears, do you not hear? And do you not remember?'"*

For the record, God takes care of what and who belongs to Him, period! Yet, if we allow our excuses to shortchange us, then how else will we take possession of what rightly belongs to us? It becomes challenging to do so when we are fighting against ourselves while at the same time laying blame elsewhere without assuming total responsibility or querying ourselves properly.

What is the purpose of dealing with our perceptual efforts? We can easily get our wires crossed if our perceptions are not Biblically Aligned or our trust in God is not established, *As It Pleases Him*. Here is what Isaiah shared with us about living a double life with one foot in the Kingdom and one foot out. *"When You did awesome things for which we did not look, You came down, the mountains shook at Your presence. For since the beginning of the world Men have not heard nor perceived by the ear, nor has the eye seen any God besides You, Who acts for the one who waits for Him."* Isaiah 64:3-4.

In developing our *Heavenly Perceptions*, there is no shame in correcting negativity. In the Eye of God, shame is unveiled when we ignore our negative thoughts, behaviors, actions, or words, allowing it to ensnare the innocent due to some form of recklessness, unawareness, or negligence, traumatizing them all the more.

As a part of Kingdom Formality, we must begin to perceive correctly to delegate or harness our Spiritual Power accordingly, based upon the instructions from the Holy Spirit. What is the reason for doing so? We must become good stewards of the Spiritual Power granted by the Heavenly of Heavens. For example, if a person is flaunting Spiritual Power, it sends up all types of RED FLAGS for me. Why? Authentic Spiritual Authority or Power does not need us to brag about it because it is ABSOLUTE.

Frankly, when bragging in such a manner and cannot Spiritually Discern another Spiritual Source of Power in the room, it says a lot in the Realm of the Spirit. What does this mean Spiritually? Spiritual Blindness or Deafness is running rampant. Here is what we need to know, but not limited to such:

- ☐ SPIRIT KNOWS SPIRIT, period!
- ☐ Spirit perceives Spirit, even if nothing is voiced!
- ☐ Spirit RESPECTS the Spiritual Level we are on; if not, we already know what we are dealing with, period!
- ☐ Deceptive Spirits are clueless about Spiritual Truths.
- ☐ An authentic Righteous Spirit heeds to Spiritual Truths and Authority naturally and instinctively, with or without being a Believer.

When operating in Spirit and Truth, we will perceive accordingly without pandering to the worldly hoopla about what God expects from us. How is this possible, especially if we are clueless about the Word of God? When we are truly ONE with the Spirit of God, using *The Spiritual Middleman Approach*, we will KNOW or become TRAINED in the know!

Here is what the Bible has to say: *"But God has revealed them to us through His Spirit. For the Spirit searches all things, yes, the deep things of God. For what man knows the things of a man except the spirit of the man which is in him? Even so no one knows the things of God except the Spirit of God."* 1 Corinthians 2:10-11. What God wants us to know about Him or the Kingdom is already within us; we only need the Bible to REMIND or ALIGN us back into Divine Order. Remember, we are Spirit first, having a human experience; therefore, it is our responsibility to connect back to God, *Spirit to Spirit*; but more importantly, *As It Pleases Him* on His Divine Terms.

What if we cannot recognize who or what we are dealing with, and we are a Spiritual Elite and Kingdomly Commissioned? We have unrepented sin, unforgiveness, lack of humility, or a hardened heart in the camp! For sure, this is similar to the lepers running around saying, 'Unclean, unclean, unclean.' Or, they would ring a bell to let us know they are in the vicinity. Well, the Holy Spirit will send this same type of alarm to our conscience, indicating a need for prayer, repenting, forgiveness, or fasting, and sometimes all four.

What if the Holy Spirit does not forewarn us? The reason will vary from person to person, situation to situation, trauma to trauma, and so on. However, one reason would be that we are in a Spiritual Classroom, and there is a hidden Lesson, Blessing, or Testing attached. So, make sure documentation is taking place to ensure we can adequately align our situations, thoughts, or feelings with the Word of God.

Why must we Spiritually Align? When God sees that we are serious about getting an understanding, *As It Pleases Him*, He ushers in Divine Wisdom to assist. Now, if we neglect Divine Wisdom, it goes into a state of dormancy until we are ready, properly seasoned to receive, or humility is set in motion.

The second reason is that we could have grieved the Holy Spirit unawaringly. How can someone grieve the Holy Spirit? According to Scripture, here is what we must know: *"Let no corrupt word proceed out of your mouth, but what is good for necessary edification, that it may impart grace to the hearers. And do not grieve the Holy Spirit of God, by whom you were sealed for the day of redemption. Let all bitterness, wrath, anger, clamor, and evil speaking be put away from you, with all malice."* Ephesians 4:29-31.

How can we reverse grievances against the Holy Spirit? We can begin using the Fruits of the Spirit and behave Christlike. *"And be kind to one another, tenderhearted, forgiving one another, even as God in Christ forgave you."* Ephesians 4:32.

Due to this type of Kingdom Astuteness, we never saw Jesus flaunting His Divine Power or Authority, even though the perception of others expected Him to be on a throne, sitting in a palace somewhere. Regardless of the mere perceptions of man, He handled His Father's business and kept it moving to the next location needing Him, *As It Pleased God*. To say the least, these simple acts of humility kept His *Heavenly Perception* intact so that He could perceive the upcoming Divine Healing or Restoration issues at hand.

According to Scripture, Jesus taught the Disciples how to perceive correctly, ensuring their *Spirit to Spirit* Connection was up to par before departing. Now, from back then to now, the Ancient of Days expects no less from us. The *Heavenly Perception* is available to all; however, it is our responsibility to get rid of the debris, specks, or planks blocking our Spiritual Eyes, Ears, and Voice to hear what the Spirit of the Lord is saying, unveiling, or planning. If not, we can succumb to having a *Slighted Perception* without realizing it and appear right in our own eyes, but it is all so wrong in the Eye of God.

Slighted Perception

As faithful Believers, it is extremely easy to think we have a clear understanding of the Kingdom of God. But what if our perception is slightly off? What if we are not seeing eye to eye with our Heavenly Father? What if we are seen as a canker sore instead of a curing remedy? With this *Slighted Perception*, not knowing the truth about the Divine Expectations from the Heavenly of Heavens can cause us to miss the mark in the Eye of God. Then again, we can miss out on the fullness of God's Divine Plan or Blueprint for our lives.

Although God's love and forgiveness are unconditional and are a FREE GIFT for everyone, they do not negate what He expects from us. Regardless of what we think, believe, or say, we are all here for a reason greater than ourselves, and if we are not doing what we were Divinely Ordained to do, we will get a side-eye from Him. Why? With the most simplicity possible, God requires selflessness instead of selfishness.

Respectfully speaking, when our perceptions are off or misaligned according to the Word of God, it is fair to say our Divine Understanding, Insight, Awareness, Knowledge, and Discernment are off-kilter, *As It Pleases God*. Spiritual Intuitiveness is of great importance in or out of the Kingdom, even when the Vicissitudes of Life press us to the max or challenge us beyond reason with a lot of trials and hardships.

For example, when we are faced with a lot of misunderstandings, confusion, miscalculations, false accusations, debauchery, foolery, dullness, lukewarmness, having a stiff neck, and so on, they are our SILENT INDICATORS of having *Slighted Perceptions* that are unpleasing in the Eye of God. All of these indicators give us an opportunity to grow, learn, revamp, extract, and reapproach, *As It Pleases Him*.

What causes colliding or *Slighted Perceptions*? It varies from person to person, situation to situation, trauma to trauma, culture to culture, bias to bias, and so on. Lacking integrity, missing transparency, avoiding forgiveness, negating repentance, and engaging in disobedience are contributing factors to exhibiting the negative characteristics God frowns upon. Not taking the time to build ourselves with the Fruits of the Spirit and developing Christlike Character, *As It Pleases Him*, we will find ourselves pulling for straws and constantly experiencing confusion out of seemingly nowhere.

Why do we become overwhelmed in such a manner, especially when our intentions are right? Negativity or positivity has a life of its own, catering to our thoughts, beliefs, words, and actions, creating a Gravitational Pull based upon the Spiritual Laws set forth. Through it all, we choose our portion of the two, stimulating the type of insight we will receive. Without a doubt, we determine our worldly or Spiritual Insights by the choices we make on a moment-by-moment basis, regardless of the season, cycle, or growth spurt encountered.

In leaning toward our *Spirit to Spirit* Relations, we must come with a wholehearted desire to have our Spiritual Eyes and Ears opened to our Heavenly Father from His Divine Perspective. If not, our perceptional understanding of the Mysteries of Heaven becomes veiled, regardless of whether we are Believers or not. Why are we deprived in such a manner? Not to discount what anyone is hearing, but if we cannot hear the Voice of God aligning with His Word, it is an indication that we are tuning into alternative voices from the inside out.

Here is what we must know: "*And in them the prophecy of Isaiah is fulfilled, which says: 'Hearing you will hear and shall not understand, And seeing you will see and not perceive; For the hearts of this people have grown dull. Their ears are hard of hearing, And their eyes they have closed, Lest they should see with their eyes and hear with their ears, Lest they should understand with their hearts and turn, So that I should heal them.' But blessed are your eyes for they see, and your ears for they hear; for assuredly, I say to you that many prophets and righteous men desired to see what you see, and did not see it, and to hear what you hear, and did not hear it."* Matthew 13:14-17.

A thwarted perception puts us on a cycle of judgment and condemnation, traumatizing folks in the Name of God. If we think for a minute that defiling a person Mentally, Physically, Emotionally, and Spiritually draws people toward the Kingdom, we are sadly mistaken. Instead, it sets the trend to follow, creating other victims of our biased or *Slighted Perceptions* of what the Kingdom of God is really about.

If we want to wholeheartedly put our *Slighted Perceptions* on blast, we should read this Scripture before we open our mouths to condemn anyone. If we are guilty of anything on this list, it behooves us to repent, casting it down. While at the same time, replacing the ones we are guilty of with a positive character trait. *"So He said to them, 'Are you thus without understanding also? Do you not perceive that whatever enters a man from outside cannot defile him, because it does not enter his heart but his stomach, and is eliminated, thus purifying all foods?' And He said, 'What comes out of a man, that defiles a man.' For from within, out of the heart of men, proceed evil thoughts, adulteries, fornications, murders, thefts, covetousness, wickedness, deceit, lewdness, an evil eye, blasphemy, pride, foolishness. All these evil things come from within and defile a man."* Mark 7:18-23.

For some, a checklist will suffice. Others may need to take their perceptional flaws to God, *Spirit to Spirit*, into their Prayer Closet for a Spiritual Overhaul, *As It Pleases Him*. Do not feel bad if you need an overhaul; I needed one to get to this point in the Kingdom...So, do what you need to do to bring forth your Divine Blueprint, *As It Pleases Him*.

Unspeakable Joy

As God has PROMISED us Joy, we often fail to understand the power hidden in it due to improper illumination. Here is what we need to know for this chapter: *"You have heard Me say to you, 'I am going away and coming back to you.' If you loved Me, you would REJOICE because I said, 'I am going to the Father,' for My Father is greater than I. And now I have told you before it comes, that when it does come to pass, you may believe."* John 14:28-29.

Unbeknown to most, PEACE and JOY go hand in hand; therefore, *Unspeakable Joy* becomes a result if we can master re-experiencing them over and over. How is it possible to relive them continuously? Simply put, it is called REJOICING. Listen, PEACE and JOY are Spiritual Commodities from within, long before making their mark outwardly through choice. *"Therefore do not let your good be spoken of as evil; for the Kingdom of God is not eating and drinking, but righteousness and PEACE and JOY in the Holy Spirit. For he who serves Christ in these things is acceptable to God and approved by men."* Romans 14:16-18.

Commonly, we typically look for the results of *Unspeakable Joy*, not understanding what it takes to obtain and maintain it, while opting for the manifested illusion instead. How do we make this make sense? With man's perception, we can create anything Mentally, Emotionally, and Soulishly without fact, rhyme, or reason, causing deception to penetrate the human psyche when left Spiritually Ungoverned. More importantly, no one is exempt from this form of deception due to the Garden of Eden Experience with Adam and Eve.

Amid all, if we continue to Spiritually Till our own ground Mentally, Physically, Emotionally, and Spiritually with the Divine Tools of Restitution, our *Unspeakable Joy* will wait for us. When wholeheartedly pleading the Blood of Jesus, AWAKENING and becoming ONE with the Holy Spirit, and placing God at the forefront of our lives, we gain Spiritual Leverage over what happened back then; without a doubt, our *Unspeakable Joy* will wait for us. While waiting, remember we will always have the option to humbly and gratefully make our requests known to God about our desire to usher in the Spirit of Joy.

As we fellowship one with another, our *Unspeakable Joy* does not abandon us! It simply lays dormant until we can avail ourselves of it. Once availed, it then spreads outwardly as a form of happiness to those who are not privy to seeing the Heavenly Manifestations of the *Unspeakable Joy* from within us.

In its simplicity, it takes a Spiritual Eye to see *Unspeakable Joy* from within another person. However, everyone can see the outward manifestations through our actions, reactions, behaviors, and spoken words. Why? Unbeknown to most, *Joy* is a SACRED inner filling from God! Blasphemy, right? Wrong! *"Now may the God of hope fill you with all joy and peace in believing, that you may abound in hope by the power of the Holy Spirit."* Romans 15:13. To be crystal clear, we need the Holy Spirit amid *Unspeakable Joy*, period.

If we do not involve the Holy Spirit, our Comforter, we may unawaringly take the Blood of Jesus and the Hand of God for granted. Why do we need to involve the Holy Spirit, especially when having free will to accept or decline? He is a package deal from the Heavenly of Heavens, designed to console, correct, guide, and discipline the human psyche. Once we are left to ourselves without Him, our psyche runs wild, doing whatever, with whomever, without Spiritual Discretion.

Frankly, this is why we often confuse *Joy* (Inner Manifestation) with Happiness (Outer Manifestation), not realizing *Joy* is connected to our Spiritual Power in and out of the Kingdom of Heaven. Listen, there is *Unspeakable Joy* hidden in the Will of God, His Word, our Divine Blueprint, the Fruits of the Spirit, behaving Christlike, and operating with a Positive Mindset.

The moment we divert to debaucherous efforts, our *Unspeakable Joy* takes a back seat until REPENTANCE takes place. What if we are not aware of what we are doing? It is time to get *In The Know*! Plus, it is written all over the Book of Proverbs regarding how to wisely conduct ourselves without engaging in foolishness. To take this a step further, by Spiritually Awakening our Spirit to become ONE with the Holy Spirit amid whatever or whomever, the Rod of Correction will naturally occur. In addition, He will help us self-correct instead of self-destruct through the use of our instincts, conscience, and senses. Thus, we must begin paying close attention to them.

What can make our *Unspeakable Joy* turn into sadness? A double, negative, unstable, or pompous mindset. Really? Yes, really! *"Let nothing be done through selfish ambition or conceit, but in lowliness of mind let each esteem others better than himself."* Philippians 2:3. Although this is what gets us into a sad state of being, it is the lust of the eyes, the lust of the flesh, and the pride of life that keep us there. What are the implications of this? For example, the way we think opens the door to sadness. And then, our lust or pride closes the door, trapping us into a corner of sadness or causing us to fight against ourselves.

Regardless of how well we paint an outward picture of who we are and why, if we fail to do a check-up from the neck up, consistently examining and aligning ourselves with the Word of God, using the Fruits of the Spirit, and exhibiting Christlike Character, we can easily fall short in the Eye of God. What makes this so important when dealing with the inner manifestations of Unspeakable Joy? Here is what we need to know, *As It Pleases God*. *"Now may the God of patience and comfort grant you to be like-minded toward one another, according to Christ Jesus, that you may with one mind and one mouth glorify the God and Father of our Lord Jesus Christ. Therefore receive one another, just as Christ also received us, to the glory of God. Now I say that Jesus Christ has become a servant to the circumcision for the truth of God, to confirm the PROMISES made to the fathers."* Romans 15:5-8.

As we meander through life, it does not mean that Spiritual Principles do not exist. We have them for a reason, and if it is not reason enough to understand and obey them, *As It Pleases God*, then we have no reason to complain, fuss, or fight, especially when we receive the mangled results or harvest of our SEEDS sown in and out of Season. *"Therefore, if there is any consolation in Christ, if any comfort of love, if any fellowship of the Spirit, if any affection and mercy, fulfill my joy by being like-minded, having the same love, being of one accord, of one mind. Let nothing be done through selfish ambition or conceit, but in lowliness of mind let each esteem others better than himself."* Philippians 2:1-3. Here is the deal: Our *Unspeakable Joy* is wrapped in a few items, but not limited to such:

- ☐ We must become hearers of the Word of God without becoming stiff-necked or developing a deaf ear.
- ☐ We must pray and forgive, repenting consistently.
- ☐ We must make our requests known to God without assuming.
- ☐ We must avail ourselves of Divine Wisdom and Understanding.

- ☐ We must walk uprightly, exhibiting the Fruits of the Spirit and Christlike Character.
- ☐ We must activate the Law of Reciprocity in the Spirit of Excellence by doing our due diligence.
- ☐ We must become GRATEFUL in all things, even if it does not appear as much.
- ☐ We must be willing to seek the Light amid receiving our Divine Blessings or Birthrights.

Here is a Scripture to glean: *"For this reason we also, since the day we heard it, do not cease to pray for you, and to ask that you may be filled with the knowledge of His will in all wisdom and spiritual understanding; that you may walk worthy of the Lord, fully pleasing Him, being fruitful in every good work and increasing in the knowledge of God; strengthened with all might, according to His glorious power, for all patience and longsuffering with joy; giving thanks to the Father who has qualified us to be partakers of the inheritance of the saints in the light."* Colossians 1:9-12.

What if we choose not to embrace *Unspeakable Joy*? We have the right to reject the Promises of God for whatever and with whomever. Nevertheless, it causes us to become worldly servants, thinking we have it going on with a Spiritual Yoke, yoking us to the core. According to the Heavenly of Heavens, a YOKE of this capacity is so heavy, weighing us down to the point where we do not know how to pick ourselves up, Mentally, Physically, or Emotionally, especially behind closed doors. Blasphemy, right? Wrong! Let us align: *"Because you did not serve the LORD your God with joy and gladness of heart, for the abundance of everything, therefore you shall serve your enemies, whom the LORD will send against you, in hunger, in thirst, in nakedness, and in need of everything; and He will put a yoke of iron on your neck until He has destroyed you."* Deuteronomy 28:47-48.

Spiritually Speaking, a Spiritual Yoke usually does not appear as such to the naked eye. How is this possible, especially when we are on top of our game? We have become conditioned to fake it or cover up things to satiate the human psyche.

In all actuality, it is imperative to pull the covers back, exposing what is slinging sludge over our *Unspeakable Joy*. Or understand what is causing us to misconstrue or misinterpret the beneficial effects of our *Unspeakable Joy* that would connect us back to the Kingdom of Heaven.

For example, in the Ancient of Days, our Forefathers dealt with Tribal Bondage, zapping their *Unspeakable Joy*. As we became wiser in our own eyes, we have upgraded Tribal Bondage to Human Enslavement for profit. Now, as we fast forward to today's day and age, Human Enslavement has progressed into Mind Control to develop hidden or open Capital Investments. Unfortunately, this form of Mind Control has now been overshadowed by Mass Manipulation of fear, panic, image, and lack, zapping the *Unspeakable Joyous* efforts of our Heaven on Earth Experience.

We can tiptoe around *Unspeakable Joy*, but it does not negate our GENETIC need for it, causing deficiencies we cannot explain unless we tap into our Spirituality, *As It Pleases God*. What is the big deal about *Unspeakable Joy*? If we find *Unspeakable Joy* from within, we will also find our hidden strengths to embrace our Blessings, becoming a Blessing to others as well. Here is what we need to know: "*Then he said to them, 'Go your way, eat the fat, drink the sweet, and send portions to those for whom nothing is prepared; for this day is holy to our Lord. Do not sorrow, for the JOY of the LORD is your strength.'* " Nehemiah 8:10.

Set Aside For Him

Of course, no one will exhibit super strength 100% of the time because we are human. However, in a moment of weakness, here is what the Bible tells us to do: "*But let all those rejoice who put their trust in You; Let them ever shout for JOY, because You defend them; Let those also who love Your name Be joyful in You. For You, O LORD, will bless the righteous; With favor You will surround him as with a shield.*" Psalm 5:11-12.

What is the purpose of knowing this Scripture? It gives us Spiritual Leverage with God, especially when we quote His Divine Word back to Him, knowing that we know! Is this disrespectful? Absolutely not! Here is how I humbly approach God in my *Spirit to Spirit* Connection with sincerity, 'Lord, You said in Your Word, ……….' 'I am claiming Your Promise of ……..' 'I Decree and Declare …….'

'I stand on Your Word, ...' 'I am Your child, therefore ....' 'This is between You and I, so ....' 'I am *Set Aside for You*, so ....'

Does quoting Scriptures back to God work? It is based upon our beliefs, mindsets, heart postures, level of selfishness, and our biased or unbiased perception. If we use Scriptures to boss God around, we will have an issue with Him. Plus, the Vicissitudes of Life will begin to read us as a canker sore due to a disruption in the Genetic Code from within, placing us in a cycle of déjà vu.

Why would we have a problem, especially when God is here for us? Simply put, this is how we become deceived! He will make an example out of us because we are *Set Aside for Him*, for our Blueprinted Purpose to feed His sheep. Here is the Scripture to develop Divine Order, *As It Pleases Him*: "*But know that the LORD has set apart for Himself him who is godly; The LORD will hear when I call to Him.*" Psalm 4:3.

In the Eye of God, although life will serve us when we are in Purpose on purpose, the Holy Spirit is here to guide us, and the Blood of Jesus is for our Atonement; we are *Set Aside for Him* to be about His Divine Business, *As It Pleases Him*. Now, keep in mind, amid all this, we have free will, but we must still make the correct choices in choosing righteousness over unrighteousness.

But for me, *As It Pleases God*, I am a living Epistle of His Word, as my Tongue is the Pen of a Ready Writer, giving back to the Divine Well I draw Heavenly Wisdom, Secrets, Mysteries, Know-How, and Creativity from. Besides, if He can work through a country girl like me, He can do anything for anyone, regardless of what we have done, are doing, or are contemplating. Yet and still, we must Divinely Align with His Will, Ways, and Blueprinted Purpose for our lives.

How can we be *Set Aside for Him* when we are in a painful place or feeling lost? Repentance, forgiveness, and prayer help us change the trajectory of the Soulish Ailments that have to do with our woes. Why must we repent and forgive, especially when we are a victim? With all due respect, victim or not, we have a responsibility to God to humbly own up to our known or unknown contributions to whatever or whomever. Unbeknown to most, doing so places a Spiritual Seal or affords us an opportunity to Spiritually Glean the Lesson, Testing, Illumination, or Blessing, preventing the cycle of déjà vu. Here is what God's Spokesman has to say about this: *"Then He is gracious to him, and says, 'Deliver him from going down to the Pit; I have found a ransom,' His flesh shall be young like a child's, He shall return to the days of his youth. He shall pray to God, and He will delight in him, He shall see His face with JOY, for He restores to man His righteousness. Then he looks at men and says, 'I have sinned, and perverted what was right, And it did not profit me.' He will redeem his soul from going down to the Pit, and his life shall see the LIGHT."* Job 33:24-28.

In seeking Light in a dark place, it is imperative to make a conscious choice to switch from negative to positive, wrong to right, unjust to just, unwise to wise, bad to good, unrighteous to righteous, and so on. What if it is difficult for us? Listen, once again, excuses have plagued us since the Garden of Eden Experience, and if we choose to continue the BIG LIE, then have at it.

In my opinion, if we can change the channel on a television, scroll through Instagram, go live on Facebook or YouTube, post on TikTok, twist a little tweet on Twitter or (X), or cash app someone, we can choose Light over darkness any day of the week. But for me and my house, we will serve the Lord in Spirit and Truth, embracing our Birthright of having the *Joy* and *Fullness* therein. How about you?

Listen, when we seek the Kingdom of God in or out of our current situation, especially in the Spirit of Righteousness, we give ourselves the leverage to play by God's Rules, *As It Pleases Him*. So, instead of living the Big Lie or playing ourselves short in the Eye of God, zapping our *Unspeakable Joy*, we should simply establish Divine Order first.

What does Divine Order have to do with our current situations? Once again, we are *Set Aside for Him*. Why should we heed the Divine Order, especially when we are already doing the right thing as Believers? *"For the LORD does not see as man sees; for man looks at the outward appearance, but the LORD looks at the heart."* 1 Samuel 16:7b. So it behooves us to establish a Spiritual Hedge, *As It Pleases Him*, for our benefit, instead of pleasing ourselves to our detriment.

CHAPTER ELEVEN
Spiritual Hedge

"This is He who came by water and blood—Jesus Christ; not only by water, but by water and blood. And it is the Spirit who bears witness, because the Spirit is truth." 1 John 5:6.

The Kingdom's Edge has a self-contained *Spiritual Hedge* protecting those who surrender to the Blueprint of their Divine Calling. What about the other Believers? We are all protected according to the level we are on. For example, what type of Spiritual Protection is needed for someone who sits around gossiping and eating bonbons all day? Little to none, right? Now, on the other hand, for those who are building the Kingdom, winning souls, breaking yokes, and transforming lives, *As It Pleases God*, they need more Heavenly Assistance than those who are destructive, negligent, and debaucherous.

When operating in the Will of God and being in Purpose on purpose, *As It Pleases Him*, He will protect us based on our Blueprinted Reason for being. Here is one of the Spiritual Seals enforcing the *Spiritual Hedge*: *"For He shall give His angels charge over you, to keep you in all your ways."* Psalm 91:11. Here is another: *"Then you will walk safely in your way, and your foot will not stumble. When you lie down, you will not be afraid; yes, you will lie down and your sleep will be sweet. Do not be afraid of sudden terror, nor of trouble from the wicked when it comes."* Proverbs 3:23-26.

Today's problem is that everyone wants Spiritual Entitlements from the Kingdom without preparation or corrective measures. Why is this considered a problem in the Eye of God? Unbeknown to most, without formal preparation, *As It Pleases Him*, we are slated to become consumed with jealousy, envy, pride, greed, and competitiveness, while thinking we are right in our own eyes.

What is the purpose of negative character traits consuming us? It is in our nature, or better yet, we are prewired to grow, serve, and become, positively or negatively. With this in mind, if we are not trained to grow, serve, and become from the inside out, *As It Pleases God*, we will allow our external conditions to define us outside of His Divine Will or Predestined Blueprint. As a result, we will find ourselves lost, contending with others about people, places, and things having nothing to do with us, without getting to the ROOT of why we are lost in the first place.

Why does the Kingdom operate with levels and stages, making us feel inferior? The inferiority complex is self-made, self-induced, self-contained, and self-maintained. Regardless of how we feel, everything in life will endure levels, stages, and phases, and if we think we can bypass growth, we are sadly mistaken. According to the Heavenly of Heavens, the Kingdom is not a quick fix. Nor does it come in a ready-made box; we are required by Spiritual Laws to step up to the plate without cutting corners.

What is the purpose of such strictness in the Kingdom? When operating in the Realm of the Spirit untrained, undisciplined, and unaware, we can cause more harm than good, leaving a trail of victims, traumatizing ourselves, or invoking a heavy Rod of Judgment. More importantly, God operates with systems, strategies, concepts, principles, and laws; therefore, some type of order must be maintained.

Listen, regardless of how the world paints a picture of the Kingdom of God or our Spiritual Levels, we must follow instructions to ensure the *Spiritual Hedge* remains untethered. Doing so gives us the Spiritual Right to say: " *'No weapon formed against you shall prosper, and every tongue which rises against you in judgment you shall condemn. This is the heritage of the servants of the Lord, and their righteousness is from Me,' says the Lord.*" Isaiah 54:17.

Unfortunately, we cannot enforce this Scripture if we are forming weapons against the innocent. Nor are we authorized to use it if we are NOT a Servant of the Lord and raising our tongues against the innocent to destroy them out of recklessness and unrighteousness. Who am I to say what Scriptures we can and cannot use, right? There is a Spiritual Contingency Clause that we overlook: *"This is the heritage of the servants of the Lord, and their righteousness is from Me,' says the Lord."* Clearly, we have free will to use any Scripture out of the Bible that we want; however, we are speaking about Spiritually ENFORCING it with Divine Authority and Power.

Then again, if we use that Scripture against someone with the *Spiritual Hedge of Protection*, we will get a rude awakening from the Heavenly of Heavens. Why? We did not use Spiritual Discernment...The Holy Spirit would have advised not to touch or interfere with someone on a Divine Mission for the Kingdom.

If we use the Word of God for darkness, with rotten fruits, or selfishly, there is still a Spiritual Penalty associated...so tread with caution! What is the penalty for using the Bible for ill will? Only God knows the true penalty because He holds the Divine Blueprint for everyone, regardless of whether we know about it or not. For this reason, it is always best to use the Fruits of the Spirit at all times. Without Spiritual Discernment, *As It Pleases Him*, we do not know who He is using. Remember this: *"Do not forget to entertain strangers, for by so doing some have unwittingly entertained angels."* Hebrews 13:2.

For example, if someone is trying to showcase their Spiritual Level or Authority, I will consider their ability to follow instructions or ask questions for clarity. What is the purpose of doing so? It reveals their level of humility, usability, and interest, which inadvertently unveils the FRUITS we are dealing with, but not limited to such. In addition, it also reveals their level of pretense or frailty.

What is the big deal about fruits, levels, and authority? Divine Wisdom, Secrets, and Treasures of the Kingdom of God do not need to brag...only immaturity in the Realm of the Spirit deems it necessary to convince another. Listen to me and listen well: The *Spiritual Hedge* does not brag about being so...IT JUST IS! And it is

ENFORCEABLE from the Heavenly of Heavens without having to say one word!

Still, if we are not trained Spiritually to See, Hear, and Speak as ONE with the Holy Spirit and cover ourselves with the Blood of Jesus, we can miss our Spiritual Cues or Concessions with the Divinely Erected Hedge. What does this mean? We can be Believers whom God uses in powerful ways and miss the mark, especially if we do not pay attention, heed instructions, become stiff-necked, dull, lukewarm, haughty, or violate our conscience.

Unfortunately, it is then that the enemy will capitalize on our slippage to ruin our credibility or hang us out to dry. For this reason, we must make sure our foundations on any level are transparently solid and fully repented, containing the Fruits of the Spirit and Christlike Character. As a *Spiritual Hedge* on our behalf, this helps seal the known and unknown cracks occurring during the natural deterioration process caused by the Vicissitudes and Cycles of Life. Doing so not only solidifies our *Spiritual Hedges* for our protection, but also creates a *Wall of Fire*, letting people know... "Saying, 'Do not touch My anointed ones, And do My prophets no harm.'" 1 Chronicles 16:22.

Wall of Fire

Can you imagine being surrounded by an invisible *Wall of Fire*? Can you fathom it keeping you safe and protected from evil and negative principalities that you cannot see with your natural eyes? Well, the *Wall of Fire* is nothing to play around with because it is a protective barrier sent forth by the Heavenly of Heavens.

In *The Spiritual Middleman Approach*, the *Wall of Fire* is a Wall of Protection, Guidance, and Anointing for those who incorporate the Glory of God into their lives without reservation. While measuring or aligning themselves according to their Divine Blueprint, the Will of God, and the Heavenly Instructions to protect the Kingdom, Decreed Promises, and Bloodline Covenants.

Before moving on, let me share this: "*Then I raised my eyes and looked, and behold, a man with a measuring line in his hand. So I said, 'Where are you going?' And he said to me, 'To measure Jerusalem, to see what is its width and* what is its length.' And there was the angel who talked with me, going out; and another angel was coming out to meet him, who said to him, 'Run, speak to this young man, saying: Jerusalem shall be inhabited as towns without walls, because of the multitude of men and livestock in it.' For I, says the LORD, 'will be a wall of fire all around her, and I will be the glory in her midst.' Up, up! Flee from the land of the north, says the LORD; 'for I have spread you abroad like the four winds of heaven,' says the LORD. Up, Zion! Escape, you who dwell with the daughter of Babylon." Zechariah 2:1-7.

Simply put, God protects what and who wholeheartedly belongs to Him, similar to Shadrach, Meshach, and Abednego being thrown into a fiery furnace, seven times hotter than the norm, in Daniel 3:16-23. The *Wall of Fire*, to say the least, is no joke in protecting us from the enemy's wiles, especially if we refuse to bow down or engage in idolatry! When using *The Spiritual Middleman Approach*, if it takes God to get in the fire with us, He will do it. If He has to send a Legion of Angels to hold back the flames, He will do it. Even if He uses our enemies to put out the fires they started, He has the power to do it.

More importantly, the *Wall of Fire* protects us from the inside out and from the outside in, depending upon our Level of Spirituality. For example, if we are a Spiritual Babe in the Kingdom, attempting to become Spiritually Righteous, the *Wall of Fire* is available for support, regardless of the naysayers. Once we are Spiritually Trained according to Kingdom Standards, we become accountable to keep the *Wall of Fire* in STANDING ORDER, *As It Pleases God*!

Is this a double standard? Absolutely not! In my opinion, this is like a grown-up walking, going, and doing whatever they like, and then turning around, getting mad at a baby for crawling or a child for walking slowly.

To become a mature adult, one must crawl before effectively walking according to their genetic design, and so it is in the Realm of the Spirit. Hence, we must not forget our early stages of development. Here is what we need to know: *"For we are His workmanship, created in Christ Jesus for good works, which God prepared beforehand that we should walk in them. Therefore remember that you, once Gentiles in the flesh—who are called Uncircumcision by what is called the Circumcision made in the flesh by hands—that at that time you were without*

Christ, being aliens from the commonwealth of Israel and strangers from the covenants of promise, having no hope and without God in the world." Ephesians 2:10-12.

Regardless of how it appears to the naked eye, by following this Spiritual Protocol, our *Fiery Walls of Protection* will become seven times hotter than the average temperature of a standalone, self-righteous, or selfish Believer. Just keep in mind, once again, we must make sure we do not smother it with unrepented sins, acts of debauchery, unforgiveness, disobedience, hatefulness, or any type of rotten fruit, creating a foothold or yoke for ourselves. More importantly, we must KNOW this information beyond a shadow of a doubt. It helps us tread with caution or get out of the way of those who are setting debauched missiles in motion while examining ourselves accordingly.

Whether we are dealing with our *Spiritual Hedge* or *Wall of Fire*, they are both riddled with Spiritual Bells, Whistles, Alarms, and Red Flags through our conscience. As a rule, when using *The Spiritual Middleman Approach*, we must make sure it is up to Kingdom Standards to ensure that when the enemy is on our trail or has set booby traps, we are forewarned of the encroachment. Really? Yes, really!

It is a Kingdom Benefit of being Spiritually Synced with the Holy Spirit and covered by the Blood of Jesus. But we must know this fact and set Divine Expectations for it, *As It Pleases God*. If not, we cannot place a Spiritual Demand on it with Divine Authority. Why? Allow me to counteract this question with another: 'How is it possible to lay claim to something we do not know about or understand?'

By approaching the Spiritual Realm without knowing who we are or without Divine Authority, we will receive mixed messages, not knowing who or what is speaking. Therefore, the Familiar Spirits come in to confuse us without convicting. To simplify this further, the Holy Spirit convicts the conscience according to the Word of God. Familiar Spirits encourage a form of Godliness with a sense of Spirituality, having a worldly twist with rotten fruits. At the same time, it keeps us questioning or justifying our righteousness and pointing the finger, especially when we know right from wrong.

Listen, no one has to tell us when we engage in debauchery; we know it! And if we are not attempting to self-correct when erring, do we think the Holy Spirit is endorsing this behavior? Absolutely not! It grieves the Holy Spirit. Please do not become deceived in this matter; it is the Spirit of Error operating!

The bottom line is that repentance is a must. We must also make a wholehearted attempt to operate in the Spirit of Righteousness using the Divine Navigational Tools from the Heavenly of Heavens to build a *Wall of Hope*. Here is what we need to know before moving on. *"Let no corrupt word proceed out of your mouth, but what is good for necessary edification, that it may impart grace to the hearers. And do not grieve the Holy Spirit of God, by whom you were sealed for the day of redemption."* Ephesians 4:29-30.

Wall of Hope

The *Wall of Fire* also creates a *Wall of Hope*, breaking the walls of separation, especially if we add the Oneness of the Holy Trinity with the Fruits of the Spirit. How is this possible in a time such as this? We must make a conscious choice to do so with peace residing in the Mind, Body, Soul, and Spirit. Really? Yes, really!

Having peace in such a manner works wonders on the human psyche, regardless of our creed, deed, or breed. Here is what we must know: *"But now in Christ Jesus you who once were far off have been brought near by the blood of Christ. For He Himself is our peace, who has made both one, and has broken down the middle wall of separation, having abolished in His flesh the enmity, that is, the law of commandments contained in ordinances, so as to create in Himself one new man from the two, thus making peace, and that He might reconcile them both to God in one body through the cross, thereby putting to death the enmity. And He came and preached peace to you who were afar off and to those who were near. For through Him we both have access by one Spirit to the Father."* Ephesians 2:13-18.

As a Word to the Wise, when using The *Spiritual Middleman Approach*, we cannot allow the enemy to penetrate the *Wall of Fire*, getting us to sabotage ourselves or destroy the *Wall of Hope*. How can we do this to ourselves, especially if we are Believers?

Unfortunately, by engaging in unrepentant unrighteousness, operating with rotten fruits, drowning in unforgiveness, being hateful, and exhibiting ungodly behaviors, we inadvertently turn on ourselves. In essence, it is recognized through the vehicle of the senses and impulses associated with the lust of the eyes, the lust of the flesh, and the pride of life.

What if we are operating in the Spirit of Righteousness, and we are under Spiritual Attack? In *The Spiritual Middleman Approach*, we must make sure we sit at the right hand of God or under His wing until He makes our enemies our footstool. However, while sitting, we cannot twiddle our thumbs in idleness, doing nothing. We must make a conscious effort to keep ourselves full of TRUST, HOPE, and FAITH without flinching an inch.

In addition, we must also protect the Mind, Body, and Soul from negative intrusions. Why? It will sedate us or cause us to fall asleep on ourselves out of fear or weariness. Here is a Scripture to repeat daily: *"He who dwells in the secret place of the Most High Shall abide under the shadow of the Almighty. I will say of the LORD, 'He is my refuge and my fortress; My God, in Him I will trust.' Surely He shall deliver you from the snare of the fowler and from the perilous pestilence. He shall cover you with His feathers, and under His wings you shall take refuge; His truth shall be your shield and buckler."* Psalm 91:1-4.

How is it possible not to flinch when vile missiles are directed toward us for no apparent reason? Regardless of whether the negative missiles are justified or unjustified, we must become THANKFUL in all things, the good, bad, and ugly, gleaning the hidden Lessons, Wisdom, or Blessings instead. If we choose not to operate in such a manner, we can quickly become vindictive, unforgiving, or angry, which is all the enemy needs to gain entry. Secondly, we must INVOKE and AWAKEN our Spirit to become One with the Holy Spirit to guide, provide, and stay on watch for us, in and out of season. Thirdly, we must cover ourselves on a moment-by-moment basis with the Blood of Jesus for the remission of our known and unknown sins.

Once again, God is weighing the heart of man. If we think for a minute that we can operate without a conscience in the Kingdom of Heaven, Spiritually Seal our Heaven on Earth Experience, or fortify our Divine Blueprint, we are sadly mistaken. He, meaning

God our Father in Heaven, is requiring more from us in the days to come to re-establish our Heaven on Earth Experiences to lead His sheep in and out of the Spiritual Folds in Spirit and Truth.

We cannot become reckless with the fragile mindset of those who are not privy to Kingdom Formality. For this reason, the Holy Spirit will do the molding and training through them with our Earthen Vessels, making it more important to cleanse ourselves of unrighteous debris that has the potential to contaminate the sheep.

How do we know what to cleanse? We should begin with the Fruits of the Spirit: Love, Joy, Peace, Patience, Kindness, Goodness, Faithfulness, Gentleness, and Self-Control. Once mastered, *As It Pleases God*, the Holy Spirit will take us to the next Spiritual Level according to our Divine Blueprint or Spiritual Capacity. So, regardless of where you are or what you are going through, "*Be kind to one another, tenderhearted, forgiving one another, even as God in Christ forgave you.*" Ephesians 4:32.

Wall of Obedience

Although we do not like talking about obedience much, it is indeed a powerful force used in success and personal growth. The act of following orders or instructions from a higher authority is crucial when dealing with the *Wall of Obedience*. There are times when obedience may seem like a passive act. Still, it requires a great deal of active engagement, critical thinking, and asking fact-finding questions to develop good habits and self-discipline.

We all desire to become strengthened in our innermost being, even if we are not fully aware of who we are or why; yet, we must first BELIEVE and OBEY. Secondly, if we begin to practice the Spiritual Principles, Insights, and Covenants documented by our Forefathers, they will revolutionize our lives, GUARANTEED. We DO NOT need to overcomplicate the Promises of God; we simply must KNOW and UNDERSTAND them, according to their intended use in the Eye of God.

In or out of our acts or the *Wall of Obedience*, we all have our kryptonite; therefore, our level of strength will vary from person to person, situation to situation, trauma to trauma, and so on.

According to the Heavenly of Heavens, humility is the first indication of Spiritual Strength hidden in plain sight. Self-control is the second, leading into the other Fruits of the Spirit. Then, our listening, learning, usability, shareability, and teachability are next in developing obedience.

Obedience is wrapped in authentic humility, but it is lacking in a state of fakeness. How do we make this make sense? When someone pretends to be humble when they possess an aura of disobedience, BEWARE! Unfortunately, this is a Spiritual Cue we most often miss, allowing the wolf in sheep's clothing to cause us to drop our Spiritual Guard or Weapon, sucker-punching or disabling us, to zap our strength. How is this possible? Those who are weak but appear strong must glean their superficial strength from others who lack understanding in this area. For this reason, we must exercise extreme caution with the loudest person in the room and those who are braggers, judgmental, hateful, cruel, bone carriers, and so on. Why? We are at risk of becoming the next VICTIM!

CHAPTER TWELVE
Divine Instructions

"And they sang a new song, saying: 'You are worthy to take the scroll, And to open its seals; For You were slain, And have redeemed us to God by Your blood Out of every tribe and tongue and people and nation, And have made us kings and priests to our God; And we shall reign on the earth.' " Revelation 5:9-10.

Have you ever wondered about the potential for receiving DIVINE INSTRUCTIONS from the Heavenly of Heavens? Are you confident in your ability to identify and interpret these *Divine Instructions*? Or have you ever felt that you are not fully equipped to receive such *Divine Guidance*? Well, the wait is over...and the *Divine Instructions* are here for a time such as this.

When you are Spiritually Prepared, *As It Pleases God*, you become more receptive to Divine Instructions, and you are more likely to recognize them or act on them. Although God has promised to *Divinely Instruct*, the question remains: Are you good with giving and receiving instructions? When God speaks to you, do you hear what He is saying? When God nudges you, do you feel it? When you do something wrong, do you feel convicted?

If we desire to know where we stand with God or in the Kingdom of Heaven, all we need to do is pinpoint our *Divine Instructions*. If they are documented, then we have our answer. On the other hand, if we DO NOT have any instructions or documentation, we also have our answer. What does this mean? Either we are not listening to God, we cannot hear Him, or He is not speaking to us for a reason. So, it is up to the individual to determine which is correct, making the appropriate changes necessary to invoke the *Spirit to Spirit* Connection needed to understand, pursue, and possess the Treasures of the Kingdom.

Will God really respond to us? Absolutely! He has indeed PROMISED to do so as long as we do not pray amiss. Yet, we must fine-tune our Spiritual Abilities to understand who is speaking to us. Why must we understand who is speaking? If not, we can get confused easily. For example, but not limited to such:

- ☐ Our inside voice speaks to us, chatting on a level of our adherence or tolerance.
- ☐ The enemy plants seeds of thought based on our level of deceivability, trauma, infiltration, or naivety.
- ☐ We have outside influences based on our insecurities, fears, conditioning, biases, and so on.
- ☐ We have the Voice of God, which needs our Spiritual Eyes, Ears, and Language quickened toward Him.

We as humans have a lot of speaking going on simultaneously; however, we need Spiritual Discernment to filter in or out whatever or whomever. What is the purpose of having a Spiritual Filter? It will vary from person to person, depending on various reasons. Nonetheless, here is a Scripture we must know about: *"But if you have bitter envy and self-seeking in your hearts, do not boast and lie against the truth. This wisdom does not descend from above, but is earthly, sensual, demonic. For where envy and self-seeking exist, confusion and every evil thing are there."* James 3:14-16.

According to the Heavenly of Heavens, we can become overwhelmed, manipulated, or confused, thwarting our perceptions or scattering our Divine Revelations without having Spiritual Filters in place. The moment we find ourselves all over the place or Spiritually Bouncing around, confusing God's sheep, there is a slight indication of unsurety from within or a fear of not meeting up to the standards set before us. To be clear, this does not make us unusable in the Kingdom; it is only an indication of the need for Spiritual Structure to build Divine Clarity when conveying.

Listen, knowing the Word of God is NOT good enough, especially if we incorporate people-pleasing into the equation instead of God-Pleasing! How can I say such a thing, right? The Word of God is a Spiritual Journey leading us and others into the LIGHT. Amid doing so, if we throw His Word out as a flash of light, it blinds the Believer instead of illuminating the Spiritual Path.

Word Pictures

In *The Spiritual Middleman Approach*, the goal is to paint Mental *Word Pictures* to connect with people on a deep and personal level. In addition, this allows us to convey complex Spiritual Concepts in a way that is understandable and relatable to the people we are speaking to. Using this approach allows others to see what we are Spiritually Seeing and not to impress them with unpainted or unconnected *Word Pictures*, confusing the flock.

However, some people think we are deep when we leave people confused and lacking in understanding. Thus, in the Eye of God, we are deep when the Well of Wisdom overflows with transferrable understanding for a Greater Good, feeding His sheep and taking them to the next level, *As It Pleases Him.*

If we lose people in the conveyance process, it means that we have not extracted the information properly, *As It Pleases God.* How do I know? The Holy Spirit will help us simplify it with what people can relate to or relate back to. All in all, we as humans need an understanding, knowing the *What, When, Where, How, Why,* and with *Whom* before moving to the next *Word Picture.*

Why do we need Word Pictures or visual analogies when dealing with Divine Instructions? It helps us develop a soft approach. In my opinion, this is similar to having a soft sales approach, but in the Realm of the Spirit. According to our Divine DNA, we secretly or openly look for the win-wins, benefits, or takeaways. If the psyche is NOT convinced, at rest, or blinded somehow, we will secretly give a side-eye, provoking deeper thoughts, positively or negatively.

How do we make understanding *Word Pictures* make sense? God has promised to Divinely Instruct and Spiritually Guide us with our Heaven on Earth Experiences with and through His WORD. For example, Jesus spoke in *Word Pictures* by telling stories and asking picturesque questions, making the Word of God palatable to the human psyche by creating an understandable and relatable flow.

Listen, if spoken words are not moving the inner man, it is the WRONG language! How do we adjust it? Frankly, this is the reason for the Holy Spirit. Really? Yes, really! He gives the instinctual *Word Pictures* to use in our Spiritual Language to reach the unreachable, quench the unquenchable, speak Divine Wisdom to the already Wise, and so on.

Here is the deal: *As It Pleases God*, in perfecting *Word Pictures*, we must MASTER asking the right questions and convey the correct answers in Spirit and Truth. Of course, this is not an overnight process, but our *Word Pictures* become more profound in or out of the Kingdom with practice. So, it behooves us to use a Mind Map to help us create powerful branches of information when conveying it in its entirety. As a Word to the Wise, repeating this process over and over until MASTERED makes our flow phenomenal, especially if we stay on the righteous side of the spectrum.

As a word of caution, if one conveys lies to manipulate, deceive, or prey upon anyone, we cannot usher in the Holy Spirit to canvas our debaucherous acts. If we do, confusion will meet us amid whatever we are doing, saying, or becoming, causing some form of turn-off, deaf ears, blinded eyes, or ungodly chatter. Therefore, Divine *Word Pictures*, guided by the Holy Spirit, requires obedience and humility, meeting people where they are. At the same time, it is important to get an understanding of the desired directions, organizational changes, or journey needed.

How do we know the difference between Divine or worldly *Word Pictures*? We can learn from both, so it is imperative to put on our thinking caps to ensure we do not reject our Teachable Moments. Once again, this is where our Spiritual Filters, Instincts, and Understanding play a vital role in determining factors of what we glean or discard. Yet, amid all, know this: *"But the wisdom that is from above is first pure, then peaceable, gentle, willing to yield, full of mercy and good* fruits, without partiality and without hypocrisy. Now the fruit of righteousness is sown in peace by those who make peace." James 3:17-18.

Divine Guarantees

Hidden within Spiritual Obedience comes *Divine Guarantees* that will naturally align with our patience and perseverance. People often ask, 'How can I place a guarantee, especially when we are all different?' Simple enough, my answer is, 'I operate through the Holy Trinity UNITED as ONE, *As It Pleases God.*'

In this Divine Union and Blueprint, if this information makes it into the hands of someone, there is a need for it, regardless of whether they admit it or not. If they connect, they will receive, and if refused, it is okay. When they are ready, the Divine Well of Wisdom will flow more fluidly upon their return. This Heavenly Information does not have a timestamp; it has a free will readiness one.

To receive a continuous download of *Divine Instructions* in Earthen Vessel, we must give THANKS to our Heavenly Creator, accept the Blood of Jesus as a formal SACRIFICE for our sinful nature, and AWAKEN our Spirit to become One with the Holy Spirit, our Comforter, the Great REWARD. With this Divine Order, using the Fruits of the Spirit and exhibiting Christlike Character, it opens the Gate of Heaven for us to become Spiritually Molded to Kingdom Standards. All in all, if we follow the Spiritual Laws, Protocols, and Principles of the Kingdom according to Scripture, Divine Wisdom is at our beck and call.

On the other hand, if we want to add a little worldliness to the equation, it taints our Walk with God, even if we are devout Believers. Here is what we need to know about the Kingdom of God, but not limited to such:

- ☐ We must **MAINTAIN** a Victorious Mindset as an overcomer. "*For whatever is born of God overcomes the world. And this is the victory that has overcome the world—our faith.* 1 John 5:4.

- ☐ We must **BECOME** an unwavering Believer. *"Who is he who overcomes the world, but he who believes that Jesus is the Son of God?"* 1 John 5:5.

- ☐ We must come into **AGREEMENT** with the Water (Baptism) and the Blood of Jesus (Sacrifice). *"This is He who came by water and blood—Jesus Christ; not only by water, but by water and blood. And it is the Spirit who bears witness, because the Spirit is truth."* 1 John 5:6.

- ☐ We must **CONNECT** to our Heavenly *Spirit to Spirit* Relationship by acknowledging our Father in Heaven, using the Word of God, and ushering in the Holy Spirit. *"For there are three that bear witness in heaven: the Father, the Word, and the Holy Spirit; and these three are one."* 1 John 5:7.

- ☐ We must **PLEAD** and **COVER** ourselves with the Blood of Jesus for repentance, forgiveness, and cleansing as a part of our Heaven on Earth Experience. *"And there are three that bear witness on earth: the Spirit, the water, and the blood; and these three agree as one."* 1 John 5:8.

- ☐ We must **BECOME** an Earthen Vessel for the Kingdom. *"If we receive the witness of men, the witness of God is greater; for this is the witness of God which He has testified of His Son."* 1 John 5:9.

- ☐ We must **AVOID** becoming a liar. *"He who believes in the Son of God has the witness in himself; he who does not believe God has made Him a liar, because he has not believed the testimony that God has given of His Son."* 1 John 5:10.

- ☐ We must **LIVE** by Example as a Testament for the Kingdom. *"And this is the testimony: that God has given us eternal life, and this life is in His Son.* 1 John 5:11.

- We must **VALUE** our lives through Christ Jesus. *"He who has the Son has life; he who does not have the Son of God does not have life."* 1 John 5:12.

- We must **USE** the Written Word of God as Spiritual Leverage for Eternal Life. *"These things I have written to you who believe in the name of the Son of God, that you may know that you have eternal life, and that you may continue to believe in the name of the Son of God."* 1 John 5:13.

- We must **ASK** Boldly, doing what it takes to **PROTECT** our Divine Blueprint, *As It Pleases God*. *"Now this is the confidence that we have in Him, that if we ask anything according to His will, He hears us."* 1 John 5:14.

- We must **TRUST** God, knowing our Spiritual Voice will reach Him beyond a shadow of a doubt. *"And if we know that He hears us, whatever we ask, we know that we have the petitions that we have asked of Him."* 1 John 5:15.

What is the purpose of knowing this information? First, *"And according to the law almost all things are purified with blood, and without shedding of blood there is no remission."* Hebrews 9:22. Secondly, it helps to tame the tongue of man. Thirdly, if we desire peace, we must understand how to obtain it, *As It Pleases God*. Here is what we must know: *"Elect according to the foreknowledge of God the Father, in sanctification of the Spirit, for obedience and sprinkling of the blood of Jesus Christ: Grace to you and peace be multiplied."* 1 Peter 1:2. How is this possible? Listen, as we all know, we can talk ourselves into and out of a Blessing. Yet, when it comes to the Promises of God, we do not want to play around or misunderstand what is DIVINE.

Plus, we want to be ever so careful about what we set in motion with our spoken words. Before we go any further, let us align this accordingly: *"Even so the tongue is a little member and boasts great things. See how great a forest a little fire kindles! And the tongue is a fire, a world of* iniquity. The tongue is so set among our members that it defiles the whole body, and sets on fire the course of nature; and it is set on fire by hell. For every kind of beast and bird, of reptile and creature of the sea, is tamed and has been tamed by mankind. But no man can tame the tongue. It is an unruly evil, full of deadly poison. With it we bless our God and Father, and with it we curse men, who have been made in the similitude of God. Out of the same mouth proceed blessing and cursing. My brethren, these things ought not to be so." James 3:5-10.

The Divine Guarantees and Instructions require us to guard our tongues, opening our Spiritual Eyes and Ears to the Language of the Kingdom. Doing so helps us see, hear, and speak differently, *As It Pleases God*. Here is what the Biblical Query that is hidden in plain sight says: *"Who is wise and understanding among you? Let him show by good conduct that his works are done in the meekness of wisdom."* James 3:13.

Spiritual Transformation

In our *Spiritual Transformation* phases, we must pay attention Mentally, Physically, Emotionally, and Spiritually, ensuring we can glean Divine Wisdom on a Supernatural Level according to our Predestined Blueprint. Why must we pay attention in this phase? The Level of Wisdom will vary, depending upon our Divine Purpose, Spiritual Tolerance, and Classroom Trainability. Thus, it is best to document, document, document to ensure we have a paper trail of information. If not, we can lose ground in this area and invoke Spiritual Limits.

Simply put, if we cannot keep track of the information, how can we properly lead in the Spirit of Excellence? No pun intended, but when dealing with the Realm of the Spirit, we cannot go on memory alone. Similar to the Bible, although it is written on the tablet of every man's heart, we must reflect on what is in black and white because our thoughts, emotions, and desires change. Plus, the psyche tends to play forgetting games, sucker punch us, and compartmentalize stuff.

Can the psyche really do this to us? It has already done a number on us. Everyone came here with their Divine Blueprint and complete instructions, but where is it? Do we remember? My point exactly...we have forgotten! In *The Spiritual Middleman Approach*, along with our *Spiritual Transformation*, you must Document, Document, Document, especially in your *Spirit to Spirit* Relations!

God will not overwhelm us with what will frighten us or shake us to the core. When dealing in the Realm of the Spirit, if we are not well-versed or adequately trained in the UNSEEN, it will traumatize the human psyche more than it will help. For this reason, God will use stages and levels in *Spiritual Transformation* or Transitioning Phases while holding us accountable in these areas.

Simply put, doing the right thing out of season or the wrong thing in season could be detrimental to our well-being, especially when lacking the understanding of who we are from the inside out. *As It Pleases God*, if we become Spirit-Led or Spiritually Synced in getting our Spiritual Oil to flow, we have less tension from the worldly edifices attempting to thwart our Divine Mission, Blueprinted Purpose, Training Process, Inherited Birthrights, Grandfathered Promises, Spiritual Rhythm, Unspeakable Joy, or DNA of Freedom.

Olive Tree Anointing

The Olive Tree has been a symbol of peace, prosperity, and *spiritual nourishment* for centuries, and it has not changed yet.

Acknowledging or calling forth our Spiritual Potential and getting our Spiritual Oil to flow is considered the *Olive Tree Anointing*.

How is it possible to get our Spiritual Oil to flow? First, we must know our Spiritual Oil is readily available from within, without second-guessing it. Secondly, due to our Genetic Design, we will autocorrect through our conscience, knowing when we are in our flow and when we are not.

Remarkably, this allows us to expand or decrease our Spiritual Peripherals by examining ourselves accordingly or doing a checkup from the neck up. What is the purpose of doing so? Beyond a shadow of a doubt, it helps us to tap into our Divine Blueprint or the Will of God, without tapping out or zapping our *Joyous Efforts* when pouring or releasing our Heavenly Oil in the Spirit of Excellence or during Divine Liberation.

As we come into agreement with the *Olive Tree Anointing*, it is crucial to understand that trial and error are needed in the manifestation of Divine Greatness, *As It Pleases God*. Without it, we become boring, redundant, dull, and lethargic while thinking the anointing of ourselves is a graced privilege for another when it is indeed a disgrace in the Eye of God.

Here is what we need to know for our Heaven on Earth Experience: *"For if God did not spare the natural branches, He may not spare you either. Therefore consider the goodness and severity of God: on those who fell, severity; but toward you, goodness, if you continue in His goodness. Otherwise you also will be cut off. And they also, if they do not continue in unbelief, will be grafted in, for God is able to graft them in again. For if you were cut out of the olive tree which is wild by nature, and were grafted contrary to nature into a cultivated olive tree, how much more will these, who are natural branches, be grafted into their own olive tree?"* Romans 11:21-24. More importantly, regardless of the level of training or state of regrafting, the *Olive Tree Anointing* has compassion, mercy, and understanding of another man's journey. They also allow their Spiritual Oil to overflow into the lives of others through their ability to LIVE BY EXAMPLE.

If we withhold our Spiritual Oil, it will inadvertently clog our Spiritual Spout (Voice). Even if we speak a seemingly good word, it will lack the IMPACT needed to penetrate to the core of another naturally. In the Kingdom, God is leveraging our IMPACT, not the hype, with zero healing from the inside out presented in His Name.

In so many words, if we are swinging it high and low without any form of restraint, depending upon grace to save us without accounting for the damage we are doing to ourselves or others, we become a victim of our own devices. How is this possible, especially when we are living the good life? We are deceiving ourselves, thinking we have the upper hand on others and the things surrounding us, when we cannot exhibit one of the most prevalent Fruits of the Spirit called Self-Control.

We can talk a good game, but when we cannot control ourselves with the lust of the eyes, the lust of the flesh, and the pride of life, our *Olive Tree Anointing* goes rancid if left unrepented.

How do we know if our *Olive Tree Anointing* is stale? It is determined by its level of bitterness, hatefulness, abusiveness, negative stench, or the sour taste of disrespectfulness. If we pay attention long enough without making excuses for ourselves or others, we can detect the rancidness without having to say one word.

Should we not point out rancidness? It depends upon the situation, circumstance, event, or our readiness. In my opinion, it is best to involve the Holy Spirit or use *The Spiritual Middleman Approach* in this matter for the lead-in or exit strategy.

According to the Heavenly of Heavens, the goal is to Live by Example, making sure we do not become paralyzed by unrepented rancidness by consciously choosing to use the Fruits of the Spirit and exhibit Christlike Character instead.

What are the benefits associated with the *Olive Tree Anointing*? It will vary from person to person, situation to situation, trauma to trauma, and so on. However, here is the Word Picture the Bible paints for us to glean, "*I will be like the dew to Israel; He shall grow like the lily, and lengthen his roots like Lebanon. His branches shall spread; His beauty shall be like an olive tree, and his fragrance like Lebanon. Those who dwell under his shadow shall return; They shall be revived like grain, and grow like a vine. Their scent shall be like the wine of Lebanon.*" Hosea 14:5-7.

What if we have a problem with believing in ourselves or God? It happens to us all at some point; we often do not share our wavering faith with others due to the fear of being ridiculed, judged, or becoming an outcast. For this reason, we must stop with the lies! King David laid his heartfelt prayers out in the Book of Psalms, riddled with Divine Instructions to help us help ourselves amid the Vicissitudes of Life. If a man after God's own heart documented his encounters, emotions, fears, triumphs, pleas, and so on, what makes us any different? Better yet, why are our encounters not documented as a Testament for the next man?

What makes documenting extremely important? It is in our nature to forget about the goodness of God, especially when something bad happens or when we are going through something. As it relates to our Olive Tree Anointing, in our *Spirit to Spirit Relations*, if we want the Spiritual Oil to flow, we must lay our truth on the table to receive the needed help from the Holy Spirit.

If we know, admit it. If we are clueless, state it. If we were wrong, repent it. If we feel some type of way, make it known. For the record, this does not mean we have to broadcast it over social media, putting ourselves on blast. We simply need to get into our Prayer Closet and let it all hang out, releasing the weight to receive the Heavenly Impact of the Spiritual Comfort needed to flow as God rightfully intended.

What is the purpose of not hiding our truth from God? Denial is kryptonic in our *Spirit to Spirit* Relations. From the Garden of Eden Experience until now, we need to know what to cover under the Blood of Jesus to ensure we do not improperly cover ourselves with what is not God Approved or Heavenly Endorsed. If we do, the Spiritual Doorpost of whatever is going on within the human psyche is left unmanned, becoming buried for an informal resurrection when we least expect it. As a result, we become susceptible to the enemy's wiles due to our lack of knowledge and understanding in this area.

For me, I choose not to take such a risk to ensure my Spiritual Armor is ready to go when the enemy comes to hit below the belt in a seemingly weak area. Humbly speaking, based upon my *Olive Tree Anointing* for a time such as this, it is not a matter of if; it is a matter of when. So, I have to stay on READY while preparing others to do likewise!

Listen, from experience, the element of risk makes us vulnerable to those who play pretend as if they operate in faithfulness 100% of the time. If we operated in such a manner consistently, we would not need prayer, repentance, forgiveness, fasting, meditation, the Blood of Jesus to cover our sins, the Holy Spirit to guide us, or a *Spirit to Spirit* Relationship with our Heavenly Father, which makes up *The Spiritual Middleman Approach*. Given that we need all of the above, it is an indication that they all work together for our good when we use them. So, do not become fooled by the hype; we will all have our moments of grief as long as the Cycle of Life continues.

According to the Heavenly of Heavens, we must work on ourselves daily, Spiritually Tilling our own ground, doing our due diligence. If we fail to use the Spiritual Tools available, we cannot lay the blame elsewhere, nor can we maximize our *Olive Tree Anointing* the way God intended. Here is a Scripture to repeat daily, "*But I am like a green olive tree in the house of God; I trust in the mercy of God forever and ever. I will praise You forever, Because You have done it; And in the presence of Your saints I will wait on Your name, for it is good."* Psalm 52:8-9.

There is hope for everyone with the *Olive Tree Anointing* if we dare to take one step at a time. Trusting God for His goodness will not disappoint, even if it appears unfavorable to the naked eye. The goal is to stay focused on the good, positive, fruitful, and productive, perfecting our charactorial skills. By doing so, whatever area we fall short, we can compensate with our strengths, creating Spiritual Balance from the inside out to overcome any form of stronghold designed to yoke us to the core. We cannot wait for someone else to do this for us; we must be willing to do this for ourselves, and if God sends another to assist, then so be it.

How can we become a disgrace when we have free will to do, say, and become whatever we desire with whomever? Whenever we bring shame to our names, God, or the Kingdom, we may forfeit Divine Grace in exchange for lustful grace, prideful grace, and merciful grace. Are they not the same? No, Divine Grace leads us into or toward our Destiny, *As It Pleases God*. The others give us another opportunity to make a wholehearted attempt to add God into the equation or change our ways from ungodly to Godly for Spiritual Refinement.

Spiritual Refinement

In the Spiritual Refining Phase, we do not know what God may use to train or equip us for our Divine Blueprinted Mission. With Divine Grace or common grace, know this: *"For the gifts and the calling of God are irrevocable. For as you were once disobedient to God, yet have now obtained mercy through their disobedience, even so these also have now been disobedient, that through the mercy shown you they also may obtain mercy. For God has committed them all to disobedience, that He might have mercy on all."* Romans 11:29-32. For this reason, let no one convince us that all hope is lost; it is NOT! We simply need to wake up from our slumber to learn and MASTER the Spiritual System governing our Heaven on Earth Experiences.

Everything is a matter of timing; some will take longer to achieve, and others may take less time to attain the Promises,

Blessings, or whatever. Yet, if we DEFINE ourselves, our seeds, or our lives, *As It Pleases God*, from the onset, we would need less *Spiritual Refinement* later.

Yet, for some odd reason, we omit the *Spiritual Refinement* of our seeds because something appears cute in its adolescent stages. But when that cute seed becomes a vestment beast, we run to God, as if we are innocent. Then, expect an overnight miracle without putting forth the effort to REGRAFT ourselves or use *The Spiritual Middleman Approach*.

What is the big deal about *Spiritual Refinement* as long as we pray for change? The big deal is whether our prayers occurred before or after the habitual beast came forth. If we had proactively DEFINED whatever, with whomever, before taking action, our outcome would have been, *As It Pleases God*.

Conversely, if we reactively pray after dishonoring God, ourselves, or others, then *Spiritual Refinement* is a justifiable reason to change our worldliness into Godliness to avoid the Kingdom Side-Eye. Please allow me to align before getting the side-eye myself: "*For if the firstfruit is holy, the lump is also holy; and if the root is holy, so are the branches. And if some of the branches were broken off, and you, being a wild olive tree, were grafted in among them, and with them became a partaker of the root and fatness of the olive tree, do not boast against the branches. But if you do boast, remember that you do not support the root, but the root supports you. You will say then, 'Branches were broken off that I might be grafted in.'* " Romans 11:16-19.

Why would the Kingdom give us a side-eye when making an honest mistake? We are all subjected to erring occasionally, and we are all a work-in-progress on a constant learning curve. For this reason, it is best to remain in a constant state of repentance, not in a constant bed of excuses. However, when beginning in the kindergarten stages of Spirituality, we do not receive the same benefits as someone with a DOCTORATE in Kingdom Spirituality. For the record, a Spiritual Elite has more accountability than a Spiritual Babe, determining the Level of Refining, Regrafting, Restitution, or Chastening.

Although God can use us at any age or stage, youthfulness is the ideal training ground for Kingdom Spirituality. Really? Yes, really!

Here is what the Bible says about starting in our youth: "*It is good for a man to bear the yoke in his youth. Let him sit alone and keep silent, because God has laid it on him; Let him put his mouth in the dust—there may yet be hope. Let him give his cheek to the one who strikes him, and be full of reproach. For the Lord will not cast off forever. Though He causes grief, yet He will show compassion according to the multitude of His mercies. For He does not afflict willingly, nor grieve the children of men.*" Lamentations 3:27-33.

The Spiritual Maturing Process is mandatory in the Kingdom, regardless of what we think or feel. With all due respect, when we approach God as a kindergarten in seed form, we must humble ourselves to become mature and trained according to Kingdom Standards. And, when we mess up, there is enough grace to sustain us in the training process, especially when we avail ourselves to the Spiritual Classroom, *As It Pleases Him*.

As we become *Spiritually Refined* according to our Divine Blueprint, here is what we must know: "*Who is wise? Let him understand these things. Who is prudent? Let him know them. For the ways of the LORD are right; The righteous walk in them, But transgressors stumble in them.*" Hosea 14:9. Yet, amid all, make sure to glean the hidden Spiritual Lessons attached to our encounters, building our experiential Repertoire of Greatness.

What is the purpose of knowing how to bring down a stronghold in the *Spiritual Refinement* process? There are two facets to strongholds in the Eye of God. First, if we are weak, vulnerable, or emotional, we can become a prime target for all types of yokes and Spiritual Attacks. Secondly, if we are not strong enough, holding ourselves back from taking matters into our own hands, we can create a God-Induced yoke or generational curse. How? It varies from person to person, situation to situation, and so on. However, it is possibly tied into some form of disobedience, lack of discretion, stiff neck, self-control, impatience, selfishness, unforgiveness, or idolatry.

For example, in David's *Spiritual Refinement* process, he held himself back from cutting off Saul's descendants or taking his life in 1 Samuel 24:18-22. We all know David would take someone out at the drop of a dime and ask questions later. Here is the Scripture on his Spiritual Growth: "*And you have shown this day how you have dealt well with me; for when the LORD delivered me into your hand, you did not kill me. For if a man finds his enemy, will he let him get away safely? Therefore may the LORD reward you with good for what you have done to me this day. And now I know indeed that you shall surely be king, and that the kingdom of Israel shall be established in your hand. Therefore swear now to me by the LORD that you will not cut off my descendants after me, and that you will not destroy my name from my father's house. So David swore to Saul. And Saul went home, but David and his men went up to the stronghold."*

To preserve our *Spiritual Refinement*, we must know the difference between the types of strongholds we are dealing with and why. If not, we can stub our own toe for not dealing with the vengeance residing within. For this reason, we must develop a *Spirit to Spirit* Relationship to determine when to hold, fold, or walk away, *As It Pleases God.*

By not knowing how to go into Spiritual Warfare alone or when to STAY our hands, we can become crushed in the meantime by those who have perfected their underhanded annihilation skills or get us to curse our own hands. Why must we go to such extremes? According to the Bible, *"For though we walk in the flesh, we do not war according to the flesh. For the weapons of our warfare are not carnal but mighty in God for pulling down strongholds, casting down arguments and every high thing that exalts itself against the knowledge of God, bringing every thought into captivity to the obedience of Christ, and being ready to punish all disobedience when your obedience is fulfilled."* 2 Corinthians 10:3-6.

All in all, when dealing with strongholds, obedience is required! Why? By operating in the flesh, we can inadvertently contend with a Vessel of God. When God is using a person according to their Divine Blueprint, it is as if we are contending with God Himself, which can cause all types of plagues to fall upon us and the people around us. Frankly, this is similar to the Plagues of Egypt when Pharaoh refused to release the Children of Israel. Can it get this serious? Absolutely!

According to our Divine Blueprint, once we are in Purpose on purpose, and operating in the Fruits of the Spirit while exhibiting Christlike Character, there are severe repercussions for unjustifiably attempting to thwart God's Predestined Plan. With this in mind, it is not wise to operate without having the Holy

Trinity at the forefront; it will cause Spiritual Blindness, Deafness, or Muteness to the Strongholds of God, as well as the self-induced or man-made ones.

Unfortunately, if we try to pull down the wrong stronghold, we can get hurt! Also, we can create an implosion if we attempt to pull down a justified stronghold without repenting of the inner sludge hanging out in the human psyche. The enemy knows this beyond a shadow of a doubt. He is banking on us NOT to be 'In the Know' regarding these Spiritual Principles. Meanwhile, it keeps us in a self-contained Egypt experience, contemplating our Red Sea experience, wandering in our Desert experience, or second-guessing our Promised Land experience.

On behalf of our *Spiritual Refinement*, the cycle of déjà vu with our experiential strongholds must come to an end. We must engage in a *Spirit to Spirit* Relationship with our Heavenly Father to decipher between the Mental, Physical, Emotional, and Spiritual strongholds from back then to now.

According to the Heavenly of Heavens, this is not a game of the fittest; it is a matter of setting the Spiritual Groundwork and Seals for Divine Righteousness, and if we desire to be in the NUMBER, we must suit up with the Whole Armor of God, *As It Pleases Him*.

When we are in Purpose on purpose, using *The Spiritual Middleman Approach, As It Pleases God*, we can boldly claim Gideon's Spiritual Seal. It says, "Then the LORD said to him, 'Peace be with you; do not fear, you shall not die.' So Gideon built an altar there to the LORD, and called it The-LORD-Is-Peace. To this day it is still in Ophrah of the Abiezrites." Judges 6:23.

The-Lord-Is-Peace

Gideon was not initially confident in his abilities because he felt the least in his father's house. Out of underlying fear, he asked God for a sign to prove that he was really the one who was chosen to lead the Israelites. In Judges 6:6:36-40, God gave him a sign by making a fleece wet with dew while the ground around it was dry, and then making the fleece dry while the ground around it was wet. This experience convinced Gideon that God was indeed with him, and he went on to lead the Israelites into battle in Judges 7 with *Divine Instructions*.

The Midianites vastly outnumbered the Israelites, but God instructed Gideon to decrease his army to just 300 men. He then gave them each a trumpet and a clay jar with a torch inside. The Israelites surrounded the camp of the Midianites at night, and at a signal from Gideon, they blew their trumpets, smashed their jars, and held up their torches. The Midianites were terrified and fled in confusion. The Israelites won a great victory, and Gideon became branded with *The-Lord-Is-Peace* until this day.

God has promised to Spiritually Liberate us with *The-Lord-Is-Peace* phenomenon. Just as it was before, it is still the case today! This undeniable truth is a TESTAMENT to the consistency of our world and serves as a reminder that we can always rely on certain constants. What is constant? The Leading of our Heavenly Father with *Divine Instructions*. In the same way that He led Gideon, He is leading us.

In times of turmoil, chaos, uncertainty, and strife, the Holy Trinity can bring peace and comfort to those who seek its ONENESS, bringing hope and strength. In the Eye of God, in this process, we are not alone in our struggles, but we must put the Mind, Body, and Soul under the subjection of the Holy Spirit.

Why must we involve the Holy Spirit in *The-Lord-Is-Peace* approach? If we desire to AWAKEN our Spirit to become ONE with the Holy Spirit, we must develop discipline in our thoughts, actions, reactions, beliefs, biases, words, emotions, and so on. Listen, our perception of being FREE does not make it so, especially when we unawaringly enslave ourselves with yokes and chains of our own making.

The Promises of God are NOT bound to a specific color, race, denomination, or whatever. Everyone has the same Spiritual Access to their Promised Land and their Egypt simultaneously, even if we think we have grown beyond these experiences or wandering in the desert. Yet, the moment we speak, it determines whether we are in the Promised Land, wandering in the Wilderness Experience, or stuck in Egypt.

More importantly, all of these experiences are determined by and through us, as God provides a Pillar of Cloud by day and a Pillar of Fire by night from back then with our Forefathers until now. How is this humanly possible? My point exactly, it is not humanly possible; it is Spiritually Possible! If we do not open our Spiritual Eyes to see, we will not recognize the Divine Illumination or Covering, regardless of how hard we try.

The Spiritual Evolution of who we are is wrapped in our growth and developmental process. In doing either or both, we have to choose between a man-made bondage diet of leeks, onions, garlic, melons, and cucumbers, yoking the Mind, Body, Soul, and Spirit, keeping us stuck in the past. Or, we can scale back to the Spiritual Manna from the Heavenly of Heavens to glean the Divine Wisdom and Provisions hidden in each experience to prepare us for our Divine Promise, Blessings, Birthrights, or Blueprint.

In the *Divine Instructions* from the Heavenly of Heavens, everything we encounter has a Lesson, Blessing, or Testing attached. If we do not recognize or understand which one it is or miss the mark, we will repeat the process with different characters and a more complex set of circumstances.

We can tiptoe around the appearance of what we have right now, but if we are not GRATEFUL for the little or much, what is the use of having it? Listen, ungratefulness contributes to all the other negative character traits, causing us to become dissatisfied with our Divine Blessings or Provisions. Frankly, it is more common to be ungrateful when material gain is not evident, or we have shattered expectations due to some form of Spiritual Blindness, Deafness, or Muteness. But the truth of the matter is that we have come too far to drop the ball now!

What does Spiritual Blindness, Deafness, or Muteness have to do with our Promised Freedom? According to Scripture, it has a lot to do with it. Here is what Psalm 146:5-10 says, "*Happy is he who has the God of Jacob for his help, Whose hope is in the LORD his God, Who made heaven and earth, The sea, and all that is in them; Who keeps truth forever, Who executes justice for the oppressed, Who gives food to the hungry. The LORD gives freedom to the prisoners. The LORD opens the eyes of the blind; The LORD raises those who are bowed down; The LORD loves the righteous. The LORD watches over the strangers; He relieves the fatherless and widow; But the way of the wicked He turns upside down. The LORD shall reign forever—Your God, O Zion, to all generations. Praise the LORD!*"

In my opinion, the last thing a person would ever want to endure is an upside-down life. What is an upside-down life? When we become rebellious, stiff-necked, doing our own thing, oppressing others as Pharaoh did with the Children of Israel. When we become a stiff-neck in the Eye of God or outright reject Him, we will feel his wrath from the inside out, with all types of chaos, confusion, control, arrogance, and debauchery, zapping one's peace with an inner hunger to take the peace of another.

To be clear, I am not God! Therefore, I cannot determine the wrath or judgment, nor do I wish this upon anyone; however, my JOB is to pay attention, understand, and bring forth an informative AWARENESS regarding what can turn our lives upside down.

What makes Spiritual Liberation so essential for us? It keeps Spiritual Oppression and Yokes from forming within the human psyche. Why? No matter how free we feel on the outside, if we are in bondage from within, it will still feel as if we are enslaved by opposing forces and ailments we may not understand. All of these are projected outwardly by unbridled actions, reactions, thoughts, beliefs, attitudes, and words.

So, to break this form of Spiritual Yoke, we must incorporate the Holy Trinity into the equation and step into the Spiritual Classroom to learn, understand, and apply Kingdom Protocols, Laws, and Principles. What is the purpose of doing so? The Divine Purpose will vary depending upon our Predestined Blueprint, but here is what we all have in common:

- ☐ We must understand God's Nature as a Believer.
- ☐ We must understand the importance of REPENTING.
- ☐ We must understand the use of the Blood of Jesus.
- ☐ We must understand how to become ONE with the Holy Spirit.
- ☐ We must understand our Divine Blueprint.
- ☐ We must understand the use of the Fruits of the Spirit.
- ☐ We must understand the importance of exhibiting Christlike Character.
- ☐ We must understand how to UNVEIL our Spiritual Eyes, Ears, and Language.
- ☐ We must understand the things God hates.
- ☐ We must understand the value hidden in OBEDIENCE.

- ☐ We must understand how to tame the lust of the eyes, the lust of the flesh, and the pride of life.
- ☐ We must understand the importance of doing a check-up from the neck up and examining ourselves according to the Word of God.

Once we are Spiritually Liberated in such a manner, here is what we must do: *"Stand fast therefore in the liberty by which Christ has made us free, and do not be entangled again with a yoke of bondage."* Galatians 5:1.

Why is Spiritual Liberation so important when Spiritually Unveiling our Divine Blueprint? It helps us to engage in the Will of God, doing the Works of the Kingdom without unknowingly interjecting debauchery or fleshly desires. Really? Yes, really! *"For you, brethren, have been called to liberty; only do not use liberty as an opportunity for the flesh, but through love serve one another."* Galatians 5:13.

"Walk in the Spirit, and you shall not fulfill the lust of the flesh." Galatians 5:16. For example, unresolved issues and untamed lusts put stains or blemishes on our Blueprint, causing us NOT to see, hear, or understand God clearly, similar to having a fuzzy reception. For this reason, it is imperative to develop a *Spirit to Spirit* Relationship with our Heavenly Father, ensuring we are queued into a Spiritual Connection instead of a worldly receiver.

What is the purpose of having a *Spirit to Spirit* Connection, especially when the Promises of God are already? There are Spiritual Contingency Clauses included with the Promises of God. In so many words, we cannot behave like an ungrateful hellion on wheels and NOT expect Spiritual Chastisement.

Listen, the Kingdom of Heaven has Spiritual Protocols, and if we desire to GLEAN from the Heavenly of Heavens, we must prove ourselves worthy of the Great Reward *In Him*. Here is the Scripture, *"For all the Promises of God in Him are Yes, and in Him Amen, to the glory of God through us. Now He who establishes us with you in Christ and has anointed us is God, who also has sealed us and given us the Spirit in our hearts as a guarantee."* 1 Corinthians 1:20-22.

In or out of our Divine Seasons, *As God Promised*, we will deal with two additional types of SEEDS outside of our good and bad or righteous or unrighteous SEEDS, which are:

- ☐ Seeds on the GIVE.
- ☐ Seeds on the TAKE.

What does this have to do with us? In varying portions or balances, we all have to govern what takes ROOT in the human psyche. We can give a little and take much, or we can give much and take less. And then again, we can give information only to fish out who or what we can take without giving back to the source. Therefore, we must become very CAUTIOUS about those who only talk about things, hoping someone will volunteer to give what they are not willing to give to themselves. Why must we exercise caution? We are dealing with a Deceptive Spirit, even if it is packaged pristinely.

According to the Heavenly of Heavens, when dealing with the Promises of God, we do not want to become a user or manipulator. In the Kingdom, this is greatly frowned upon because the Promises of God come with their own set of Divine Provisions from the least to the greatest.

How is this possible, especially when we are between a rock and a hard place? It is dealt out in stages or levels when dealing with Kingdom Capital, ensuring we can MASTER where we are before moving on. Why is it dealt in such a manner? We will naturally gravitate toward ungratefulness or unrighteousness, especially if we cannot MASTER where we are Mentally, Physically, Emotionally, or Spiritually. Regardless of what we possess or who we are, this character trait is wrapped in a typical package called SELFISHNESS. Unfortunately, when this becomes our normal, it goes unrecognized unless we constantly examine ourselves with the Fruits of the Spirit and Christlike Character.

As God Promised, the Tree of Life or Death is within everyone through their own choosing, and both are subjected to the REGRAFTING Phase, positively or negatively. So, if we control our SEEDS, we can better determine the TREE and FRUITS we possess.

On the other hand, if we are full of lies and debauchery, we will always have to develop all types of cover-ups or masks to control the trajectory, eventually resulting in some form of breakdown in formality. What does the Tree of Life or Death have to do with us? Unbeknown to most, it is more connected to us than we think.

For example, according to our Divine Design, an unborn fetus is similarly connected to a Tree of Life called the Placenta. Although it looks a little gory, no one is exempt from this process. Furthermore, if I take this a step further, a Placenta even looks like a Tree as well, giving us a bird's eye view of how we are Divinely Connected to our lifeline.

Whereas, once we are born, breathing the Breath of Life, and disconnected from the source of nutrients, we then must become Rooted and Grounded back to our Spiritual Tree of Life through our Character Traits, Fruits, and Seeds that are sown in and out of Season. Really? Yes, really! So, please allow me to align: *"Blessed are those who do His commandments, that they may have the right to the tree of life, and may enter through the gates into the city."* Revelation 22:14.

We can tiptoe around our Genetic Makeup, yet the Secrets are Hidden in Plain Sight if we dare to take the time to understand ourselves from a Spiritual Perspective. Why do we need to understand ourselves in such a manner? Our Promises from God are connected in our Earthen Vessels for our Heaven on Earth Experience and not Earth in Heaven. Due to this misunderstanding on our behalf, we inadvertently use our tongue to sever ties with our very own Spirit to our detriment. How is this possible? Let us take this one to Scripture: *"The tongue of the wise uses knowledge rightly, but the mouth of fools pours forth foolishness. The eyes of the LORD are in every place, keeping watch on the evil and the good. A wholesome tongue is a tree of life, but perverseness in it breaks the Spirit."* Proverbs 15:2-4.

In the Kingdom, once we become transparent, we can allow ourselves to work on regrafting our dark seeds into Seeds of Light, giving life to ourselves and others. What does all of this mean for us? Simply put, we must determine if we are building the Kingdom, ourselves, and others positively or negatively, *As It Pleases God*. And, if we please ourselves only, then we automatically know what type of seeds we are dealing with, and it is left up to us to regraft them or allow them to bear fruit after their own kind.

What do we do if we try to help others and are rejected? In the Spiritual Building process with ourselves, or when sharing our Spiritual Journey of Divine Wisdom with another for Kingdom Edification or Revelation, we must pull back if our hand is rejected. *"And whoever will not receive you nor hear your words, when you depart from that house or city, shake off the dust from your feet."* Matthew 10:14. To be clear, we do not pull back in a rejective manner; we pull back with tough love and zero tolerance if Divine Wisdom is falling upon deaf ears.

In conclusion, in *The Spiritual Middleman Approach*, *"The manifestation of the Spirit is given to each one for the profit of all."* 1 Corinthians 12:7. From me to you, you do not have to force what God has given to you upon anyone. *"A man's gift makes room for him, and brings him before great men."* Proverbs 18:16. Remember that everything you need is already. Your Greatness is already. Your Divine Blueprint is already. And what belongs to you will be, while what is not meant for you will inevitably fall by the wayside because it cannot remain. From this point forward, the only thing that can hold you back is the limitations you place upon yourself. Now is the time to embrace your full potential with confidence, tenacity, and determination. May you be BLESSED abundantly with Divine Peace in your endeavors.

Dr. Y. Bur

www.ingramcontent.com/pod-product-compliance
Lightning Source LLC
Chambersburg PA
CBHW071715160426
43195CB00012B/1685